Citizen
and
Pariah

Citizen and Pariah

Somali Traders and the Regulation
of Difference in South Africa

Vanya Gastrow

WITS UNIVERSITY PRESS

Published in South Africa by:
Wits University Press
1 Jan Smuts Avenue
Johannesburg 2001

www.witspress.co.za

First published 2022

http://dx.doi.org.10.18772/12022037397

978-1-77614-739-7 (Paperback)
978-1-77614-740-3 (Hardback)
978-1-77614-741-0 (Web PDF)
978-1-77614-742-7 (EPUB)

Project manager: Catherine Damerell
Copy editor: Alison Lowry
Proofreader: Lisa Compton
Indexer: Sanet le Roux
Cover design: Hothouse
Typeset in 11.5 point Crimson

For Camaren, David and Myer

Contents

List of Illustrations

Preface

This book is the product of a significant number of fortunate coincidences. My first interest in the Somali community in South Africa arose in 2009, when I was carrying out my articles of clerkship at a law firm in Cape Town. One morning, while I was seated in my office cubicle, a senior colleague placed a copy of the *Cape Times* on my desk. In a rushed voice she instructed me to set aside my work, and rather spend my day helping her write a response to an article. I looked closer and read the article below the headline 'Somalis Refuse to Sign "One-sided" Deal for Spaza Owners'.[1] It was about an informal trade agreement governing Somali-run shops in Gugulethu township. My colleague was alarmed at the anti-competitive nature of the agreement's terms, and the failure of the Competition Commission to take any action over the arrangement. I took up her request and worked on an opinion piece analysing the agreement from a legal perspective, which was published in the *Cape Times* that month.[2] However, the matter continued to linger in my mind, as I struggled to understand why authorities had responded that way.

The following year I by chance came across an advertisement for a research position at the African Centre for Migration & Society (ACMS) at the University of the Witwatersrand to study crime affecting foreign shopkeepers in the Western Cape and their ability to access formal and informal justice mechanisms. I applied and was selected for the project. The data I collected during the course of the project informed my PhD dissertation and, later, this book.

My fortune in the field of migration studies continued. In September 2010 I met Mohamed Aden Osman (known more commonly by the name 'Xadiis') of the Somali Association of South Africa. He accompanied me to interviews, acted as an interpreter where needed, and alerted me to news, meetings and other key events involving the Somali community. Over the years he shared many of his life experiences with me, some of which are featured in the book.

These events – completely unplanned – led me to specialise in the field of immigrant entrepreneurship in South Africa, a topic that has preoccupied me ever since.

The ACMS study entailed conducting 194 qualitative interviews between September 2010 and August 2013, with findings published in three separate reports.[3] The field sites chosen were Philippi, Khayelitsha and Kraaifontein. Parties interviewed included 73 Somali retailers and 65 South African township residents, as well as police, prosecutors, community leaders, legal aid attorneys and local councillors.

The vast majority of Somali retailers I interviewed were men, most of them between 20 and 35 years of age. Few Somali women operate spaza shops in Cape Town's townships due to the high rate of crime that affects these businesses. Instead, they tend to work in more formal central business districts, and operate enterprises such as street stalls, small shops and Somali restaurants. While many male shopkeepers were single, all the women I encountered in the spaza market were married and worked in partnership with their husbands.

After completing the project I embarked on a PhD in migration studies and worked as a researcher on several other migration studies projects in South Africa.[4] During the course of these subsequent studies (between 2014 and 2018), I conducted approximately 40 further interviews with parties including immigrant retailers, municipal law enforcement officials, city planners, provincial government officials, informal business associations and migrant community leaders.

My recording methods varied. When conducting my initial research for the ACMS, I recorded most interviews using written notes, and a large number via a voice recorder. Early on in my research I was reluctant to use a voice recorder, as I felt the device was intimidating and would put interviewees on edge, but as my research progressed, I gained more confidence and increasingly relied on voice recordings. Some of the informal conversations with Mohamed featured in this book are based on my recollections of events, not on notes I wrote or voice recordings. Where this is the case, I asked Mohamed to check the relevant sections and confirm that I had remembered those conversations accurately.

The book draws on the above qualitative studies in its exploration of the experiences of Somali retailers in South Africa. The names of the research participants who appear in the book have all been changed, as almost all the interviews I conducted over my career were under the condition that participants' identities would remain anonymous. One exception to this is Mohamed, who gave informed consent to his name being used in the book.

The book is a narrative account of South African law and society. It investigates violent crime affecting Somali shopkeepers, their ability to access informal and formal justice mechanisms, and efforts to regulate their economic activities. The events as described shed light on how Somali and other foreign retailers are perceived and treated as social and political pariahs, and comment on the state of democracy, rights and citizenship in South Africa today.

Acknowledgements

This book was written between 2018 and 2020 while I was carrying out a postdoctoral research fellowship at the University of Cape Town's public law department. For two years I enjoyed the privilege of being awarded the space and time to write a book on a matter of key interest to me under the insightful supervision of Dee Smythe. It was a rewarding experience and I am incredibly grateful to Dee for her helpful reviews of chapter drafts, her patience and her constant support and encouragement. My fellowship was generously funded by UCT's University Research Council (URC) as well as the South African National Research Foundation (NRF) Chair of Security and Justice. The Centre for Law and Society at UCT and its funders contributed towards the publishing costs of the book.

The research for the book relied on the critical help and work of Mohamed Aden Osman ('Xadiis'), who opened the doors of his life to me and introduced me to his vast network of Somali friends and colleagues in Bellville, Cape Town and Mitchell's Plain. He accompanied me to most of my interviews, assisted when I had follow-up queries or just random questions, and has been highly supportive of my work over the past decade. Knowing him has made me a more generous and thoughtful person and I am incredibly grateful to him.

I am greatly indebted to Roni Amit for overseeing my research and reading over my early reports with a fine-tooth comb. I learned a lot from her rigour and keen eye for detail. Both she and Loren Landau of the African Centre for Migration & Society encouraged me to undertake a PhD on the topic, which later became the foundation for this book.

I am immensely appreciative of key individuals who assisted me in carrying out my research. Thank you, Toto Gxabela, for your sensitive reflections; Abdikadir Mohamed, for your support and presence for so many years; and Abdiahmed Aden, for your clear and frank opinions. Wanda Bici, Mohamed Abshir Fatule, Fundiswa Hoko, Omar Hassan, Abdullahi Ali Hassan, Dahir Mahamed Ali, William Kerfoot and Miranda Madikane also contributed invaluably to my research through their assistance and advice.

I would like to thank Caroline Skinner and Theresa Alfaro-Velcamp for their friendship and camaraderie. Stacey Moses and Jemima Thomas at UCT were immensely helpful in administrating my postdoctoral fellowship and ensuring that my experience at the institution ran smoothly. I wish to thank Mark Massoud for reviewing my early work at a workshop held by the Centre for Law and Society at UCT in partnership with the Law and Society Review.

I am very grateful to Jonathan Crush for enabling me to conduct further research as part of projects carried out by the Southern African Migration Programme which allowed me to gain important further knowledge in the field. I would also like to thank Jaco Barnard-Naudé for introducing me to the work of Hannah Arendt, and encouraging me to explore her thoughts and writings.

I would not have been able to write the book had numerous individuals not generously volunteered their time to me. I cannot name all these people for reasons of anonymity, but they include many members of the South African Police Service, prosecutors, township residents, Somali shopkeepers, NGO and community activists, city officials and legal aid attorneys, all of whom allowed me to gain insight into contemporary South African society and its challenges.

I thank Petra Krusche for being the first person to draw my attention to the topic of Somali retailers in South Africa.

I thank my family for investing in my education, showing me how to enter unconventional careers, and their interest in my work.

Lastly, I thank my husband, Camaren Peter, for his support, guidance and love, and for always encouraging me unhesitatingly to pursue my interests and trust my intuitions.

Part I
Arrival and Reception

1 | Introduction: Law, Justice and the Pariah

You are pariahs. You have to live on tenterhooks lest anyone
deprive you of your rights or property.

Theodor Herzl, *Gesammelte Werke*

The meeting hall at Khayelitsha Resource Centre is mostly empty.
Plastic chairs are arranged in uneven rows across the room. They
face an elevated platform, where seating has been set out for several
speakers. It is 7 March 2012. A golden late-summer light shines through
the windows and illuminates the dust particles moving slowly through
the air. Most attendees are still gathered at the entrance area greeting
each other and engaging in polite chatter. But their civil conversations
mask more than they disclose. Eyes and smiles are tense. Handshakes
are stiff and clasping.

Having opted out of the fraught introductions, I sit down on one
of the vacant seats. A few minutes later casually dressed shopkeepers,
neighbourhood representatives and civil society members drift into the
venue and a hum of chatter reverberates across the room. I notice two
Somali representatives across the hall smiling at me and beckoning me
to join them. I smile back but shake my head. I am not willing to make
myself their visible acquaintance in the tense surroundings.

When the hall is almost full, a tall man dressed in a suit with a priest's
collar takes the podium. Reverend Mbekwa's eyes dart pointedly around
the audience and the banter quickly subsides. Seated behind him on the

platform are two South African and two Somali retailers' representatives. One of the Somali representatives is wearing a tight-fitting dusty black blazer. In the afternoon heat he is perspiring profusely. Beside the retailers' representative sits Sibongile Mbotwe, the special adviser to the national minister of police. I do a quick headcount of the attendees. Of the 79 people in the room, 75 are South Africans. Four are Somali. Later on, a group of six Somali shopkeepers discreetly enter the hall and seat themselves towards the back of the venue.

Mbekwa, who has chaired meetings between traders in Khayelitsha for several years, commands the attention of the audience: 'On 22 May 2008 xenophobic riots took place in Khayelitsha. In November 2008 it was therefore agreed that no new shops would open.'

The room is silent. Attendees are all familiar with the agreement of four years ago that he is referring to. The agreement was the outcome of negotiations between the Somali Retailers' Association (SRA) and the Zanokhanyo Retailers' Association (ZRA). It stipulated that no new spaza shops could open in Khayelitsha without both bodies' approval.

Spaza shops are small informal grocery shops and they are found in most of the country's largely low-income black township neighbourhoods. Many South African residents in these townships convert portions of their properties – be they front yards, garages or sections of their homes – into business premises, which they then rent out to foreign shopkeepers. The presence of foreigners in this market has in turn attracted the ire and hostility of their competitors, namely, South African shop owners. Agitating against the presence of these foreign shopkeepers is not something new.

The reverend is shaking his head disappointedly. The post-2008 agreement has not been properly managed or monitored, he says – 'It is now just a piece of paper.' Somalis and Ethiopians have continued to open shops in the township without any regard for the peace-keeping measure. These new shops not only breach the agreement, Mbekwa asserts.

'Also by law they must have permits. The by-law to limit the influx is not working.' Despite being given notice by law enforcement officials, shops had remained open. This left South African retailers with no other option but 'to take it upon themselves' to close down foreign shops.

Mbekwa speaks with an air of moral authority and self-belief that leaves no room for compromise or critical reflection. Yet what he describes as official 'law' is largely fictional. Spaza shops may be informal, but that does not mean they are illegal. No law in Cape Town requires spaza shops to possess permits. Likewise there is no by-law limiting the so-called influx in the neighbourhood or city. But no one in the room – including representatives from the South African Police Service who are there – seems willing to question Mbekwa's construction of a parallel legal reality. Two seats away from me I recognise a member of a local refugee rights NGO who greets me with a brief nod but, like me, maintains their observer status.

The South African ZRA members who had taken it upon themselves to close down foreign spaza businesses in Khayelitsha were not engaging in extraordinary action. 'Self-help' was commonly deployed in the area when formal legal avenues appeared insufficient. The dry, expansive township on the fringes of Cape Town is meticulously organised from the street level upwards. Street committees convene regularly over anything from domestic disputes to housing delivery to crime. Unresolved matters are referred on to area committees, and thereafter escalated to ward or township committees.

Together these structures fall under the South African National Civic Organisation (SANCO), a large national umbrella organisation that is heavily invested and engaged in township governance. SANCO does not only enjoy popular support. It is also closely allied to the country's leading political party, whose assistance and resources it draws on when grappling with local issues. The trade-off is that the voices and opinions of those who are not aligned to the party are often overlooked.

The power and authority that popular township groupings exercise at the local level can both compete with and override those of the state. They generate rules and customs that tightly control and manage everyday township life. For the person on the street, ignoring these regimes can mean risking injury or death, as the punishments that are meted out can be violent. Lack of formal authority is often little hindrance to these regulatory systems. Community leaders are not afraid to enforce their 'laws' themselves, whether that means adjudicating crimes and punishing offenders or, in the matter under discussion in this hall today, closing down new foreign national shops. Government and political party representatives often watch from the sidelines, not wanting to provoke violent protest or endanger their already fragile legitimacy among key political constituencies.

But informal regulation has its challenges. SANCO in Khayelitsha is backtracking on the spaza trade agreement. While many SANCO leaders are sympathetic to South African shopkeepers, others have sided with landlords who rent out premises to foreign traders. This mixed support proves to be a headache for South African shopkeepers. Attempts to close down foreign shops had initially seemed promising. A few days prior to the meeting 30 South African shopkeepers had driven in convoy to Somali businesses in Harare, Khayelitsha, and ordered them to close down. Traders who protested were hit, kicked and pushed around. Yet the protest had not immediately drawn widespread popular support, and some landlords had threatened counter-protests.

But new foreign traders were not entirely off the hook as, overall, the trade agreement in the township held. While police did not close down new migrant shops, neither did they act against the South African retailers who had driven in convoy. A Somali community leader described that when migrant traders tried to lay complaints with the police, the police retorted that it was not in anyone's interest to arrest people, as this could 'escalate the whole thing'. The turmoil eventually led to a temporary impasse. The new shops remained open, but foreign traders were left in no doubt that the establishment of any further businesses would be at their peril.

Although the principle of the rule of law is weak if not largely absent in Khayelitsha, few foreign traders would in any event view this notion as some form of salvation or justice. Formal laws lack the flexibility of informal rules, which can be negotiated, adapted or side-stepped. Although formal laws could protect foreign businesses by recognising their entitlement to trade and punishing those attempting to expel them, demands for stricter application of laws could just as easily backfire. Police and law enforcement officials are only too eager to step up quasi-militarised operations against foreign national businesses via searches, confiscations of stock and arresting undocumented traders. The formal law can also change according to society's whims. The current legal framework is relatively lenient towards informal township traders.[1] But overly relying on legal provisions that favour them could result in these laws being amended. While fragmented and devolved legal systems can prove capable of spurring injustice and even brutal violence, for many they are still less menacing than the offerings of the modern bureaucratised state.

The reverend's speech is followed by further discussion. One participant likens breaching the agreement to breaking the law: 'People know about the agreement, but it's like selling drugs. It's illegal, but we do it because we are hungry.'

Mbekwa then invites Mbotwe to speak. Despite his title as senior adviser to the national minister of police, Mbotwe does little to correct Mbekwa's misrepresentation of the law: 'The beauty of Khayelitsha post 2008 is this agreement. We must ask the Somalis to give an audit of shops in 2008 and we start from there,' he tells the audience. He pledges police support. 'The police will come and make sure the agreement is enforced in each and every community.'

Mbotwe calmly takes his seat. His speech has left little doubt over the police service's stance on shop regulation in the township. The room remains still and Mbotwe looks across to the chairperson to continue. Then a hand goes up. Mbotwe looks at the audience member – an unassuming Somali man – and nods. 'Is it legal for an agreement to limit the shops of one minority group of people and not apply to other people?' The question pierces the carefully managed calm in the room.

'He is trying to side-step the agreement, so we are not going to entertain his question,' the chairperson interjects. Mbotwe nevertheless responds: 'Here we signed to accommodate the Somali community. We want Somalis to abide by the rules for peaceful coexistence. We understand why you are here, but we need your assistance. Arrogance will not help you or us.'

But Mbotwe's answer does not seem to have satisfied all audience members. Some Somali attendees have further queries. The Somali representative seated on the platform – now more at ease and perspiring less – asks curiously, 'What if your shop opened after 2008 but has a licence? Also, why do you come now, but not earlier? There are 200 new shops. Are you going to close down all of them?'

Instead of resolving ambiguity about the law, Mbotwe's attendance has backfired. His presence unexpectedly invites questions by those seeking legal clarity. He concedes that he cannot answer the questions: 'I do not come here with all the solutions.'

Noticing the change of direction of the meeting, a member of the SRA comes to Mbotwe's defence. 'The main problem in Khayelitsha is the new shops,' he says. 'We need government to assign a task team on this thing. We need implementation.'

Another Somali community representative fails to toe the line. The man stands up in the crowded room and argues that a peaceful solution to the conflict should not violate the rights of South Africans or foreigners. The room begins to rumble with disapproval, tension and unease. The reverend is beginning to lose patience. 'You missed the agenda of this meeting,' he says. 'It says: "How can we work together to control the overflow of influx?" As a leader of the Somali community you should know better.'

South African retailers mutter among themselves and shift around in their seats. 'That Somali man is arrogant because they have money to buy their way,' one of them angrily claims. Another in the audience, a tall thin man, raises the spear he holds in his hand and furiously threatens the Somali speaker with assault. Loud commotion erupts in the hall, and participants shuffle about. Mbekwa is incensed and frustrated. Aware that he has lost control of the meeting, he prematurely concludes it by shouting over the cacophony.

Carefully avoiding eye-contact with anyone, I make my exit.

According to German sociologist Max Weber, 'pariah people' can be found throughout the world.

> These people form communities, acquire specific occupational traditions of handicrafts or of other arts, and cultivate a belief in their ethnic community. They live in a diaspora strictly segregated from all personal intercourse, except that of an unavoidable sort, and their situation is legally precarious. Yet, by virtue of their economic indispensability, they are tolerated, indeed frequently privileged, and they live interspersed in the political communities.[2]

One could say pretty much the same about Somali migrants in South Africa today. In most cities in South Africa Somalis have established neighbourhood enclaves where they live in tight-knit communities that are largely cut off from mainstream South African society. They either set up shop in these enclaves or venture out to low-income neighbourhoods or small isolated rural towns to start up small businesses. They rarely socialise in these environments, however.

Their most common form of township enterprise is spaza shops supplying surrounding neighbours with basic household necessities such as bread, milk, cold-drinks, vegetables, sweets and cosmetics. Working in a spaza shop means no 'leisure time'. Traders wake up early and work throughout the day. South African residents who comprise their customer base tolerate them largely because of their low prices and the range of services they offer. Most Somalis in South Africa are asylum seekers or refugees who can legally live and work in the country.[3]

However, these rights are tenuous. Asylum seeker permits must repeatedly be renewed by the country's largely corrupt, inefficient and erratic refugee reception offices.[4] At the same time paperwork is no guarantee of protection.

Weber's term 'pariah' originates from the pariah caste in India, and it was later adopted by Hannah Arendt in her reflections on the position of Jews in nineteenth- and early twentieth-century Europe. Arendt believed that the defining feature of pariah people was not that they engaged in petty trade or were legally precarious, but more fundamentally that they were political and social outcasts. They belonged 'neither to the common people nor to its rulers'.[5] In this sense the pariah has wider relevance to a mobile and plural age, in which increasing numbers of people struggle to find a secure location in society.

The quandary of the pariah – unable to leverage elite power or the basic entitlements of common members of society – has relevance to those who fall outside of both elitist establishments and popular masses. Their experiences shed light on how those living on social and political peripheries seek dignity, freedom or, more modestly, the simple enjoyment of a 'plain normal life'.[6]

What does the meeting on the balmy afternoon of 7 March 2012 say about the condition of the pariah in post-apartheid, democratic South Africa? Examining how a pariah group encounters and navigates social, political and legal orders in contexts of poverty and informality is a window into how life on the margins is experienced. In these spaces social desires and anxieties are often at their most elevated and urgent, and formal laws at their weakest and most distorted. Rights and entitlements ebb and flow along the lines of what society and those in power desire. Here, the pariah sees legality unravel, and various political groupings enter into conflict over competing values, interests and identities. These fault lines reveal elements of broader political values and logics across the country which, if not addressed, may ultimately come to affect those who do not clearly reside on the margins.

This book is an examination of how Somali spaza traders have found themselves in a foreign country as modern pariahs, and as such have been problematised and confronted by South Africa's myriad and conflicting legal orders and increasingly hostile sociopolitical spheres. Given this reality, how best should the marginalised seek out justice?

2 | Getting Started: A Tale of Three Cities

Bellville station shopping centre is a beige two-storey building on the corner of Durban Road and the train station parking lot. Shops selling clothing and electronic goods spill out onto the pavement, which is assailed by a steady stream of hurried pedestrians who dodge trollies, mannequins and boxes as they go about their daily business. The ground floor smells like a combination of disinfectant and incense and contains more small shops and a busy cafeteria. Grey tiled steps lead up to the first floor, which houses an office belonging to an imam. This is where I find myself one afternoon in September 2010. I am here with Mohamed Aden Osman, the Western Cape co-ordinator of the Somali Retailers' Association (SRA) of South Africa.

I am in Bellville to conduct my first interview for the project I am doing for the African Centre for Migration & Society (ACMS) at Wits. My recruitment was unexpected. One morning, while experiencing problems logging onto my university email address, I came across a job advertisement on the university's website. At the time I was a master's student at the University of Cape Town, with limited funds to support my studies. The post looked interesting. The ACMS was looking to hire a researcher to investigate the ability of foreign shopkeepers to access justice when they were victims of crime. The research focused on the Western Cape Province, where many incidents of violent crime had occurred, and also where I happened to live. I applied, and before long I was appointed to the position. Shortly thereafter I made my first trip to Bellville, where I found myself parked outside Bellville train station waiting to meet Mohamed.

Bellville is a historically white, mainly Afrikaans suburb located 25 kilometres north-east of Cape Town. Today it serves as a key business and transport node between the city, outlying suburbs and nearby agricultural regions. Somali shops line the end of Durban Road, which descends into Bellville train station, and turns up towards Bellville taxi rank. 'Shops in Bellville's business district are equally as profitable as in the city centre, but pay 30 per cent less rent,' a resident business owner later tells me.

I am interested in Mohamed's feedback, as Somali shopkeepers seem particularly vulnerable to violent attacks. Most crime affecting foreign shopkeepers in Cape Town occurs in the spaza market, where Somali businesses are highly concentrated. In fact, Somalis are so prevalent in the city's spaza market that most foreign-owned spaza shops in Cape Town are operated by Somalis.[1]

Figure 2.1: Durban Road in Bellville with hatchback cars and bakkies lining the street (2018). Photograph by Vanya Gastrow.

The imam's office offers respite from the commotion on the street. It is cool and airy and has a large bookshelf filled with books, pamphlets and collections of religious texts. The racket outside fades to a din and I sit facing Mohamed and an associate of his in the centre of the room. Mohamed is medium height and dressed formally in a white, collared shirt and black trousers. He speaks with a calm, soft voice and chooses his words carefully. He appears to be in his early 30s – only a year or two older than me. Mohamed's younger colleague defers to him; he is more of an observer than a participant in the meeting.

I cast a quick eye over my interview questions. 'What is your general impression of the response of the justice system towards attacks on foreign shopkeepers?' I ask. In a measured, diplomatic fashion Mohamed explains that the government is trying hard to combat xenophobia and crime affecting foreign nationals, but it is not doing enough. Police often do not protect traders' properties from looters, and more efforts need to be made to tackle business robberies.

But not all townships in Cape Town are the same. Mohamed describes Philippi, Kraaifontein and Delft as crime 'hotspots' and says foreign retailers venture into these areas with trepidation. In contrast, Khayelitsha, he says, although 'previously dangerous', since 2008 is 'the best township in the province'.

Having little other data to go by, I decide to focus my research on these areas. The South African Police Service (SAPS) does not publish any statistics on crimes affecting foreign nationals in the country, and although violent attacks are reported in the media, these accounts are often brief and sporadic. Philippi and Kraaifontein could shed light on heightened levels of crime, and Khayelitsha could serve as a peaceful comparison. The research entails interviewing foreign traders as well as South African residents, police, prosecutors, community leaders and local councillors. Through these multiple perspectives I will hopefully find out more about how formal and informal justice institutions respond to crime that affects foreign retailers.

I thank Mohamed for his time. While we're descending the grey tiled staircase, he offers to show me around the area and introduce me to shopkeepers I could interview. It is 5.30 pm and the sky outside is dusty peach and deepening to blue. Nightfall will be arriving soon – not an opportune time to conduct interviews in an unfamiliar neighbourhood, I think to myself. I envision awkwardly showing up unannounced at someone's house, just as they have settled down for a quiet evening. Or alternatively – and revealing my own prejudices – of being accosted by wayward Somali bandits in some desolated cul-de-sac. I shake my head. 'It's getting late and I need to go back home.' Mohamed stares at me, perplexed by my response. He presses on, explaining that he knows someone who was injured in Philippi who lives just around the corner. I look up the chaotic street full of rush-hour commuters, reflecting on the fact that key research subjects are just within reach. But then I come to my senses again. He must be crazy to think that I will carry out research at this hour, I reason; I tell Mohamed that I will return another day.

Driving home that evening along the N1 highway back towards the glittering lights of Cape Town's city centre, I reflect on Mohamed's offer more than on the interview itself. Something about it strikes a chord within me. For Mohamed, the evening does not symbolise a retreat into one's atomised private space, cloistered safely behind burglar bars, watching television for a couple hours before retiring to bed. For him, the evening seems almost as continuous as day. Rather than winding down, Somali life in Bellville appeared to be getting only busier into the evening, with residents swiftly walking to mosque, eating and socialising at local cafeterias, and catching up on the news in brightly lit internet cafés. In fact, on closer reflection I realise that 5.30 pm is probably an ideal time to carry out interviews in Bellville. After work people are more likely to be available to meet and engage in community affairs. I feel struck by Mohamed's invitation, but in a good way. I have rarely encountered such social ease and ongoing activity in my everyday life.

Figure 2.2: Mohamed drinking tea at the Blue Café in Bellville (2010). Photograph by Vanya Gastrow.

I meet Mohamed two weeks later at the Blue Café on the ground floor of the Belmed building in Bellville. It is informally known as the 'Borama' building, after a town with the same name in Somaliland. The structure is a former hospital but is now filled with dozens of shops and other businesses. Signs displayed at the entrance advertise Qurxiye Tailors, Belmed Building Cash and Carry, Xawaalada Bakaal Express Airtime, and Cape Internet II.

Our table is in a quiet passageway outside the café. Inside, a rowdy crowd of Somali men animatedly watch an international football match on a giant flat-screen television, applauding or bemoaning their respective team's play. Somali women, although active in business and community matters, do not frequent Somali restaurants. I order a cappuccino, which arrives fresh from the café's large espresso machine, a likely legacy of Somalia's former Italian colonial rulers. Mohamed orders milky black tea. We are here to discuss how he can help me with my research. I had told him I would like to take up his offer to introduce me to some shopkeepers that he knows.

I feel relaxed and comfortable in the Blue Café, despite being female and a newcomer to Bellville. Although I clearly do not blend into my surroundings, restaurant patrons, while polite, do not pay too much attention to me. There is also an air of informality and familiarity in the venue. People come and go, greeting each other, patrons loudly cheering on their football teams together. At prayer time a man places his prayer mat at the entrance to the café beside us and kneels to pray, seemingly unperturbed by my presence. The café has the atmosphere of a living room housing close friends and family rather than mostly strangers.

I realise that I am going to require significant help with my research. Truth be told, I have little idea of how to locate Somali victims of crime or introduce myself to them. I don't speak a word of Somali. Mohamed will be an excellent facilitator. He is sociable and outgoing without being overly pushy or intrusive. He also has experience in the spaza market, having been a shop owner himself in the past, and he knows the ins and outs of Cape Town's Somali community. I invite him to be my paid assistant on the project, and he enthusiastically agrees.

Mohamed recommends the imam's quiet office as a venue to conduct interviews. I quickly learn that traders would prefer not to meet me in their shops. Some are wary of criminals and do not wish to draw any unwanted attention to themselves. Others are more concerned about customers – they worry about being distracted or overheard by them. These concerns are not unfounded. Most of the interviews that I later carry out in shops are awkward and difficult. Customers purchasing packets of chips, chewing-gum or loose cigarettes constantly interrupt us. Discussing community responses to crime directly in front of community members is also not ideal, if not dangerous. In one case a trader gets cold feet and asks to be interviewed more discreetly in my stuffy hatchback car. In another instance we retreat to a trader's landlord's house, only to have to talk in whispers out of fear that the landlord can overhear us. On a few occasions, we are fortunate that business is either slow or traders feel less threatened, and we typically retreat to small living quarters behind shops to converse. Overall Bellville is the preferred venue. Here we can speak undistracted and in relatively secure and familiar surroundings.

In return for travelling to Bellville to meet with me, I offer traders R50 to cover their transport costs. It is a reasonable reimbursement, I think to myself, as it should compensate traders for their bus, taxi or train fare. I also bring along refreshments for participants – bottles of water and soft drinks. But my plan does not play out as expected. All traders turn down my R50 offer. They wave their hands in embarrassment on their and my behalf. The general explanation given is that their travel costs are just 'small money'. In the same vein Somali participants politely refuse soft drinks, and waiters turn down tips from me at restaurants. Instead, interviewees return from daily prayers with tea, coffee and other refreshments for me, and insist on buying me lunch at local cafeterias. There is a clear etiquette of making guests feel welcome. All the Somalis I encounter, without variation, exhibit this hospitality.

As the days come and go, I meet other Somali community activists. Bellville houses a plethora of community organisations. Apart from the Somali Association of South Africa, there is the SRA, the Somali Community Board, the Somali Student Association, the Ogaden Youth and Student Association, and the Somali Refugee Aid Agency, to name a few. Many are interested in my work as a researcher, as they themselves aspire to pursue tertiary education.

As Mohamed and I sit in the imam's office carrying out interviews, passersby poke their heads through the door and greet us. Some join us while we wait for interviewees to arrive. Subjects of conversation are broad. One day a trader I had met the day before storms into the room. A police officer had tear-gassed him in the face on the street for no reason at all. When he went to lay a complaint, he was brushed off. Police explained that the officers who attacked him had been provoked because a Somali man had assaulted a policeman at the taxi rank that evening. At other times we dwell on current affairs, or discuss future life plans such as studying, marriage, starting a business or travelling abroad. Most of those I meet are my age or younger, having left their home country fresh out of their teens in the early 2000s or later. Coffee cups forgotten on the floor are constantly knocked over, and have Mohamed rushing to fetch a broom to mop up, joking about how he's been forced to modernise in South Africa and undertake women's tasks.

Over time I realise that relations between Somali community members are not always harmonious. As with all close-knit social circles, relationships are often fraught with rivalries, fallings-out and acrimony. A major point of contention was the collusion of some community leaders in corruption carried out by the office of the United Nations High Commission for Refugees (UNHCR) in Cape Town.

I begin to regard Bellville as a second home. Considering interviewees' general tardiness, interruptions for prayer times, and mutual interest in current affairs, one interview in Bellville can easily take half a day. The imam leaves the keys to his office at an adjacent shop, where I wait for Mohamed and chat to the shop's manager. Many faces become familiar – from that of the imam himself, to those of nearby shopkeepers, community activists and various people I've interviewed. Yet at the same time I am not bound by Somali cultural rules and customs. Few of the social expectations and gendered norms that govern the community apply to me. I enjoy basking in the security and structure provided by new relations, while at the same time I am not tied by their corresponding obligations and expectations.

Bellville differs markedly from the world I normally inhabit. I live a peaceful, comfortable life with my partner on the slopes of Devil's Peak. I see friends and family on weekends – not to discuss urgent community matters but to socialise and recuperate from long hours of work. If I have an opinion, I share it passively from the vantage point of a comfortable armchair, rather than deliberately convening and acting with others. I live in my head. I mainly focus my attentions inwards on myself and my close and immediate relationships.

In contrast, in Bellville my thoughts feel relevant and appear to have impact; my skills and knowledge are put to use. My time in the neighbourhood starts to exceed what is necessary for my research. I become drawn into community meetings, I volunteer at a local school and occasionally I meet up with people for lunch or tea when I am in the area. I encounter a source of collective support and fellowship there that I find grounding and restorative. At the same time, I suspect that the Somali colleagues, acquaintances and friends I get to know enjoy the opposite – an escape from rigid social rules and the overfamiliarity of their social network.

My largely seamless introduction to Somali community structures in Cape Town cannot only be due to Somali hospitality and Mohamed's skills as a research assistant. Although those I meet hardly mention it overtly, I also happen to be a relatively privileged white South African. My social location draws people towards me. Many of the Somalis I come to know ask me for assistance in various matters. Requests are minor and realistic. They mostly entail me harnessing the power of my accent. A five-minute telephone enquiry enables me to obtain information that would likely take them an entire morning or day to acquire and with difficulty. Matters include contacting a hospital to find out someone's patient number and booking a consultation with a specialist doctor who treats throat cancer. I also contact the University of Cape Town's library to find out what they do with old computers, phone NGOs to enquire about assistance, and in one case telephone a landlord to find out how much he is renting his property for. 'His secretary won't want to speak to me if I make the call,' the shopkeeper explains. I thereby leverage my racial and class privilege in support of my newfound relations – both confronting and affirming the systemic inequalities that prevail in post-apartheid South Africa.

In contrast, my experience of Cape Town's townships is poles apart. I do not familiarise myself with township neighbourhoods to the same extent as I have done in Bellville. This is not because of any cold reception. As in Bellville, I also recruit South African assistants to

Figure 2.3: RDP houses in Khayelitsha (2012). Photograph by Vanya Gastrow.

accompany me when I am interviewing South African township residents in Philippi, Khayelitsha and Kraaifontein. Township residents
are generally happy to speak to me and share their views. However, I
am not always certain that their accounts are accurate. I sometimes get
the sense that versions of events and personal sentiments are adjusted
for me, with some township residents possibly underplaying levels of
xenophobia and distrust towards foreigners. By the same token foreign
nationals sometimes appear prone to highlighting their victimhood and
underplaying their levels of agency.

My general lack of familiarity and arm's-length distance with the
township neighbourhoods that I visit stems from other factors. The
Somali district in Bellville comprises only a few busy streets and office
blocks. Places and people quickly become recognisable. The sprawling
expanses of Khayelitsha, Philippi and Kraaifontein extend over a much
bigger area. The 2011 census estimated the population of Khayelitsha

alone at almost 400 000 people – the size of a large city. The population of Philippi comprises approximately 200 000 people, while together Bloekombos and Wallacedene townships in Kraaifontein are slightly smaller at 40 000.

My method of research in townships is also different. While I am happy to draw on Somali social networks and friendship circles to ascertain traders' experiences of crime, my interviews with South African residents involve deliberately seeking out people who do not know each other. I cannot rely on the views of one social group in seeking to understand general community perceptions of foreign-owned shops. I therefore go out of my way to more randomly identify potential participants. I do this by driving around neighbourhoods and approaching individuals sitting on street corners or in their yards, in the hope that they might have the time and inclination to chat. Weekends are best so that I can also encounter people who would otherwise be at work.

I also do not wish to linger in townships for very long. Local community workers fear that my research may re-ignite latent conflicts and spark new bursts of violence against foreign-owned shops. In all three township areas that I enter, foreign traders have encountered mob lootings and organised mobilisations against their businesses. I therefore move as quickly and seamlessly as possible in and out of township neighbourhoods to eschew generating broader popular awareness and discussion about my research. I also avoid interviewing South African traders altogether; instead I attend community meetings in Khayelitsha to listen to their views. These meetings lead me to broaden the scope of my research. 'Regulation' is the pivoting call for how to deal with crime against these shops – more so than heightened patrols, investigations and prosecutions.

Unlike Bellville, I do not find the township neighbourhoods that I visit 'restorative'. In fact I find them utterly depleting. This is to a large extent simply due to heat exhaustion, something that doesn't affect me significantly in Bellville. Bellville's densely occupied apartment and office blocks offer some respite from the dry summer heat. Tall buildings and broad trees provide shaded cover to the streets. Shops, restaurants and apartments located inside are relatively cool and well protected from the sun. Bellville's density also means that I do not have to drive very far (if at all) to get from one place to another.

The township sites – satellite towns set up during apartheid to house the city's black residents – could not be more different. Here, thousands of tiny single-storey houses dot the parched, flat earth. Grey, sandy roads and pavements lack almost any trace of greenery or shade. I interview people on street corners or in their yards under the dizzying white glare of the sun. Much of my day is also spent climbing in and out of my car which, after a few minutes of being parked on a pavement, feels like a sauna.

But I cannot pin my exhaustion only on the intense and persistent heat. My fatigue is also fed by the interactions that I have. Many of these engagements leave me disorientated and in shock. Apartheid policies and their legacies have sheltered me from social hardships for most of my life. I have never witnessed violence, been subjected to frequent indignity or had to endure hunger or poverty. My normal is abnormal in South Africa. I cannot immediately relate to many of the feelings, opinions and events that are detailed to me. The full extent of many interactions only dawns on me months or years later.

The degree of my divergent world strikes me on my first day of conducting research in Philippi, when my research assistant and I visit Thabo Mbeki, a small informal settlement lodged between Govan Mbeki Road and the N2 highway. Thabo Mbeki is also known as Lloyd, allegedly after an irate landowner who repeatedly threatened determined residents with eviction. The settlement feels like a rabbit warren of tiny winding paths and homes built almost on top of one another. Yet, despite exhibiting many features of a neighbourhood with high crime rates – unemployment, poverty and no street lighting or proper roads – crime is almost non-existent in the settlement. My research assistant, who is active in civil society in the area, introduces me to an acquaintance of his, whom he met through a neighbourhood development programme. She is a short delicate woman in her mid-40s. Her home is a small shack with large windows facing a winding pathway outside.

'There were no xenophobic attacks in Lloyd,' the woman tells me, referencing the widespread riots that swept Philippi in 2008. 'In fact, Lloyd has never had any attacks against foreigners at all. I saw the attacks on TV, but not in my area.' The reason for this, she explains, is because of strict community control over the neighbourhood. Landlords wishing to rent their premises to foreigners first have to obtain permission from community representatives. Thereafter residents will accept and protect foreign traders as equals. This, I later discover, is not entirely true. A nearby neighbour tells me: 'Foreign traders are not involved in any community happenings, so we cannot protect them.'

The woman describes that a committee of 13 people govern Lloyd and investigate and adjudicate crimes. All accused are granted a hearing where they are given an opportunity to defend themselves. Punishments usually take the form of lashings or beatings. 'If a person has been beaten once or twice already,' she says, 'the whole family will be chased out of the area.' Once culprits have been punished, they are handed over to the police. 'The police don't mind if a youth has been beaten ...' As we end our interview, she stammers something, then stops mid-sentence. After a moment she says she has another example for me. 'Go ahead,' I encourage her.

She recalls that there was once a problematic youth in Lloyd who repeatedly committed crime. The youth was apprehended, and the committee called a meeting to discuss his fate. Residents in attendance were frustrated and at their wits' end. After some discussion, community leaders at the meeting requested that all women leave the venue.

The woman shakes her head as she thinks back. At the time she found the request odd, she says, but she followed through with the instruction and left. The men who remained behind apparently surrounded the delinquent youth and beat him to death. This, however, was only the first element of his punishment. Residents thereafter took to his shack, dismantled it and collected all of the youth's meagre belongings. They laid these items alongside his broken corpse on an open field outside of the neighbourhood – his final banishment. This dramatic illustration is difficult for me fully to absorb and I drive home in numbed shock. I narrate the story to a relative in a comfortable suburb the following day, but their matter-of-fact response ('That's what we need in *our* area') does little to alleviate my bewilderment.

On a follow-up trip to Philippi I approach two casually dressed youth sitting outside a Bangladeshi spaza shop. One looks thin and dishevelled; the other sits upright on a red plastic Coca-Cola crate. The dishevelled youth describes the many problems facing young people in Philippi. Gangsterism prevents them from being able to move around the township, and many quit school because they do not want to 'listen to teachers speaking crap all day'. Foreign shopkeepers, he says, are partially responsible for crime affecting them 'because they play angel'. 'There are people looking to commit violence, so you must not be left behind. That's why life is a battlefield.'

The second youth, though, believes that crime cannot provide a long-term solution to poverty. 'People need to change how their minds are conditioned,' he says.

Meeting bored and wholly dejected youth sitting on street corners, and hearing descriptions of violent vigilante action, are not uncommon encounters for me. Some speak with compassion and clarity about complex social and political challenges that are beyond my lived experience. One thing that strikes me is how their accounts are not neatly censored or repressed. There is a bluntness and transparency in their narratives that I am not accustomed to in my usual middle-class social interactions. Anger, hope, admiration and depression all come across directly and unfiltered. From depictions of beating suspected criminals with 'half-bricks' to one Philippi youth confessing his dependency on methamphetamine, to frustrated complaints over corruption and lawlessness, interviewees are frank and straight-talking. They do not couch their words in phrases and insinuations that could make my interviews more comfortable. They confront and present their social hardships and injustices head on.

My interactions with Somalis in Bellville are markedly different. Here ceremonious etiquette and courtesy act as buffering from raw emotion or reality in general. It is not only Mohamed who chooses his words carefully. There is a disposition towards diplomacy and vague generalities. I put this polite avoidance down to a subtle uncertainty towards outsiders. Researchers and journalists cannot be trusted at face value. Traders are overly cautious for fear of somehow putting themselves or others at risk. This, I think, speaks partially to levels of repression in home countries such as Somalia and Ethiopia. At the same time their dislocation from mainstream South African society, com-bined with widespread animosity towards them, does little to quell such reservations.

But there is a broader avoidance of reality. Renderings of traumatic experiences of violent crime are often accompanied by a polite joke or pleasantry. There is an unwillingness to dwell on and grapple with one's present reality, a preference for hastily moving beyond the present and focusing instead on the future. Traders emphasise their prospec-tive plans – studying at university, moving to another city, expanding their businesses or emigrating overseas. A worldview underpinned by uprootedness and impermanence offers a comfort and reassurance that nothing need stay the same. No one is obliged to accept their current position except in the short term. A grand aspirational future softens the blunt reality of the present, and the trauma of the past. Whether or how long the buffer will last is another matter. Somalis seem geared towards outrunning their reality and pursuing the hope of greener fields elsewhere – via work, imagination or travel. In contrast, South African township residents are staying put and preparing for a fight.

3 | The Unwelcome Guest: Flight and Arrival in South Africa

'It was so peaceful. If you wanted to, you could leave a suitcase filled with cash in the middle of a busy market and nobody would take it. Lots of people were considering going back. *I* even thought of going back.'

Mohamed is speaking of Mogadishu. Not of its early democratic era, when the city, with its pastel arabesque buildings, was known as the 'white pearl' of the Indian Ocean, but the Mogadishu of 2006, when it came briefly under the control of the Islamic Courts Union. At the time, clan-based warlords' divisive 16-year-long control of the city caved under the unifying power of religion. The courts brought together competing clans and expelled private militias. But stability was short-lived. The Union soon rivalled the internationally recognised and pro-Western Transitional Federal Government, which was based in the southern inland town of Baidoa.

In December 2006, Ethiopian forces, with backing from the United States, invaded Mogadishu with the intention of bolstering the transitional government and preventing the Union from expanding its control. Unlike more familiar street battles fought with small arms in contained precincts of the city, the Ethiopian invasion entailed widespread rocket bombardment and shelling of the city's run-down and bullet-ridden buildings on a scale not seen before. By the time Ethiopia withdrew its forces two years later, more than 16 000 civilians had been killed and over a million people displaced. But the renewed violence had further consequences. While the leadership of the Union had quickly dissolved into the rubble of the city or surrounding towns and countries, a radical youth militia associated with it, al-Shabaab – meaning the 'youth' or the 'boys' – refused to accept defeat. As a result, Somalia entered a renewed period of violence and instability that continues to plague the country today.

'Ethiopia will never want a strong Somalia. So long as there is a civil war in Somalia, Somalis won't be able to lay claim to the Ogaden,' Mohamed tells me one afternoon at the Blue Café. Mohamed's family are originally from the disputed Ogaden region in eastern Ethiopia. He draws a rough map of Ethiopia on a crumpled piece of paper with a small circle in the corner indicating the Ogaden. I later look up the region online. The Ogaden makes up roughly a quarter of the country's landmass, and comprises Ethiopia's iconic eastern horn. Mohamed's parents fled the region in the 1970s and settled in Afmadow, a small rural town near the port city of Kismayo in Somalia.

'Afmadow is to Kismayo the same way Paarl is to Cape Town,' he explains.

'An hour's drive from Kismayo?' I remark.

'More like a three-day walk.'

Mohamed recalls his life in Afmadow as idyllic. He grew up as the eldest child with eight younger sisters on a plot of land near the town's centre, where his parents still live today. His upbringing was rudimentary, but happy. His home comprised a yard with a mud hut and two small wooden buildings called *baraakos*. The hut was for sleeping in, while the *baraakos* were for eating and preparing food. These structures were later replaced with brick buildings. Mohamed's father is an imam. He describes him as a humble and reserved man, possessing a quiet and contemplative nature. His mother is more of an extrovert. She operates a small clothing shop to support the family. She phones her son faithfully every second month when she travels to Kismayo to collect stock. Although Afmadow is small, arid and difficult to reach, Mohamed assures me that the town is far from dull. It contains several restaurants and the market serves as a hub of social activity where friends and family regularly meet, socialise and exchange news.

Yet, by the mid-1990s the war had taken its toll on the town's institutions, and nearby high schools had become defunct. Mohamed's family chose to send him to Jijiga in the Ogaden to complete his schooling. When he returned to Afmadow several years later, it was clear that the town was no place for a young adult. Although in many respects it had remained the quiet sleepy haven that he had known growing up, youth Mohamed's age were expected to join violent warring factions engaged in the country's prolonged civil conflict. Mohamed's talkative and outspoken nature was also no asset in a time of war and civil strife. As he saw it, the cosmopolitan city of Nairobi, Kenya, offered far greater opportunities for a new high school leaver. At 720 kilometres distance from Afmadow, it was far enough away from Somalia's conflict yet still close enough for relatives periodically to pay a visit. Mohamed also had friends and relatives there who could help him find his feet.

Unlike Ethiopia, Kenya was democratic. After years of living in Ethiopia, where the disappearance of classmates, friends or relatives was routine, Kenya offered the prospect of a free life. 'In Ethiopia the military can come to your home and rape your sister in front of you,' Mohamed states bluntly. 'And there's nothing you can do about it.' For him living under an authoritarian regime was not something he could willingly stomach.

When Mohamed arrived in Nairobi at the age of 22, the congested city bore almost no resemblance to the rural towns and remote cities that he was used to. His new home was a cramped apartment in Eastleigh, a chaotic and densely populated Somali business and residential quarter. Office blocks, shopping malls and apartment buildings overlooked gridlocked traffic on narrow streets and a constant flow of pedestrians. Mohamed spent the next 18 months navigating Eastleigh's packed lanes and frenetic pavements, but despite his best efforts things did not pan out for him in the city. Finding work was not the problem.

Eastleigh was flooded with Somali businesses and new and reliable staff were in demand. Mohamed's dilemma was that he became frequent and easy fodder for corrupt police officials. 'I didn't have a Kenyan ID,' he shrugs. 'Police repeatedly arrested me, and I struggled to find money to pay their bribes.'

He recalls how one day, while walking in a busy street, police appeared and asked him to show them his identity document. Nervously he admitted that he did not possess one. They immediately handcuffed him and took him to a police station. A friend of his, who witnessed the encounter, arrived at the station moments later and offered 300 Kenyan shillings loaned from Mohamed's relatives for his release.

But it was not the end of Mohamed's hassles. One afternoon, while he and two friends were eating in a cafeteria, police entered the venue and arrested them all. Once more, Mohamed was bailed out by a relative. Although these incidents caused Mohamed consternation, it was the third incident that left him properly shaken. One night he was returning home from a nearby market when he stumbled across a group of police officers, one of whom was notoriously known among Somalis in the areas as 'Ciijiye' or 'strangler'. As he eyed Mohamed, he dispensed with typical state officialdom, and instead grabbed Mohamed directly by the neck, choking him. 'Where's your ID?' he demanded. When he loosened his grip, Mohamed confessed that he had no papers. 'Organise something,' the officer instructed him. Luckily, Mohamed had 100 Kenyan shillings on him, and he paid the officers to set him free.

Over time Mohamed sensed that his relatives were becoming weary of his presence. He could not hold down a job and was a constant source of anxiety for those around him. 'Every week or every day I was having to ask people for help. I was ashamed,' he told me. There was also no prospect of resolving his legal dilemma. 'If you are a refugee you have to be in the camp,' he said. He would need to make a further plan. This time his choice of destination was more distant and even less familiar.

Many Somalis gravitate towards the southernmost tip of the continent for similar reasons. Somalia has been in a state of civil war since the early 1990s. Kenya houses large numbers of Somalis fleeing the conflict in expansive refugee camps where they are provided with basic food and shelter, but few are granted permission to reside in urban areas. Many of the more ambitious, hoping to live a life free of camp restrictions and malaise, thus choose to travel further. While significant numbers head north to Europe or America to seek asylum, others try their luck going south. Apart from being a middle-income country with a progressive democracy, since the mid-1990s South Africa has also had a favourable refugee policy. Asylum seekers and refugees are permitted to work and move around the country unhindered.

Other Somalis settle in South Africa for different reasons. For some the country serves as a platform for emigrating to the United States or another third country. A handful of Kenyan Somalis travel to the country to further their education, and thereafter return home.

For most the journey to South Africa is not easy. They travel via land and sea, relying on informal networks of smugglers to see the journey through. One Somali youth who fled al-Shabaab recruiters in Mogadishu described dodging bullets of Kenyan security officials near the Somali border, and seeing the corpses of two co-travellers being taken from the truck he had been transported in. He survived the journey with only a few items of clothing, having abandoned his worn-out shoes while climbing steep hills in Malawi, and being robbed of all his valuables by border officials.

Somali immigrants' first taste of South Africa is usually the shrubby banks of the Limpopo River along the country's northern border. From there they find their way towards ethnic enclaves in cities and small towns across the country and apply for asylum. This is no simple task. Since 2010 the state has closed down a number of key refugee offices across the country, and backlogs mean that applicants can often wait for more than a decade for their cases to be finalised. Asylum seeker permits, 'the newspaper', as one holder disparagingly put it, are printed on flimsy A4 sheets of paper and need to be renewed every few months. They are frequently not recognised by institutions and their short duration of validity makes tasks like opening bank accounts or applying for employment extremely difficult.

Cape Town is the most popular destination. The Somali Association of South Africa estimates that there are about 80 000 Somalis in South Africa, of whom approximately 30 000 reside in the Western Cape Province, and 20 000 in the city. Somali neighbourhoods in the city exist in the traditionally white Afrikaans suburb of Bellville, or the coloured suburb of Mitchell's Plain. In Bellville – the largest hub – their businesses have rejuvenated a previously abandoned strip of the neighbourhood. Streets are packed with enterprises ranging from wholesalers, restaurants, internet cafés, clothing stores, fabric shops, electronic shops, DVD stores, laundromats, tailors, salons, guest lodges, accountants and travel agents.

The imam's quiet and musty office in Bellville shopping centre is my first introduction to a number of other community-based institutions and initiatives. A faith-based organisation, Al Bayaan, operates two local mosques and a madrassa, and recently set up a crèche to support working parents. Somali NGOs grapple with issues such as crime, legal rights and integration. The Somali Association of South Africa, whose office is not far from the mosque, offers skills development and English classes to community members, and after-care facilities for school children. It also hosts workshops, paralegal advice sessions and support groups. Clan structures complement these activities by carrying out extended family roles – visiting the sick in hospital, intervening in community conflicts, or settling members' bad debts. There are also intermediaries, some of whom provide essential services such as translating for patients in hospitals. Others act as gatekeepers (*mukhalas*) who extort funds or solicit bribes from community members in return for access to Department of Home Affairs documents or, until a few years ago, UNHCR resettlement opportunities.

Few of these activities and initiatives existed more than two decades ago. Somalis began migrating to South Africa in the mid-1990s. 'Youth arriving today have it easy,' a middle-aged Somali clothing shopkeeper in Tulbagh advises me. When he first arrived in Cape Town in the late

1990s, he was completely alone, without any support. He initially spent his days selling clothes and sandals outside social welfare offices in Cape Town and surrounding towns on pension days. At the time he was homeless and slept under highway bridges. 'I used the clothes I sold as blankets,' he reflects, thinking back. 'Bellville was empty. There were only homeless people and stray dogs.'

Older generations of Somalis in South Africa are distinguished from their younger counterparts in another way. Although they may have lacked initial support, they enjoyed the benefit of having grown up in the context of a weak but relatively functional state. The social fabric of communities was still generally intact in Somalia during their child-hoods, and many had the good fortune of having gained basic education and work skills. It is not uncommon to find former electricians, teachers and civil servants among this group. A clothing shopkeeper in Prince Alfred Hamlet with a degree in agriculture told me that after he fin-ished university he was employed by the government. The war changed his trajectory. 'I was first just a happy citizen living in his home coun-try, working hard, had ambition, had a good future, and then one time everything gets upside down. Then I have no other choice but to run.'

As the generations progress, narratives of destabilisation and struggle in Somalia increase among younger Somalis. Eventually one encounters what one trader jokingly termed 'the Somalians' – the youths who fled Mogadishu in the aftermath of Ethiopia's invasion in December 2006. 'It was like the cattle had been let out of the kraal,' a community leader said sardonically. For older Somalis these youth were not real 'Somalis'. Growing up in a failed state had caused them to lose touch with entrenched Somali cultural etiquettes, norms and values. The Somalis who arrived in the aftermath of the escalation of conflict in 2006 were a largely bewildered and traumatised generation lacking many of the most basic educational and psychological tools to navigate their way in a new country. This generation increasingly filtered into the spaza market, which lies on the frontline of South Africa's harshest social conditions.

The rush from Mogadishu spiked between 2008 and 2011. It tapered off in 2012, when a new government was elected in Somalia, and al-Shabaab was, for the most part, driven out of Mogadishu. Today Bellville has a slower, calmer feeling – it is no longer the hotbed of new arrivals and activity.

As with migration trends, migrant economies are dynamic. Somalis venturing to Cape Town did not always operate in the spaza market. When they first began arriving in Cape Town, at the dawn of democracy, most Somalis worked as hawkers. Some traded in clothes such as socks, belts, sandals and underwear, selling their wares on sidewalks or by patiently going door to door in far-to-reach neighbourhoods. Others sold snacks and cigarettes at transport interchanges. Over time a few managed to open formal clothing shops, but it was not easy. 'You need nice premises in a business area with air-conditioning and other infrastructure if you want to open a clothing shop,' one spaza trader explained to me. The grocery market was more accessible. Former hawkers found that opening convenience stores in low-income areas was relatively straightforward and inexpensive, and they enjoyed a busy and expanding trade. These shops were particularly in demand in the city's satellite township neighbourhoods, which had for the most part been neglected by the large retail chains. Start-up costs and regulatory requirements were low, and relaxed township zoning schemes permitted businesses to operate from residential properties. Grocery shops could flourish from people's garages, front yards or living rooms.

These informal spaza shops were already a common fixture in local township economic life by the time Somalis first entered the sector. The spaza shop is largely an outcome of apartheid spatial planning. Townships – designated 'black areas' by the apartheid regime – were not envisioned to accommodate or encourage local business enterprise. Their residents were intended to serve as the city's labour force, and commute daily to urban centres to perform low-paid menial tasks for white employers.

Far from encouraging black entrepreneurship, the apartheid government deliberately enacted legislation undermining black South

African business activities in cities and township areas.[1] In the 1950s and 1960s black businesses that reached above a certain level of capital and expertise were obliged to relocate to distant 'homelands' created by the government – discouraging expansion. Other restrictions included prohibiting black South Africans who did not qualify for urban residence from trading, limiting the forms of business that black people could operate, and barring people designated as black from forming companies or partnerships or operating more than one business.[2] Most of these restrictions remained in force throughout the 1970s, slowly eroding only in the aftermath of the 1976 Soweto riots.

It is unclear how the earliest South African spaza shops emerged. The anthropologist Andrew Spiegel has observed that the term 'spaza' resembles the Zulu word *isiphazamiso* and the Xhosa word *isiphazamisa*, meaning 'a disturbance or hindrance.'[3] He believes that shops might have sprung up during the anti-apartheid consumer boycotts of white-owned businesses in the 1970s and 1980s, with new informal black-owned shops viewed as part of a programme of countering the country's white-dominated economy.[4] South African spaza shops relied primarily on a business model that leveraged convenience. Larger supermarkets, which tended to offer lower prices and a wider product range, were difficult for township consumers to reach. At the same time, many residents did not have their own means of transport, resulting in them having little choice but to shop locally. Residents were therefore prepared to pay higher prices for the convenience of shopping nearby, saving them time and transport fares.

However, the competitive practice of relying on pure convenience was turned upside down with the arrival of Somalis and other foreign nationals in the spaza market, who introduced a radically new approach to conducting business. These shops functioned as partnerships rather than sole proprietorships, enabling shopkeepers to raise higher amounts of investment. Partnerships also meant that traders had an extra set of hands on board, as partners could delegate roles to each other, such as serving customers or collecting stock. In the event that businesses succeeded, partners would often open one or two additional shops together, splitting the shareholding between them and hiring additional employees. The partnership comprises the basic foundation of almost any new Somali business.

Somali traders in Cape Town also introduced new means of procuring low-priced goods. Rather than shopping at the nearest wholesaler or supplier, Somali retailers would shop at several different wholesalers, targeting special offers and low prices. In order to do this, traders would share transport to save on petrol costs. Despite common perceptions that migrant traders pool funds to access bulk discounts, in reality shopkeepers purchase goods individually. A Bangladeshi shopkeeper, whose extended family owned a number of spaza shops in Philippi and Mitchell's Plain, explained to me why group purchasing would never work in practice. Different shops had different stock requirements that all needed to be met quickly. It was unfeasible for all his relatives to meet together in advance to arrange collective purchases.

Somali traders across the board also believed that collective purchasing was unrealistic. Shops were individually managed, and joint procurement could also lead to accounting difficulties and in turn lead to conflict. In their opinion bulk discounts were low and did not justify the effort that would be entailed in collective buying. A Somali translator at Philippi Cash and Carry gave this example: 'If you buy R6 000 or more, you get two per cent off non-promotion stuff.'

When Somalis entered Cape Town's spaza market, their competitive edge was founded not only on low prices, but also on broader service offerings. A resident in Pola Park, Philippi, said Somalis' shops were not only cheaper, but their service was 'first class'. He explained that at South African shops, customers would have to wait at the shop counter, while 'Somalis are rather waiting for you'. Other residents cited other beneficial offerings such as wider product ranges, shorter queues, interest-free credit, correct change being given, and longer operating hours. Somali shops also sold 'hampers' – bulk collections of goods sold at a discount – and offered goods in flexible quantities, such as a single egg or tea bag as opposed to having to buy by the box. Because they already had a wealth of knowledge, skills and experience to draw on, foreign traders were easily able to introduce these new retail methods to the spaza market.

As social pariahs Somalis lived in ethnic enclaves cut off from mainstream society. For such communities, making a living demands a degree of entrepreneurship, as finding formal employment is difficult. Somali traders, many of whom have no background in business in Somalia, usually start out as shop employees, and learn the ropes of operating a business through first-hand exposure. After gaining experience along with some basic business skills, they invest their savings in opening their own shop. Among Somalis, such risk taking is not the exception, but the norm. Traders embrace uncertainty and the possibility of failure. 'Business is mainly about luck,' one trader acknowledges when I ask about his business strategy. 'You open a shop and you try your luck.'

These local economic activities have enabled an immigrant community to become economically self-sufficient, but they have also garnered animosity – not only at the grassroots, but also from the country's political elite. In 2011 the Western Cape Province's outspoken premier Helen Zille stated at a 'Business Meets Cabinet' function that foreign nationals operating in the city's spaza market were mostly not genuine refugees, but economic migrants. Apart from being in the country fraudulently, these traders, she also argued, did not pay taxes, did not employ South Africans and were pushing local retailers out of business.[5] Since then the refrain has only increased and gathered momentum. In 2015, an Inter-Ministerial Committee on Migration, which was established in response to widespread xenophobic violence in 2015, complained that foreigners were using illegitimate practices such as forming monopolies and tax avoidance, and were 'dominating' trade in certain sectors. This, it believed, negatively impacted on unemployed and low-skilled South Africans.[6]

Another version of events is that foreign-owned spaza shops have had almost no impact on South African spaza shops, and were simply – in a sense – in the wrong place at the wrong time. Andrew Plastow, who marketed consumer goods to the spaza market in the mid-2000s, believes that South African spaza shops were already in decline by the time migrants arrived in the sector.[7] This was due to the expansion of corporate retail chains into South Africa's townships in the post-apartheid era. Traditional spaza shops could not compete with large supermarkets, resulting in many traders renting out their shops to immigrants. These new shopkeepers resuscitated the spaza market through new business models centred on consumer needs.

Township economies are multifarious and complex. Key stakeholders include landlords, who rent their premises to foreigners, wholesalers, deliverers, suppliers, employees, customers and manufacturers. Not to mention the transitionary potential that shops have due to many Somali traders later exiting the market to establish businesses in the city's formal economy.[8] No study has examined the economic footprint of spaza shops in light of these various parties and linkages, making their overall economic contribution almost impossible accurately to quantify.

Irrespective of how events in the spaza market have unfolded in reality, what is apparent is that many sectors of South African society perceive Somali shops as economically detrimental and harmful. Governance actors intervened to curb immigrant enterprises in many ways, eventually culminating in new legislation, passed in 2017, which barred asylum seekers for the most part from establishing businesses in the country.[9]

At the same time, state organs have done little to address rampant robbery and other crimes that affect foreign shops. Many Somali traders fled unrest in their home country only to encounter yet more threats in South Africa. Traders are routinely attacked by robbers and other criminals, who often leave their victims shot or stabbed. On some occasions, shops are petrol-bombed and set alight. Just operating a spaza shop can be a form of psychological warfare. 'I couldn't sleep at night,' a former Khayelitsha trader confided. Three of his friends were murdered in separate incidents in his vicinity. While lying restlessly in bed at night, his mind would jitter with thoughts of assailants lying in wait.

Somali migrants are largely unwelcome guests in South Africa and criminals target their businesses with relative impunity. With little access to the documentation that they need or legal rights to secure their livelihoods, they are left in a legal quagmire. Over the past decade Somalis have responded by slowly exiting the spaza market. I hear the same thing from several shopkeepers: 'We sell off our shops to Ethiopians.' Some eye new opportunities in connected markets such as the wholesaler and delivery businesses. Others pack their bags yet again and head for new destinations, having recognised that their aspiration of living a simple and unassuming life in South Africa is largely out of reach.

4 | Crime and the Fluid Migrant

Mohamed and I turn right into a quiet open-air parking lot in Mitchell's Plain town centre. 'It's not safe here,' he remarks as I park beneath a twisted wind-swept eucalyptus tree. As we climb out, I suddenly feel exposed – though I'm not sure to whom or what. We walk briskly across the parking lot into a busy business complex. Once inside I breathe a sigh of relief. Along the narrow, pedestrianised streets of the town centre are the familiar ramshackle Somali shops and businesses that I recognise from Bellville. Trickles of grey water, accompanied by the sharp odour of raw sewage, leak across the street. Faint wafts of incense and disinfectant mask it, but not entirely. Mohamed and I climb a dark stairway, which leads us up to an apartment located along a dimly lit corridor. 'The person I want you to speak to knows a lot about Khayelitsha,' he has told me.

Hassan opens the door. He's thick-boned with dark glowing skin and twinkling eyes. He enthusiastically welcomes us into his sparsely furnished one-bedroomed apartment, chatting constantly, bursting with thoughts and opinions. In the process I forget to take my shoes off, as is customary in Somali homes, and follow Hassan straight into his bedroom, which he shares with two housemates. I guiltily think of the sewage-laced street outdoors as I seat myself awkwardly on one of three single beds in the room, trying to ensure that my shoes barely touch the ground. My host is too polite to ask me to remove them, and I am too embarrassed by this time to offer. I hope that by ignoring my lapse, it will be less noticeable.

After settling down and introducing ourselves, Hassan opens up about his experiences of life in Khayelitsha. 'I can give you everything from A to Z,' he says, and proceeds to fire off words in rapid succession. In many respects Hassan has fond recollections of life in the township. 'Khayelitsha is the only area where at least we have a friendship with the black people. At least it's somewhere I can go any time.' However, unlike Mohamed's depiction of Khayelitsha, the peacefulness that Hassan describes has less to do with the absence of violent crime, and more with his relationship with local residents. Hassan had sold his shares in four shops in Khayelitsha a few years earlier due to repeated incidents of robbery. 'The problem of gun pointing was on and off like a daily routine. In a day, two times, you will be gun pointed,' he tells me.

Robbers would usually wait outside his shop and enter unexpectedly as soon as customers left. 'When the customer come out of the shop, then they would start robbing. If you talk to them, they will start shooting bullets. You understand me? Then you have to go under seat cover so that you may not get hit by so many bullets.' These events prompted Hassan to take flight: 'Out of 100 per cent of people coming to the shop, 35 per cent were gunmen.' Eventually, he closed shop: 'I decided that I should not lose my life.'

Foreign shopkeepers' susceptibility to violent crime in South Africa has become so widely publicised in local and global media that it has come to be regarded as a truism. But opinions vary as to the exact nature of such crime. While many insist that crimes are 'just crime' – as opposed to 'xenophobia'[1] – others maintain that the violence exhibits xenophobic dimensions.[2] This tension is aggravated by broad uncertainty as to what 'xenophobic' violence actually entails.

Most understandings of xenophobic violence in South Africa associate it with forced expulsions of foreign national residents from township neighbourhoods and the mob lootings of their shops. These forms of attack reached national consciousness when riots broke out against foreigners in Alexandra township in Johannesburg in May 2008 and spread across the country. Groups of marauding residents ransacked foreign national homes and businesses in a show of nationalism, violence and hate. In the process tens of thousands of people were displaced. According to official records, 62 people were killed, including 21 South Africans, and 670 injured.[3] In response the government hurriedly set up temporary camps to house displaced persons over the country's cold winter months. The words 'xenophobic violence' still conjure up these events in the public imagination more than 10 years later.

Recollections of mob attacks differed slightly among Somalis in Cape Town, whose collective memory of pillaging crowds began two years before the 2008 unrest, in the small seaside township of Masiphumelele, just outside Cape Town. Here, in August 2006, violent mobs hacked down shop doors and shattered windows in desperate efforts to loot and expel foreign traders from the neighbourhood, forcing the township's 71 Somali residents to evacuate the area. Today, local unrest towards foreign national shops still routinely sparks up throughout the country, like bubbles in a simmering pot. Occasionally these bubbles boil over and extend into regional-and national-level violence against foreign nationals or their homes and businesses.

Although these crimes have certainly wreaked havoc on the lives of many foreign nationals and exposed heightened social tensions in the country, they make up a minority of violent attacks affecting foreign shopkeepers. Most incidents of violence experienced by Somali spaza traders in Cape Town did not come in the form of mob attacks. As early as 2006, when Masiphumelele experienced their period of rioting, police had already highlighted an alarming murder rate amongst Somali shopkeepers, with up to 30 Somali shopkeepers being killed in the city between July and September that year. But these individuals had not fallen victim to angry crowds of looters. They had died during the course of seemingly ordinary business robberies.

Robberies affecting Somali traders did not dissipate after the media attention on the 2006 riots had subsided; they continued to escalate. Many traders reported how in the midst of busily attending to sales, they would look up only to find that the customer in front of them was a robber armed with a handgun. Sometimes robbers were accommodating with their victims and left shopkeepers shaken but physically unharmed once cash and goods had been handed over. Other robbers would blandly shoot at their victims in a detached fashion irrespective of whether they complied with requests or not. In some instances traders found themselves being robbed by the police officers charged with protecting their shops.

Anti-foreigner riots resurged in Cape Town in the aftermath of the 2010 FIFA World Cup. This time thousands of shopkeepers averted harm by temporarily closing down their businesses and seeking refuge in packed apartments and guest lodges in Bellville. Many of the shops that did remain open were once more emptied of products and stripped of their infrastructure. But again, in the shadow of these events, other forms of crime were rife. Notably, foreign traders began experiencing an up-tick in hijackings en route to wholesalers. Traders were robbed, shot at and sometimes killed by armed gangs targeting their characteristically white and rusted hatchback bakkies. Key intersections near wholesalers became life-threatening locations, and the mundane task of re-stocking came to feel like a dreaded game of Russian roulette. Police believed that foreign shopkeepers were being specifically sought out, with these crimes making up a significant portion of provincial carjacking figures.[4]

Some attacks against Somali traders were more ominous, however. In late 2009 mysterious assassinations of shopkeepers began occurring in the city. Traders found themselves awakening in the early hours of the morning to lit paraffin bottles being thrown into their premises. A few described having been shot by gunmen without any items taken from them. These crimes lacked the characteristics of typical robberies. Assailants were not interested in stealing valuables, but were more preoccupied with destroying businesses through terror, arson and murder. Shopkeepers and police suspected that competing South African business owners were behind these attacks. While none of the incidents was ever successfully prosecuted, in 2010 police in Kraaifontein arrested five South African shopkeepers connected to 33 cases involving attacks on foreign shops. Errors with ballistics evidence and the refusal of a key witness to testify saw the case collapse.

Although police believed that most crimes against foreign shops were carried out by South African nationals, some crimes were attributed to conflict between foreign shopkeepers. Khayelitsha crime intelligence officials knew of three cases involving 'foreigners fighting', though these made up 'not even one per cent of cases'. Police investigators knew of several incidents where suspects were foreign nationals. For instance, a Philippi East investigator spoke of a case where a Somali trader had laid a charge of intimidation against a Somali competitor who had threatened him at knifepoint and instructed him to close down his new shop.

In Harare, Khayelitsha, a police investigator had come across a matter where two Somali traders had had an argument, which resulted in one trader laying a charge of attempted murder against the other. The complainant later withdrew the matter, explaining that he and the accused were 'brothers' and the dispute had been resolved. 'They sort out problems between themselves,' the officer said. 'Their headquarters are in Bellville and that's where they sort it out.'

By 2012 the general feeling among many Somalis was that Cape Town was no longer drawing new Somali migrants. Fewer were venturing to leave Somalia, as the election of a new government in that country had raised local optimism. Also, tales of violence and xenophobia in South Africa had filtered back home. A South African diplomat recalled meeting a group of women in Somalia to discuss gender-related matters, but was instead bombarded with the question 'Why are you killing our boys?' At the same time the South African government deterred migration to Cape Town by shutting down the city's refugee reception office. In July 2012 it ceased processing new applications for asylum.

The frequent occurrence of violent crime affecting foreign traders in Cape Town does not in itself point to the phenomenon of xenophobia. Somali spaza shops happen to be located in some of the most crime-ridden neighbourhoods in the country. While some sections of the township neighbourhoods I visited were relatively peaceful, others were crime hotbeds where not even police were willing to venture. Violence in these precincts was a common occurrence. Khayelitsha police station, for instance, recorded 251 murders in its jurisdiction between March 2019 and April 2020 alone.[5] Somali traders could therefore have simply been experiencing the same high levels of crime to which surrounding inhabitants were prone.

Understanding xenophobic dimensions of violence, I realised, would require deeper probing. Deeper probing, however, proved difficult. For one, SAPS' annually published crime statistics do not disclose the nationality of victims. Secondly, assessing foreign traders' vulnerability to crime could not be carried out by local surveys comparing foreign national and South African experiences of crime in a set area. Such an effort could run the risk of cloaking real degrees of violence rather than shedding light on them. This was because Somali traders (who operated most foreign spaza shops in Cape Town) were for the most part people on the run.

Flight and relocation were the two frequent responses among Somali traders to challenges posed by hostile and unwelcoming environments. Somali shopkeepers' recollections of crime matched their often vivid accounts of zigzagging movements across neighbourhoods, cities, provinces or the country. While some sought refuge in small towns, others explored new opportunities in neighbouring townships or large cities where they had contacts. Movements were not always sparked by crime, however; some traders closed shop and relocated due to bankruptcy, business stagnation or lack of opportunities for growth.

I never enquired into the apparent ease with which traders seemed willing to cut their losses and seek greener pastures elsewhere. On the one hand, my impression was that they saw life as a gambling act where the more attempts one made, the higher one's chances of success. The words 'business is mainly about luck' echo in my mind, as though repeated effort is the key to good fortune. On the other hand, many Somalis' association with Somalia's rural nomads might have normalised the anxieties about movement and change that restrain more settled communities. Nomads were perceived not as backward vagrants, but almost as holy aesthetes. They were the embodiment of authentic and untarnished Somali values, having chosen a life of simplicity roaming the country's barren shrubland, rejecting the vanities and ambitions of modern life.

Routes chosen by traders were usually unique and unpredictable, with new locations being selected by happenchance, rumour or recommendations by friends or relatives. One trader described starting off in the lush green northern border town of Nelspruit, then relocating to the busy streets of Mitchell's Plain town centre, and a few years later setting up a shop in rural Prince Alfred Hamlet. Another arrived in Cape Town, moved to the coastal town of Hermanus, then established a spaza shop in the mountainous town of Tulbagh, only to return thereafter to Cape Town once more.

'They called us *amakula* in the Free State,' a Somali community organiser whom I knew very well once remarked. I was surprised by his

Figure 4.1: A Somali-owned spaza shop in Velddrif, West Coast (2012). Photograph by Vanya Gastrow.

statement, not only because this was a derogatory term usually reserved for Indians, but also because I had up until then not even known that he had once lived in the Free State. The stories of movement and transience were a strong common thread. Gradually the lines started spreading further and reaching beyond the country altogether – Angola to Brazil to Mexico and America; or north to Libya and across the sparkling azure Mediterranean to Europe; or back to Kenya or Somalia. Some were fortunate enough to find formal methods of travel via passenger flights to America, Australia, Scandinavia and the UK. Most of the Somali students, activists and township traders that I met in 2010 in the imam's office or while sipping coffee in the Blue Café have since left the country. Memories of them continue to hover like ghosts, haunting the ever-changing streets and refurbished shops of Bellville's central business district.

One of the implications of these movements is that compiling an accurate historical picture of crime affecting Somali – and possibly other immigrant – shopkeepers in a specific area is nearly impossible. Somali shopkeepers' tendency to flee in the aftermath of crime means that many new shopkeepers with little experience of crime could very well be residing in key crime hotspots abandoned by previous owners. Shopkeepers reporting the least crime could thus be occupying shops that had experienced the most. Where respondents are either relative newcomers or when victims have fled areas, there is little to go by in trying to assess crime trends other than past police records. But, as stated before, official crime statistics are aggregated and do not disclose the nationality of victims. Assessing rates of crime affecting foreign spaza traders seemed almost as elusive as shopkeepers themselves.

5 | A Window on Statistics Opens Up

How does one ascertain crime rates affecting foreign shopkeepers when victims have fled and official public records on crime affecting them do not exist? I had more or less resigned myself to having to rely on foreign traders' repeated accounts of relentless violence to highlight their susceptibility to crime when unexpectedly a window of opportunity opened, yielding a significant new and interesting insight.

In October 2011, the SAPS Western Cape office emailed me with the good news that an application I had submitted to interview police officers in Cape Town had been approved. I had almost given up on receiving an outcome, having sent the application eight months prior, and receiving little feedback from my several follow-up enquiries. I contacted the office in reply, which then set to work immediately. It put me in touch with relevant station commanders who promptly met with me and introduced me to police officials who could help. Police sector managers happily included me on patrols and put me in touch with community leaders they knew. SAPS' initial evasiveness was now inverted, and the organisation opened its doors to me in welcome. This was a far more effective strategy than the initial response I'd been met with. It made it more difficult for me to paint the police with a broad brush, and allowed for a more varied and complex picture of their roles and predicaments to emerge.

On the morning of 25 October 2011, the station commander of Khayelitsha police station guided me eagerly through the face-brick station building and led me to a small bright office. A police officer

48

peered up at me from behind a bulky desktop computer. A large clear window opened up on the room. A backdrop of Table Mountain and the dilapidated homes and green spring shrubbery of the Cape Flats shone through it. I sat down and introduced myself in a friendly but neutral manner, trying not to seem nonchalant on the one hand or overeager on the other. I was afraid that if I spoke in the wrong tone or pitch, this would somehow raise suspicion and possibly dash an opportunity to obtain crucial data.

But my concerns were unwarranted. 'Yes, we have records of crime affecting foreign shopkeepers in Khayelitsha,' the officer advised enthusiastically. 'You will get a heart attack if you see the numbers.' The officer began reading out computer records: 'In April 2011, there was a 1 500 per cent increase; May 2011, a 12.5 per cent increase; June, 33 per cent decrease.'

I could not believe my luck. Had all my apprehension over crime data been unwarranted? I scribbled down notes as fast as I could.

'Could you email these statistics to me instead?' I asked as I struggled to keep up.

'I can, but they are also on the SAPS website,' the officer advised.

'Really?' I was dumbstruck at SAPS' apparent turnaround in publishing statistics on crime affecting foreign nationals.

'Just look up business robberies,' the officer said, still staring transfixed at the computer screen. 'All SAPS' crime statistics can be found on the website.'

Confused by the reference to business robberies, I asked: 'Do the statistics specifically relate to foreign nationals?'

'No, but almost all business robbery victims *are* foreigners, so you can use business robbery statistics to track crime affecting them.'

I was stunned by the claim. Although Somali shopkeepers had continually spoken of business robberies, these crimes were not what I had had in mind when contemplating violence against foreign traders. My dominant focus had been angry mobs, and late-night assailants setting shops alight, not disaffected youths clutching handguns.

When I returned home, I searched the SAPS website and down-loaded several years of records of business robbery crime statistics.[1] These indicated that business robbery cases at Khayelitsha police station had increased by over 1 000 per cent over the past seven-year period. The same spiralling trend was reflected province-wide, with business robberies increasing from 109 reported cases in 2003/2004 to 1 309 in the 2010/2011 financial year. Robbery rates in the Western Cape have plateaued since 2012 up until the present, but they remain high, with at least 217 Somalis having died of unnatural causes in Cape Town since that year.[2] At the same time robbery rates across other provinces have continued to climb.

A few months later, in May 2012, I contacted the officer again. 'What in particular did you mean by "almost all" business robbery victims are foreign nationals?' I asked.

'Hold on.' There was a brief silence at the other end of the phone. I pictured the officer leaning over and squinting at the large archaic computer screen. 'Our latest data shows that 96.5 per cent of business robbery victims are foreign nationals, almost all spaza shopkeepers,' the officer finally said.

Furthermore, according to the station, South Africans owned approximately 50 per cent of spaza shops in Sites B and C, and for-eigners owned the other 50 per cent. Crime intelligence officials at the neighbouring Harare police station also described that almost all spaza robbery victims in the station's jurisdiction were foreign nationals. Some South African businesses had also been robbed, but these were primarily in the shebeen (informal tavern) sector. According to their 2011 audit, foreigners owned 90 spaza shops (67.7 per cent of shops), while South Africans operated 43 spaza shops (32.3 per cent of shops). Although foreign nationals operated a larger share of township spaza shops at the time, rates of business robbery affecting their businesses were even higher than their relative portion of the market.

I later learned that high robbery rates involving foreign national shops were not limited to Khayelitsha. In 2014 I attended a sentencing hearing for three men found guilty of a crime spree against foreign retailers in the picturesque Western Cape town of George. In court, a police captain revealed that 18 out of 19 business robberies reported at Thembalethu police station in 2011 had occurred at shops belonging to foreign nationals.[3] In the same vein, a 2015 national study by SAPS found that foreign nationals made up 47.6 per cent of business robbery victims in the country.[4] Those targeted were primarily Ethiopian, Somali, Bangladeshi and Pakistani nationals. In the North West Province the percentage was as high as 77 per cent of business robbery victims. Yet foreign-born residents roughly make up between 2.8 per cent to 5.8 per cent of South Africa's overall population.[5]

Although police data can be notoriously unreliable, these statistics still suggested that something was askew.[6] Foreign traders seemed particularly prone to robberies no matter how one looked at it. Official statistics did not shed light on the reasons for this, however. While many instances of violence against foreigners do vividly exhibit extreme xenophobic prejudice towards victims, robberies tend not to be one of them. Assailants in Cape Town's townships were usually youth, whose actions most shopkeepers believed were motivated by economic gain rather than violent hostility. At first glance there appeared to be little relation between traders' perceived foreignness and the robberies they were experiencing, despite their propensity for being targeted.

6 | Fortress South Africa: Informal Justice and Control

A youth sitting with some friends in a dusty parking lot in Philippi East laughs when I ask him about his perception of foreign shopkeepers. 'When I see a foreign shop,' he says, grinning, 'all I see are dollar signs and the potential for quick cash.' Despite this casual reply, surprisingly he holds little overt hostility towards traders; his friends who are listening in are in apparent agreement. 'They are of use to the community,' he explains. 'Their prices are cheaper. You can get a scoop of sugar for two rand. They are also more convenient because they open early in the morning and close late at night.'

The more I probed, the less it seemed as though robbers were particularly motivated by fierce misgivings towards their victims. Police believed that spaza shops were popular targets for robbers because they were cash businesses that traded in easily conveyable goods, such as cigarettes and airtime. To a degree this made sense. An Angolan shoe repairer operating from a wooden shed in Philippi told me that his business had never been affected by crime. 'What are they going to take?' he said. 'I only have old shoes!'

Robbers' economic motives were one thing, but there had to be more to why they selected the targets they did. Robbers' lack of clear malice was accompanied by a particular nonchalance towards their victims. Gradually, I began to comprehend why.

South African township residents are no strangers to violent crime. Many narrated incidents of rape, muggings, assaults and murder either affecting them directly or individuals they knew. But how residents dealt with these crimes differed markedly from the tactics foreign traders employed. In contrast to the flux and disorder that characterised Somali responses to attacks on their shops, residents painted a picture of entrenching themselves, of mustering communal power and fighting back. While foreign traders seemed actively to pursue risk and uncertainty, South African residents sought to confront and overcome it. One particular method of doing this was by closely monitoring and controlling their immediate environments.

Many township communities, I began to understand, were tightly organised, not only on neighbourhood levels, but also on micro block and street levels. Regular street-level meetings were conducted not just on an annual basis, but often on a weekly or even bi-weekly basis. Street committees reported to area committees, who in turn took unresolved matters to ward committees and township-level representatives. These groupings usually fell under the SANCO banner, the umbrella body that represents township civic structures across the country. Unlike seemingly aloof and bureaucratised police stations, community structures such as informal and close-knit street committees were more intimate spaces where victims could build solidarity and draw on communal support.

As a result of their close yet also vast and intricate networks, local community leaders were a force to be reckoned with in many township neighbourhoods. They had the authority to set curfews, close down businesses, resolve disputes, allocate jobs and houses, investigate crimes and oversee the punishment of offenders. 'We are not being governed by the police but by SANCO,' a Pola Park resident in Philippi remarked. Some street committees carried out their regulatory and quasi-judicial roles in a careful methodical manner, while others could unleash extreme violence against suspects without any semblance of due process or proportionality.

Figure 6.1: A field in Khayelitsha identified by police as having been the site of a recent killing by necklacing (2012). Photograph by Vanya Gastrow.

Punishments ranged from extracting an apology and imposing a fine to more severe ones, such as beatings with batons or bricks, necklacing – when a tyre containing paraffin is put around an alleged culprit's neck and set alight – and banishment from the area. A legal aid attorney handling cases arising in Kraaifontein described having come across penalties such as pouring melted plastic on suspected criminals or sjambokking (whipping) them and leaving them in cages in the sun. In Khayelitsha violent forms of retribution were so widespread that data collected by the Khayelitsha Commission of Inquiry in 2012 showed that they accounted for almost a fifth of all murder cases in the township.[1]

To a great extent violent vengeance was as much a means of gaining a sense of control over local surroundings as it was a way of pursuing justice. Several residents cautioned that many of those targeted had been 'just suspects', not conclusive criminals. Residents' committees sometimes inflicted punishments as a way to consolidate their local authority and demonstrate their ability to act. The degree of brutality in many instances also suggested that actions went beyond basic penalties for the commission of a crime. Meting out violence against criminals, suspects or 'skollies' seemed more like a purging, an attempt violently to remove what was perceived as wrong or corrupt within society. Through such acts residents were able to vent deep-seated feelings of social and personal frustration and disaffection, and create a renewed sense of order and control.

When it came to crime, police often played a supplementary role to community structures. Sometimes local residents would turn suspects over to the police once they had completed meting out their own penalties. Other times, alleged perpetrators would pay compensation to victims to avoid a police investigation. Most police officers I spoke to said they received little community co-operation in the investigation of crimes, irrespective of whether the victim was South African or foreign. This was because residents did not trust them with sensitive information. People believed that assisting the police would lead to them being targeted by criminals themselves. The general response of witnesses at the scene of a crime was 'Andazi' (I don't know), even when attacks had occurred in broad daylight.

Community efforts at addressing crime seemed to serve as a deterrent for many criminals. A police investigator at Kraaifontein police station assured me that informal justice mechanisms in Wallacedene and Bloekombos struck terror into the hearts of many potential criminals. 'They attack with pangas, knobkerries and sjamboks,' he said. 'The police pick up bodies along the road. Therefore you do not sommer rob a South African shop.'

Such joint action and aggression seemed not to be the case when the targets of criminals were foreign nationals, however. Community response was subdued – foreign shops did not fall within their fortress walls. 'Life just goes on,' as one Somali retailer put it. Police I spoke to agree with this sentiment. Crime affecting foreigners was not something that residents reacted strongly to. One officer summed up residents' attitude as 'It's fine – you can rob *them* but not a local.' On the other hand, when a South African was affected by crime, as one youth in Philippi described it to me, the street committee would 'deal with you quick-quick and leave you there'. When Somalis were attacked it was different. There was no response from the community because 'they are not our flesh and blood so we don't care'. Another resident stated that when South Africans died – even from natural causes – local residents would come together and hold a prayer ceremony to honour the person, but this did not happen when the victim was a foreigner. Residents heard about robberies from friends and neighbours – sometimes they would walk past burned-down and vacated shops on their way to work – but their focus was on getting on with their own lives. They saw little point in investing time and resources in matters that were none of their concern.

A man sitting in his front yard in Philippi one morning recalled the recent petrol-bombing of two Somali shopkeepers in their shop. The street committee 'did not act at all', he told me, and the Somalis had packed up and left shortly thereafter. But in all fairness, he added, 'the street committee does not have the authority to act alone'. It relied on local outrage and mobilisation. When these were present, the committee would respond and bring order. In this case there had been no outrage from the community, no mobilisation. A Gugulethu youth believed that people did not care when foreigners were attacked 'because of old stigmas about foreign people'. Somali traders said their attempts to seek street committees' assistance had been met with little support apart from polite condolences.

The dormant response of surrounding households enabled youth to rob foreign-owned shops indiscriminately. One I spoke to, who was sitting chatting with his friends on the gravel at the Philippi car wash, admitted that he frequently robbed foreign-owned shops, the same shop more than once, and was not put off if traders recognised him. Robbing these shops was easy, he said. 'Not much will happen because they do not lay charges and the community will not respond.' In contrast, it was 'riskier to commit a crime against a local' as they or their relatives could have links to community leadership. Residents also reasoned that foreign shops were easy pickings for robbers 'They are weak,' was how one resident described it, adding: 'When the Somalis next to me were attacked they ran away.'

At first the overall community passivity towards violent attacks confused me. Somali shopkeepers described most of their customers as 'good' and 'friendly' people. Many residents were at pains to emphasise that they harboured no ill feelings towards traders and appreciated their services. But the generally harmonious interactions described by traders and customers did not mean that traders were fully accepted into the neighbourhoods where they worked. Underlying resentments towards shopkeepers still existed. Many passing interactions as described to me by some of the traders, although these were in the minority, suggested that traders were not completely embraced by the broader society in which they lived and worked. Bored children playing outside shops sometimes taunted foreign shopkeepers and threw stones at their makeshift premises. Every now and then unassuming customers would suddenly deliver hate-filled vitriol – such as over an argument regarding correct change – addressing them as 'fucking kwerekwere' or telling them to 'go back to Somalia'.

On one occasion, while I was seated quietly in a Somali street stall on a hot lazy afternoon in Cape Town's city centre, a middle-aged female customer ordered a bottle of still water from the shopkeeper. 'I want still water,' she emphasised. When she was given the bottle, she asked, 'Is this water still?' 'Yes, it is,' the shopkeeper politely replied. The woman paid for her purchase and then looked him in the eye and said, 'If this water is sparkling, I'll shoot you.' And with that she turned and left. The trader, a composed man in his mid-20s wearing a buttoned-up shirt and jacket, turned and looked at me, alarmed. 'Did you see that? She said that she would shoot me!' he exclaimed. 'This is what we go through.' I regretted that I had barely taken notice of the encounter, having quietly observed the interaction from the corner of the stand without much thought.

Shopkeepers felt they had to walk on eggshells, accepting frequent derision and intimidation for the sake of continued peace. Sometimes their alienation from general society came across in more subtle and unintentional ways. 'Hey, Somalian' was a constant greeting of passersby, recognising traders but also reminding them of their alienation.

Even traders who claimed to have formed close relationships with local residents acknowledged that they were nevertheless outcasts to a degree. Hassan, who spoke enthusiastically of his 'friendship with the black people' of Khayelitsha, told me he'd made significant efforts to get to know his neighbours. Before opening his first shop he'd organised a party for local residents, paying the landlord R1 000 to make traditional beer. 'You know, in every place where you go you can't just pop in,' he told me. 'You have to knock.'

These efforts enabled him to form close relationships with his neighbours, but they were of little assistance to him when it came to crime. The only assistance he had received was from a neighbour who sometimes shot at robbers targeting his shop. But general community support was absent. 'There is no one time where the African people will help you, telling you the truth,' he conceded.

'No, what does that mean?' I enquired.

Hassan continued. 'There is what we call "Andazi" in Xhosa, you see. Whatever they see, they will tell you "Andazi". Even if it is your best friend. Even the owner of the house.'

'And why is that?' I pressed.

'I don't know. It's one thing I'm asking myself up and down.'

Residents for the most part believed that community structures overlooked crimes that affected foreign shopkeepers because they did not attend local community meetings. They surmised that this was due to security concerns, feelings of not being welcome, working hours, language barriers, as well as the fact that traders were tenants and not property owners. 'They keep to their shops,' one resident said, 'and it's better that way.' Somali shopkeepers gave similar reasons for their absence. Many felt afraid of participating in community structures. 'I don't think they would welcome someone like me,' said a Somali trader in Lower Crossroads. Some also believed that they would be extorted for donations and money – 'everyone demands money, even police officers' – while others said they did not have time to participate in meetings because these clashed with shop operating hours.

Hassan and other Somali community leaders had attempted to work with SANCO in Khayelitsha, but the relationship did not work out. 'They are greedy,' he told me. 'They used to have a lot of stories like donations. You have to make a donation for a funeral, which is taking place in PE.' When he and others resisted demands for funding, one of his colleagues received a telephone message suggesting that he not 'play with fire'. He interpreted the message to mean: If you don't contribute to us, then we will kill you. 'They talk shit, man,' was Hassan's conclusion. 'We realised they are the big enemy to us.'

Apart from their absence from community meetings, cultural, religious and linguistic barriers also played a role in preventing the full integration of foreign traders into surrounding communities. Most Somali families lived far beyond township perimeters in Somali enclaves set up in centralised business districts in Bellville or Mitchell's Plain. Traders mainly came to know their neighbours from behind their counters rather than in their living rooms, on sports fields or at school meetings.

As a result, in spite of the constant quiet hum of customers exchanging cash for goods throughout the day, relations between traders and their South African neighbours were far from simple and straightforward. This had a bearing on how they were perceived by the bored youth who stalked their shops, waiting for the right moment to brandish their weapons.

7 | Elusive Justice and Xenophobic Crime

Mohamed introduces me to Mr Rooble by his surname, rather than his first name. I assume it is probably because of his age. Mr Rooble appears to be in his late 50s. He sits quietly in his chair, his face blank. He has come to talk about his shop, in particular the fate of his nephew Ibrahim, who worked behind its small worn counter. The lethargy that I sense from him makes the imam's office feel uncharacteristically dark and sullen. He keeps his account brief and sparse. Mr Rooble's nephew Ibrahim had survived an arson attack on the shop in January 2010. At 2 am assailants had thrown a lit bottle of petrol into the shop. Mr Rooble was not there at the time, as his primary role in the business was to collect stock in Bellville, where he lived. The fire destroyed everything inside, but fortunately all three shopkeepers in the shop managed to escape. Two months later, just as it appeared as though life had returned to normal, robbers descended on the shop again. This time Ibrahim was shot and killed.

There was a faint hope of justice, Mr Rooble said, when the police notified him that they had a lead. They suspected that Ibrahim's neighbour could be implicated in the murder, as witnesses had seen the assailants' vehicle parked in this person's driveway. When Mr Rooble followed up with the police they told him that the suspect was in hiding, but assured him that they would apprehend the man once they found him. When he subsequently tried to follow up again and the investigating officer did not answer the phone, he decided to pay a visit to Philippi

East police station in person. After making enquiries at the front reception desk, police officials told him that they could not assist him unless they received a letter from his attorneys. He subsequently procured a letter from public interest attorneys and returned with it to the station. To date, he told me, his efforts had still not produced any results.

A few months later I queried a police investigator at Philippi East police station about the murder, hoping to provide some feedback to the anxious shop owner. The investigator reluctantly typed the case number into his computer and after a brief pause a record came up. I then understood the officers' reluctance. The investigation had been unsuccessful due to lack of evidence. I enquired about the victim's neighbour, but the police officer shook his head. 'He did have an argument with his neighbour,' he confirmed, 'but there was no evidence or eyewitnesses to link the crimes.'

While the doors of neighbourhood forums were mostly closed to foreign traders, the gates of the formal justice system seemed to lead frustratingly to dead ends. With the exception of a hijacking ring, none of the Somali traders I spoke to about crime had ever experienced a case being successfully prosecuted in court. Most shopkeepers viewed police as well intentioned but ineffective and under-resourced. Police would open cases, but after that traders would never hear from them again.

Police gave many reasons for the failed outcomes of their investigations. Robberies were difficult cases to take on. 'It's easier to solve murders than robberies,' one detective claimed. Murders usually involved people in a relationship with each other. With robberies, suspects were much harder to pinpoint. Police also found that foreign shopkeepers made poor witnesses. Officers arriving on the scene of crimes often struggled to communicate with the victims. Instead of quickly pursuing attackers, they would become embroiled in confused gesturing and broken speech with bewildered shopkeepers. Language barriers led to witness statements that were vague and incoherent, leaving prosecutors with little to go on.

Police also highlighted that foreign traders were not familiar with formal police procedure. Community members would swarm onto a crime scene and remove bodies for burial even before police arrived. 'Sometimes they take the body away because they wish to bury it within 24 hours. As a result, no post-mortem is conducted. It's a nuisance,' was how one officer put it. Some traders would continue working straight after an attack had happened and contaminate evidence. Foreign shop-keepers were also often new to an area and could not identify suspects at an identity parade. 'Foreigners blame anyone,' another investigator complained. 'They point out anyone at ID parades.'

One would think that such challenges would be enough to undo any case, but there was more. Traders' tendency to relocate – 'They move around a lot' – further undid their cases. Not only was this very frus-trating, one police officer told me, but it could sabotage their efforts. 'You must have a witness for there to be a case,' he said. 'We've had some breakthroughs, but when you go back there's another Somali in the shop.'

Criminals were aware of this fact, that traders moved frequently. A legal aid attorney who represented many suspected robbers in Philippi and Khayelitsha said that, basically, criminals took full advantage of this situation. Continual delay tactics, knowing that victims would likely relocate before proceedings were finalised, was something they relied on.

Police and other formal justice strategies are founded on assump-tions of populations as fixed, permanent and familiar with local environ-ments. They are ill-prepared for grappling with groups whose existence is defined by transience and social isolation. At the same time formal state actors show little interest in developing cohesive plans to over-come these barriers. Police used interpreters only on an ad hoc basis and doggedly expected shopkeepers to reappear at their shops when summonses were issued, sometimes years later. Prosecutors shrugged off requests by traders who had relocated to other cities or countries to testify remotely.

Policing efforts showed more vigour towards finding strategies to clamp down on foreign shops rather than to protect them. Police con-ducted frequent raids to search for unregistered firearms, and imposed

fines on operations aimed at penalising businesses that could not pro-
duce licences. Police also hosted and oversaw informal discussions and
agreements between foreign and South African spaza retailers aimed at
curbing the number of foreign-owned shops.

The overwhelming propensity for police cases to collapse – or not
even get off the ground – my research showed me, meant that many
Somalis simply did not report incidents to the police. Despite the high
prevalence of crime affecting his shops, Hassan – who formerly owned
shares in four shops in Khayelitsha – had never reported any cases.
'There is nothing like law in Khayelitsha,' he reasoned, 'so there is no
need.' In his view the most that the police could do was arrest suspects,
and thereafter release them, placing victims in an even more precarious
position.

Hassan had only dealt with police on two occasions. Once, when
'there was too much shooting in the shop – the shooting was going for
the last 30 minutes, 40 minutes' – his neighbours phoned the police.
In the midst of the battle Hassan saw a police vehicle arriving and he
breathed a sigh of relief. But rather than intervene, the police officers
quickly reversed their vehicle and disappeared into the surrounding
streets. 'After the situation was calm they came back,' Hassan said. 'They
try now and have an interview with me. I say to them, "Fuck you."'

Hassan's second encounter with the police occurred when a nearby
Somali shop was attacked. 'There was a day there was serious gun
shootings in one of my neighbour's shops. I went there and one guy was
injured.' The police arrived three hours after the incident. 'The guy was
already taken to the hospital. He managed his own transport, everything.
No ambulance came.' While standing at the scene, Hassan asked a police
officer what the police were doing to help the people of Khayelitsha. 'He
said to me, "My friend, you people you don't have discipline and man-
ners." And I tell him, "Why? You mean that we are doing wrong to have
businesses here?" He said, "Yes. Go to areas which is secure."'

Instead of approaching police, Hassan sought ways to build and
restore relationships with the attackers themselves. 'The guy who was

gun-shotted me, I know him, he's next door. He's so small boy. He's underage,' he told me. Hassan approached the parents of the boy, who apologised for their son's actions. He then confided directly with his attacker: 'Whatever you've got a problem just come to me rather than coming with other guys, new faces, and starting shooting the shops and starting to rob.'

A common thread running through traders' narratives was that they frequently abandoned cases they had reported to police not because they couldn't recognise the culprits, but because culprits or their relatives had approached them either to intimidate them or to strike a deal. One shop-keeper in Philippi detailed how four youth who lived nearby had set his shop alight. Police arrived at the scene while the youth were still there and assaulted them. Despite the suspects being caught red-handed, the trader chose not to pursue the matter. Instead, he met with the youths' parents, who apologised. In many instances, traders believed it wiser to engage directly with suspects than to seek prosecutions because, when cases fell apart, traders were left in a worse position, having 'just created an enemy rather than being a friend to someone'.

A Western Cape police report confirmed a similar picture. It found that: 'Youths from the very community who "hang" around in the neigh-bourhood all day, have been identified as the main culprits robbing Spaza shops.'[1] Traders were reluctant to testify due to fears of retribution 'as the perpetrators in most instances are from the same community and that owners sleep in their shops putting their lives at risk'.[2]

This is not to say that traders were without any recourse at all. Apart from fleeing or negotiating with attackers and their relatives, traders sometimes illegally acquired firearms to defend their shops. As mostly refugees and asylum seekers, they were not in a position to be regis-tered firearms owners; this was the preserve of citizens and permanent residents only. A police captain in Khayelitsha described that a Somali trader 'shot one of my most wanted suspects. The Somali disappeared, but we found the suspect in hospital.' But reliance on firearms also had its downside. Police in the city stepped up efforts to search foreign shops and confiscate firearms. And so possessing a firearm to repel criminals at the same time opened the trader up to the risk of arrest and prosecution.

Somali efforts at arming themselves also garnered a mixed response from local residents. One Philippi resident was of the view that Somali shopkeepers were 'fighting back', that they were 'tired of being the soft targets'. He believed that this would help to quell violence because 'maybe some people will start to respect them'. But other residents were wary of foreign nationals resorting to self-help methods. The idea of having armed foreigners living and working in their neighbourhood was a source of anxiety and fear. In some cases, the use of force by foreign nationals elicited intense public outrage. A Kraaifontein policeman described the aftermath of a fatal stabbing of a South African youth in the area by a Somali trader as a 'war situation'. The stabbing – which was in self-defence – resulted in the eruption of violent rage amongst angered residents: 'The community got involved, they burned tyres, shops, cars, wanted to kill people.' The Somali traders implicated left the area, returning only to meet with the family and contribute money for the funeral. Force therefore also had serious potential drawbacks for traders, as their attempts to resort to violent means were not as easily condoned as South African residents' own vigilante actions.

Other methods of defence used by Somali shopkeepers included less violent protections such as familiarising themselves with local youth who would help them to identify suspects and stolen property. Sometimes they paid youth to keep an eye on their premises, which may have contributed to a more recent flourishing of extortion rackets in Cape Town.[3] Occasionally criminals avoided targeting shops located on premises belonging to influential landlords who wielded local power. But overall, Somali traders' methods of recourse were weak and their attempts few in number. Their inability to garner community support or leverage formal justice avenues left their spaza shops largely exposed to criminals and vulnerable to many different forms of attack.

As a result, even in the absence of direct animosity, traders' isolation and uprootedness rendered them easy pickings for criminals. Locked in

Figure 7.1: A Somali-owned spaza shop in Kraaifontein (2011). Photograph by Vanya Gastrow.

their shops, fearful of robbers, and largely bound by cultural and religious rules that inhibited their socialisation with 'locals', they generally fell outside of the township's social and political circles and the protections these offered. At the same time police difficulties in taking on cases and foreign traders' frequent relocations heightened their exposure.

The varied and often subtle ways in which Somali traders were rendered vulnerable to attacks raises questions about common notions of xenophobic crime. 'Xenophobia' has been defined as 'the fear or hatred of others based on ethnic, national, or racial background'[4] or 'highly negative perceptions of non-citizen groups on the basis of their citizenship and foreign origin'.[5] Most academic analyses of xenophobic violence in South Africa tend to focus on the 'violent orgy'[6] and furious 'scenes of knife-and-stick-wielding aggressors'[7] that characterised the 2008 xenophobic riots.

But the root of the word 'phobia' is fear – not hatred. And fear need not always manifest in aggressive or hostile ways. An equally if not more common response to fear is unease and avoidance. Most violent crime affecting shopkeepers was linked to the social and political discomfort towards and evasion of foreign traders. Residents in the surrounding areas maintained a stable distance from shopkeepers, and community groups were hesitant to intervene in the aftermath of an attack. Police interventions – which were focused more on closing down businesses than on investigating crime – treated shops as hazardous and in urgent need of curtailment rather than protection.

Robbers and other criminals were reassured and in turn motivated in part by these pervasive apprehensions and hesitations. Youth robbed shops with abandon. But rather than seething hate or acute fear, their attitude was more one of cool indifference. Robbers who targeted foreign shops did so with a sense of casual impunity, a belief that their victims were pliable (and largely unprotected) and their lives easily expendable. Such an attitude was not equally afforded to South African counterparts, who, although also subjected to violent crime, enjoyed a greater degree of community belonging, respect and recourse. This fear-driven alienation of traders at the same time generated a widespread sense of fearlessness towards them. Fear and its absence thus emerged as two sides of the same coin, both consistent with the condition of being a pariah.

The structural forms of xenophobia, so prevalent in the neighbourhoods where traders worked, also created a fertile environment for other forms of lawlessness.[8] The ability of local political actors to incite residents to raid and loot foreign shops was not unrelated to foreign traders' social estrangement and their weakened capacity to draw on arms of justice or community vengeance. At closer inspection business robberies and other seemingly 'normal' crimes affecting foreign traders revealed a more comprehensive picture of xenophobia and its varied configurations.

8 | An Ordinary Crime: The Politics of Denial

On 19 January 2015, a 14-year-old South African boy, Siphiwe Mahori, was shot and killed in Snake Park, Soweto. Versions of the incident vary. A crowd had gathered outside a Somali (or, as other reports allege, a Pakistani) spaza shop intending to either loot or rob the business. Feeling threatened, the shopkeeper shot into the crowd. His bullet struck the teenager in the neck and fatally injured him. It is not certain how the teenager came to be there. Accounts range from the youth being a robber, a looter or just an innocent passerby. The killing sparked fury. Over the next few days many shops were looted across Soweto. Seven people were killed, and more than 100 arrested.

The riots in Soweto had barely subsided when attacks broke out in KwaZulu-Natal in early April. Foreign shops were looted and torched, and over 1 000 people were displaced from neighbourhoods surrounding Durban and nearby towns. While condemning the violence, political leaders and state officials were quick to assert that xenophobia was not involved.

A few days after violence first broke out in Soweto, the province's Community Safety MEC Sizakele Nkosi-Malobane assured journalists that 'The actions are pure criminality ... For now we won't declare it xenophobic attacks.'[1] Provincial premier David Makhura similarly attributed the attacks on foreign shops to criminality rather than xenophobia: 'What we saw in Soweto was not xenophobia, but criminal activity. And crime must be dealt with as crime because crime has no colour, class or gender.'[2]

Two years later, when confronted by a planned 'March Against Immigrants' in Pretoria held on 24 February 2017, the political refrain remained the same. The marchers' pamphlet alleged that 'Nigerians, Pakistanis, Zimbabweans, etc. bring nothing but destruction; hijack our buildings, sell drugs; inject young South African ladies with drugs and sell them as prostitutes.'

The then state president, Jacob Zuma, labelled the protests as 'anti-crime' not 'anti-foreigner'[3] and doubted that the march against immigrants could be understood as xenophobic. Instead, he believed, South Africans were protesting because foreign nationals 'open a lot of businesses. It becomes so obvious that the numbers are too big. And with time, people begin to feel "what is this?".'[4] He illustrated the absence of xenophobia among South Africans by describing how the 2015 Soweto riots were sparked when a foreign shopkeeper had shot a South African youth attempting to rob him and 'that became the problem'.

Political leaders in the country have largely veered away from acknowledging the presence of xenophobic sentiment in society when offering explanations for violence against foreigners. Even mob attacks specifically targeting foreign shops are frequently downplayed as 'naked criminal activity'[5] or 'crimes of opportunity'.[6]

In making their assertions, political leaders overlook both overt forms of xenophobic prejudice in the country as well as the subtle every-day process of marginalisation. They avoid tackling popular depictions of foreigners as job takers and criminals; instead, they condemn foreign-ers for provoking South Africans' anger. Such denials reinforce fears and hostilities and enable them to fester. In the spaza market, traders remain exposed and isolated behind their tills, and residents continue to politely shop while harbouring lingering resentment and suspicion. Social dynamics and their outcomes continue unchanged.

Over time, however, political denial generates even more problem-atic outcomes. In particular, when it comes to crimes affecting foreign shopkeepers, responsibility for the bloodied tills, the hijacked bakkies and the burned-down shops becomes increasingly placed on foreign victims themselves. A 2014 Western Cape police report attributed increased robbery rates largely to foreign traders. It stated that these groups were 'essentially economic refugees', who came to the country 'empty handed', rented the 'cheapest premises, which were never intended for business purposes', with 'none or inadequate security measures'.[7] A later police report found that the growth of informal businesses, their 'unusual business hours' and poor security measures were 'a direct contributor to the increase in the incidence of robbery at non-residential premises'.[8] Upsurges in business robberies were pinned on the 'influx', 'mushrooming' and 'spread' of foreign national spaza shops, and shopkeepers were repeatedly described as 'illegal' and 'unregistered'.[9]

By framing traders as primarily responsible for their predicaments, they also become perceived as a social threat and menace. 'Foreign owned businesses are a potential crime generator,' as one SAPS document put it.[10] By entering townships and opening shops, foreign traders lure and foster criminal elements within society. Traders' quest for profit, as it is often perceived, is thus viewed as generating social ills, be they up-ticks in robberies, conflict over competition or provocation of local residents. The proposed solution to the threat becomes less about addressing crime affecting shops and more about acting against foreign national shops themselves as the way to reduce social instability and curtail violent attacks, purportedly provoked and generated merely by the foreigners' presence.

This argument is not simply a political tactic by expedient leaders. It is also to a large extent a genuine belief. The post-apartheid era was one of many 'post' eras that came about in the 1990s. Across the world, responsibility for social discontent, high crime and economic hardship is difficult to pinpoint in a period largely devoid of clear ideologies and visions of how to eliminate these conditions. Post apartheid, South African citizens emerged disorientated from decades of isolation into a globalised and globalising world, encountering new neighbours at their doorstep. This experience was compounded by internal movements to urban areas that had previously been off-limits to many black

South Africans. Newly settled communities perceived foreign arrivals as symptomatic of an uncertain, uncontrolled and overwhelming world, and their anxieties towards them were indicative of their own sense of victimhood in the face of a foreign pariah.

Hence political leaders, spirited somewhat by this same anxiety, believe that varied forms of targeting of shopkeepers, be they attempted evictions of traders or their maiming by robbers, can be explained by foreign traders' own actions. Identifying structural and overt forms of fear and prejudice against shopkeepers will do little to allay local fears when it comes to unfamiliar minorities, and could undermine political efforts to target and contain pariah groups. And so, implicit biases towards foreign traders are not addressed; instead, they are emboldened and further entrenched. Instead of examining the nature of society, political leaders stress the social threat posed by foreign shops. They raise concerns about hygiene, regulation, crime and competition, but only in relation to foreign shops and not their South African counterparts.

By succeeding with this narrative – that is, stripping crimes of their prejudicial features and overlooking deeper societal divisions – political leaders, supported by sections of the country's civil society and intelligentsia, create a space to problematise the foreign shop. Through this process victim and pariah become perpetrator and aggressor. Removing them from society – either formally or informally – becomes one more means of purging and ridding South African society of disruption, uncertainty and malaise. Leaders calling for the curtailment of shops, and their stricter 'regulation', view these efforts as contributing towards a cleansed, stable and cohesive society. Instead of South Africans engaging in deeper internal social reflection, the task at hand becomes solely an external charge of removing the threat.

Part II
Regulation and Containment

9 | The Masiphumelele Shop Threat, 2006

Mohamed peered out of his shop door. Small groups of warmly dressed pedestrians meandered down the sandy dirt road leading past his premises. It was almost 8 pm, and a cold winter's darkness had settled on Masiphumelele's small brick and corrugated metal homes. He was tempted to keep his shop open, as customers often frequented his small, ramshackle business as late as 10 pm. But today was not an ordinary working day. The deadline for foreign shops to close down in the township had passed two days earlier, and despite the apparent peacefulness of the evening, Mohamed was fearful. 'One of the things I remember very clearly was that they said that they would "send their dogs" against us,' he recalls. 'The other thing that I remember was that it was the 28th of August. I will never forget that date.'

Mohamed chose to keep his shop open. He was struggling to afford his R2 500 monthly rent, so ceasing operations could spell eviction. In any event, local police had assured him that he could remain open, as he was permitted to trade by law; they'd told him they would patrol and protect his shop against any danger. He had arrived in Masiphumelele two months earlier, in June 2006, having become one of the two owners of Mandela Cash Store. His 50 per cent shareholding in the shop had cost him R35 000. R20 000 came from personal savings earned over four years working as an assistant in spaza shops in Cape Town and in Upington. The remaining R15 000 had been loaned interest-free from his former employer in Upington, who was also a close relative. 'We help each other, you know,' Mohamed said. 'It's just normal. If the business is successful and he wants to borrow money, then it's my turn.'

Mohamed's shop was a simple corrugated iron structure connected to his South African landlord's house and was stocked with basic food and household items such as bread, milk, cold-drinks, vegetables, sweets and cosmetics. He, his business partner and a shop assistant all lived and worked on the premises together, surviving mostly off simple brown bread and butter sandwiches. Occasionally they would cook dinners comprised of canned curry and bread, or chicken fried with onion and potatoes, served with rice.

Mohamed purchased stock from a variety of wholesalers in the distant industrial district of Epping, where he sought out low prices and special offers, sometimes arriving at outlets as early as 5 am to get the best deals before they sold out. Price discounts were passed on to customers. He generally placed a low mark-up on his goods: 'If you get R6 for 1 kg sugar, that's just for example, then you need to sell for R7 or R8, while some other people sell it for, like, R10.' Although these practices helped to attract customers to his business, many competing South African spaza traders perceived his and other foreign traders' low prices as undermining their own viability.

Whenever Mohamed ran out of stock or change, his first port of call was to run across the street to Buya Buya, a small spaza shop or 'tuck-shop' operated by a short gregarious Somali woman named Hooda and her Ethiopian husband. The couple lived on the same premises with their three children. Hooda and Mohamed developed a good rapport, and readily assisted each other whenever needed. On quiet mornings when customers were at work or at school, they would enjoy brief exchanges about family life and shop activities. His regular discussions with her were a breath of fresh air, an escape from the dark and often isolated recesses of his small store.

On most evenings Mohamed worked until the gradual flow of pedestrians outdoors came to a halt and the street lay dormant. He would then close up his business and walk to a nearby friend's store to watch football. But the atmosphere of Masiphumelele had changed since South African shopkeepers had sent out letters two weeks prior demanding the closure of foreign-owned shops. A number of contentious meetings had followed, where South African spaza shopkeepers, police, community leaders and landlords vigorously debated the fate of foreign shopkeepers. At the same time, shop customers, or even complete strangers walking past him in the street, would warn him that his time in Masiphumelele was soon coming to an end.

Mohamed locked his shop's metal burglar gate and tended to a few more customers through the iron bars. He feared potential danger, but at the same time the night looked quiet and ordinary. While still weighing up his options he noticed the outline of Hooda, her robed chador flickering while she hurried across the street towards him. She reached his shop out of breath, panicked, with no time even for greetings. Looting had broken out in Masiphumelele, she stammered, listing the names of shops in the area that she had heard had already been attacked. Without elaborating further, she turned and ran back into the winter's darkness towards the dim light of her small shop entrance. Mohamed immediately shut his front door, grabbed his phone and dialled the police. A distracted and flustered voice answered the phone. Police were in the process of responding to the looting in the area, he was told, and would come to assist Mohamed as soon as they had the time.

On hearing the news, Mohamed and his colleagues darted around the shop, looking for potential makeshift weapons. They settled on two empty glass soft-drink bottles and a panga. Mohamed sat on a chair, fidgeting with his bottle, and glancing at his colleagues sitting opposite him. Unsure of what to expect, they began making suggestions about how to reinforce the shop, and trying to estimate when the police would arrive. In the midst of discussion, Mohamed's partner cocked his head and the three traders fell silent. In the distance came the soft sound of chanting voices, laughter and chatter. The voices gradually became louder until Mohamed could discern the chant as 'Hamba, Baraka' (go away, Somalis).[1] Shouts and calls soon surrounded the shop, until Mohamed sensed people's presence only metres away from him. Mohamed and his colleagues remained frozen, holding onto the vain hope that the crowd would somehow overlook the silent shop and continue down the street.

This was not to be. Like the start of a hailstorm, a lone stone struck the shop's corrugated iron wall. Before its echo had faded, an avalanche of stones, bricks, pangas and axes descended on the shop's fragile structure. Mohamed could hear thumping, pushing and kicking against his door, and clanging against his burglar guards. Glass shards fell through the window, and hands and arms stretched in, grabbing anything within reach. Mohamed's assistant struck at people's fingers with his glass bottle, which elicited a sharp yell of pain – 'Voetsek!' Seeking alternative ways in, members of the mob climbed onto the shop's roof. In response, the shopkeepers began hitting the roof and shop walls with their makeshift weapons to signal that they were armed and prepared to fight back.

The sirens of two police vehicles abruptly interrupted the chaos. The cars halted outside the shop and police called out and fired rubber bullets to scatter the crowd. Gatherers ducked and ran in different directions, dissolving into the township's dark network of houses and narrow streets. Ten police officers surrounded the shop and checked up on Mohamed and his colleagues. Relieved that they were being rescued, the shopkeepers began to assemble their stock for transport, but the police interrupted them. 'Look, we have a report that some of your brothers are stabbed and you know we have life-threatening things, so we cannot save the property,' they said. Mohamed, resonating with fear and panic, glanced at his shop shelves, still for the most part neatly lined with canned goods, chips, vegetables, flour, cooking oil and the like. As though caught in a dream, he and his colleagues collected a few personal possessions, climbed into the police vehicle, and left. Mohamed was never to return to the shop again. All that remained of the business the following day was a battered and empty corrugated iron shell.

The night of 28 August 2006 momentarily shocked the city and the country. Over the following months dozens of news articles tried to account for why the small, peaceful seaside township had been rocked by violent anarchy. A few days after the attacks had subsided, the Western Cape Premier's Office, alarmed by the display of violent rage, established a peace-building intervention aimed at reintegrating evicted foreign shopkeepers into the township.[2] Government mediators and NGOs descended on the area. Quickly they went to work to address local tensions, arranging meetings, workshops and training sessions with shopkeepers, community leaders, street committee members and political party representatives.

While the Premier's Office acknowledged the harm experienced by shopkeepers, there was something askew in its narrative. Traders – in spite of their trauma and loss of livelihoods – did not seem to be viewed as regular victims of crime. Instead of being portrayed as vulnerable targets of criminal perpetrators, traders were cast as being complicit in their own persecution. A report by the office on the peace intervention process described the mobs as reacting to 'unfair' competition by Somali traders, who charged low prices; it likened their entry into the township to an 'invasion'. It asserted that 'communities in the Western Cape are up in arms over a perceived take-over by Somali refugees and a noticeable threat to their economic survival'.[3] Somalis were 'newcomers' living on 'borrowed space' who 'were not particularly welcome'.[4] Landlords who rented property to them 'had an attitude of oblivion'[5] to ordinary people's aspirations for social and economic justice.

By implication, in the eyes of provincial officials South African residents were the legitimate occupiers of the township; foreigners did not have the automatic right to enter, reside and work there. In this sense the riots were presented as merely a misguided form of self-defence against foreign intruders.

But what marked the Masiphumelele conflict intervention was not only its surprising narrative of events, but also its end product. To ensure re-entry into the township a new peace-keeping endeavour was established in the form of an 'agreement on future business arrangements'.[6] Existing Somali shopkeepers were permitted to return to the township, but on one condition. No new foreign-owned spaza shops were allowed in the township, the number of foreign-owned shops being capped at 15.[7] This agreement stood in clear opposition to South African law. In 2006, asylum seekers and refugees in South Africa had the right to work and to open businesses. The country's constitution enshrined the right to equality, which included the right not to be unfairly discriminated against. Now the state appeared to be intent on opening up a new exception to its own laws.

10 | In the Shadow of Masiphumelele

By 2007 the anguish that had erupted in Masiphumelele the previous year had subsided. The township's conflict intervention process came to a close on Human Rights Day with a programme of festivities and dancing at a nearby school. Foreign retailer representatives had agreed that their countrymen would not open any new shops in the township and South African traders accepted their promise in exchange for peace. No further uprisings were reported in the city or province that year, making 2007 seem relatively free of social conflict and anti-foreigner violence.

But the events of 2006 were not so easily overcome for those who had been adversely affected. After escaping the angry crowds in the seaside township, Mohamed took up employment at a small Somali wholesaler in Bellstar Junction, located next to the Bellville train station platform. When not spending his time politely negotiating sales of bread and bags of peanuts with customers hurrying on and off trains, he became increasingly engaged in community activism. He found a cramped three-bedroomed apartment to rent, which he shared with eight other tenants. Life felt safer, but his ambition of operating his own business to support his intended further education had been stalled. His pursuit of movement, change and advancement had become suspended.

Despite the absence of tumultuous riots in 2007, the year was far from a period of calm. Reported business robbery rates in the Western Cape Province leapt several-fold, from 197 robberies between April

2006 and March 2007 to 635 robberies between April 2007 and March 2008.[1] Nationally, reported business robberies increased by 47.4 per cent. Violence against foreign retailers reached new levels, but the public's awareness of this increase did not. Nor, for that matter, did SAPS'. SAPS had yet to link these surges in robberies to the spaza market, let alone foreign-owned shops. Its annual crime report for that year notes a dramatic increase in business robberies.[2] It describes these robberies as occurring usually in central business districts such as Johannesburg Central, Durban Central and Pinetown. The report cautioned that increases in aggravated robbery were particularly troublesome, as they engendered negative perceptions of security in the country. It called for tough action on the culprits: 'Seen in this light, the criminals committing these crimes deserve the harshest possible punishment. They play an active part in sabotaging the development prospects of South Africa.'[3]

The following year, business robberies were overshadowed by another form of violence. On 11 May 2008 in Alexandra, Gauteng, a community group by the name of Umphakathi organised a lunchtime meeting in the township to discuss a recent spate of crime in the area. During the course of discussion, participants began to raise complaints about the presence of foreigners in Alexandra and their alleged role in criminal activities. These people, residents argued, were taking jobs and houses away from South Africans. Participants in attendance soon became increasingly incensed and embittered, and decided to meet up again later in the evening. Their intention: to expel foreigners from the area forcefully. At 10 pm, when darkness had set over the township, residents armed with traditional weapons, guns and steel bars descended on Alexandra's streets, looting and setting alight shacks suspected of hosting foreign occupants. One South African who refused to join the mob was shot and killed, and a Zimbabwean who was identified through his accent was stoned to death.

The violence in Alexandra did not subside with the break of dawn but continued to rage. Within a few days other townships in Gauteng reported similar violence, and by the end of the month riots had erupted across the country. The attacks shocked the nation and the international community, which had until then perceived the country as a beacon of tolerance and diversity. The attacks left 62 people dead, and displaced over 100 000 people. The state responded by evacuating fleeing foreigners and hurriedly resettling them in temporary shelters and camps.

After the May 2008 violence had died down, a veneer of stability returned to the afflicted areas. Cars and pedestrians filled streets once more. Uniformed children walked briskly to school in the early morning, and residents hung up washing in their yards. With the appearance of peace, foreign traders gradually began to return to their former premises, re-stocking their shelves or starting over from scratch. Although it seemed innocuous enough at the time, their return marked the beginning of renewed crisis.

'Our problem is simple: We are hungry. We are angry. And the Somalis are undercutting us,' Sydwell Citwa of Khayelitsha explained to a journalist in early September 2008.[4] His organisation, the Zanokhanyo Retailers' Association (ZRA), had distributed letters to Somali spaza traders in Khayelitsha a few days earlier, which ordered them 'to close your shops as of 25 August 2008 to 14 September 2008 ... where all matters regarding your existence in our communities are being discussed'.

The return of foreign spaza shopkeepers to Khayelitsha was what had triggered hostility, this time not so much among residents, but from competing South African traders. As in Masiphumelele two years prior, political leaders, state officials and hired mediators descended on the township, the catastrophe of the May events still fresh in their minds. They eagerly went about organising meetings to address local tensions. Foreign traders were accused of opening too many shops and charging low prices, making South African businesses unfeasible. As in Masiphumelele, after lengthy talks Somali representatives agreed that Somalis would cease opening new businesses in the township in return for their safety.

Trade conflicts between South African and foreign spaza shopkeepers were of critical concern to political leaders and state officials at the time. They did not wish to see another outbreak of violence. But soon these fears over the presence of foreign traders in the spaza market were compounded by another concern. By 2009 police finally caught wind that there was a robbery problem in the spaza market. For the first time the SAPS annual crime report of 2008/2009 identified 'spaza shops' as key targets of business robberies. The report argued that 'emphasis on the more sensational shopping mall and supermarket robberies created an idea that these are the only business robberies. In reality most of the business robberies occurred at small to medium businesses.'[5] Robberies were a growing scourge to smaller businesses operating in urban peripheries, rather than for the large, shiny malls and air-conditioned supermarkets in city centres.

Foreign-owned shops, in particular, in these areas were becoming serious targets of robbers. In 2012, SAPS made it known that business robberies affected foreigners disproportionately in the spaza market. Its analysis of 2011/2012 national crime statistics[6] contained the first official mention that robbers were largely targeting foreign spaza shops in the country's townships. But the reason provided in the report for this was that foreigners did not 'bank their money in the conventional manner'.[7]

By the following year the police service was losing patience. Its 2012/2013 annual report struggled to contain SAPS' disdain towards the victims of these crimes. The increases in murder and attempted murder in the country pointed to robbers targeting 'economic refugees'.[8] These robberies contributed to the heightened levels of aggravated robbery rates. More specifically, when it came to business robberies, the report complained that 'the spread of foreign-owned businesses that are also utilised as residences and the utilisation of these residences for cash storages and the lack of minimum or basic security measures on the small business premises' contributed to crimes.[9]

Proposed strategies in dealing with rising rates of business robbery differed markedly from the days when these crimes were thought to affect South African businesses in urban centres. Rather than meting out the 'harshest possible punishment' on culprits perceived as 'sabotaging' the country, the SAPS 2012/2013 report recommended that business and government work together 'to ensure that proper business processes are followed by all businesses'. Tighter regulation of enterprises was prioritised. Read between the lines, this time it was shops, not robbers, sabotaging the country.

At the same time calls by South African retailers against the presence of foreign-owned spaza shops in the country's townships continued to grow, joined by political leaders and state officials. By 2012 informal curtailments on foreign-owned spaza shops had been agreed to in most of Cape Town's townships. New foreign shops were informally prohibited in Khayelitsha, the Strand, Gugulethu, Philippi and Kraaifontein, as well as further afield in towns such as Paarl and Saldanha Bay. Restrictions on foreign spaza trade also arose in towns and cities in the Eastern Cape Province.

Since the mobs of angry residents first marched down Masiphumelele's dark streets that August evening in 2006, foreign-owned shops have been a source of political anxiety and frustration in South Africa. These businesses not only infuriated South African competitors, and potentially triggered xenophobic attacks; they were viewed by many state officials as responsible for the skyrocketing rates of robbery. Without their influx and growth, officials believed, local communities would be safer. The solution to this dilemma was to push back and stem their trade. But in order to do so, policies would need to be identified and developed. This would be easier said than done.

11 | The Shifting Problem and Changing Narratives

The Western Cape Premier's Office report on Masiphumelele depicts the problem posed by foreign retailers in the township in 2006 in clear and simple terms. It asserts that 'the undercutting of prices on goods by Somali-owned businesses' and the 'further arrival of Somali-owned businesses in an existing compact trading space' caused heightened anger among South African retailers in the area.[1] In other words, the problem was a matter of price and numbers. This dilemma was mirrored in Gugulethu in 2009. When South African retailers in the township sent out more threatening letters to their foreign counterparts in June that year, their grievances were more or less the same: Somali prices were too low and their shops too many.[2]

In the view as expressed frequently by South African retailers, state officials and members of civil society, the charging of low prices by foreign retailers was an 'unfair practice' as opposed to a competitive boon. Foreign traders' bargain offerings posed an economic threat to South African shopkeepers, who were not able to keep up with the competition, which was not fair. But over the years complaints expanded and became more elaborate. These adaptations and evolutions in argument were in part fed by the realisation that South African law encouraged rather than prohibited businesses charging lower prices than their competitors. Furthermore, the country's laws did not regulate or limit the number of shops that foreigners could open in townships. Because of these things there was no clear legal remedy to compensate for the alleged unfairness. It soon became apparent that, in the words of the former minister of trade and industry Rob Davies, the government could only deal with foreign shops 'in terms of whether or not people are involved in illegal activity or not … We can't deal with it because people are from a particular national-ity'.[3] New mischiefs therefore needed to be found and identified.

New reasons for antagonisms towards foreign traders emerged. In May 2011, five years after the eruption of violence in Masiphumelele, an organisation called the Greater Gauteng Business Forum delivered letters to foreign spaza traders in nine areas in Gauteng ordering them to close shop. The letters received by astounded shopkeepers differed in a significant way from those delivered in various parts of Cape Town. This time there was a departure from the typical complaints of low prices and too many shops. Specifically, the notice read: 'As from this day … you are served with this notice to close your so-called business, which in terms of the SA rules and regulations is an illegal trading prac-tice'.[4] When interviewed by a journalist, the forum's chairperson stated that 'foreigners who entered the country illegally or don't have a busi-ness licence to run spaza shops should leave'.[5] The espoused threat now posed by foreign shops related to their skirting of trading laws – not just their numbers and competitive practices. This spelled the beginning of a new discourse centred on problematising the foreign shop in terms of illegality rather than economic competition.

The framing of shops as engaged in illegal trading became appar-ent in Cape Town over the same period. Between November 2011 and February 2013 police raided foreign spaza shops in townships through-out the city and fined traders between R1 000 and R1 500 in terms of the 'Local Authorities Act of 1974' for trading without a licence. By 2012, arguments relating to regulatory non-compliance were well entrenched among political actors in the city. At community meetings in Khayelitsha local and national leaders, as well as South African traders, alleged that foreign traders were in breach of municipal by-laws, did not apply for licences and did not possess tax certificates.

On 26 July 2012 the provincial commissioner of police in Limpopo issued a directive ordering police to close down spaza shops that were operating without licences in the province. The consequent raids led to the closure of over 500 foreign-owned shops in the province. Police confiscated traders' stock and equipment and arrested them and their employees. According to foreign shopkeepers, few if any South African retailers were targeted.[6] By 2015 claims of illegal trading were openly being made by senior political leadership. Responding to concerns over violence against foreign national traders in 2015, the minister of small business development, Lindiwe Zulu, claimed that South African business owners had valid frustrations because foreigners did not trade according to the law.[7]

But again – as was the case with complaints about competition – criticisms over unlawful trading often did not align with South African legal precepts. When asked during a television interview in 2015 about which laws foreigners were breaching, Zulu gave a vague and evasive response: 'That's why I'm saying we need to fast-track that, because the regulations are falling short in terms of ensuring that there's proper re-zoning, there's proper infrastructure.'[8]

In actual fact the illegality claimed rested more on perception than legal reality. 'Khayelitsha is a free trade area,' the station commander of Khayelitsha police station informed me in 2011, 'therefore you do not need re-zoning to open a new shop.' He was quite correct. Practically all zoning schemes governing black townships in Cape Town permitted the opening of businesses on residential premises, so long as the dominant nature of the property remained residential. At the same time the City's Department of Environmental Health held that shops did not require business licences because they sold 'pre-packed food', not food that was prepared on site. Nor did shops require business 'permits', which only applied to businesses situated on demarcated municipal trading bays. A representative from the City's law enforcement department summed things up at a meeting in Khayelitsha by clarifying: 'I want to stress. We should start pointing fingers at ourselves. They are not setting up shop on city land, but in your yards.'

SAPS' input into the 2015 National Informal Business Upliftment Strategy echoed the same message. A major hurdle to 'strict compliance', it stated, was that some informal businesses operated on private premises. As a result, they 'cannot be charged in terms of contravention of the by-law on Street Trading'.[9] In any event foreign traders who had been fined by police in Cape Town elected to disregard their fines, and it turned out that the 'Local Authorities Act of 1974' cited on them did not exist.

In contrast to Cape Town, spaza shops in Limpopo did need licences and many foreign retailers did not have them. At the time Operation Hardstick was initiated in July 2012, municipal offices were refusing to issue licences to asylum seekers and refugees. Police raids were consequently more effective in clamping down on foreign-owned spaza shops in that province than in Cape Town. But these interventions petered out after the Supreme Court of Appeal declared that the closure of asylum seeker-and refugee-operated shops was unlawful and ordered the municipality to cease withholding licences on the basis of traders' nationality.[10]

Governance actors came to realise that the application of trading laws was not the quick and effective solution they had hoped for. Although illegal trading still remained a rallying call, with President Cyril Ramaphosa declaring as recently as January 2019 that 'everybody just arrives in our townships and rural areas and sets up businesses without licences, permits', it could not engender effective state action. With this growing awareness in mind, political emphasis slowly shifted to new alleged menaces. Alternative and wider contraventions needed to be identified, and this time with corresponding legal sanctions. But this was not a straightforward task, as any concerted efforts to dislodge foreign shops risked entangling South African retailers in the same expanded legal net.

Pressure mounted on public officials in 2015 in the aftermath of renewed xenophobic violence in Soweto and KwaZulu-Natal. In response to the attacks, President Jacob Zuma convened an ad hoc

Inter-Ministerial Task Team on Migration on 21 April 2015 aimed at identifying and dealing with the underlying causes of the unrest and finding a 'lasting solution' to varied grievances.[11] The task team came up with a new holistic approach to tackling the 'criminality' they believed had provoked South Africans into carrying out attacks on their foreign neighbours. Comprised of 14 ministries, it problematised foreigners in the country as well as their shops from a myriad of legal angles. The result was Operation Fiela-Reclaim. 'Fiela is a Sesotho word for sweep,' the committee announced on 28 April. 'We want to sweep our public places clean so that our people can be and feel safe.' By allegedly breaching a wide range of laws, foreigners sullied the country. To cleanse society and reclaim spaces, the operation evoked multiple laws relating to a broad range of illegal activities. These included the selling of contraband, undocumented migration, the illegal possession of firearms and the running of unlicensed businesses.

The operation relied on the public order provisions of the South African Police Service Act to empower state officials to search premises and confiscate goods without a warrant. Implicitly, Operation Fiela was a promise to rid neighbourhoods of unclean foreign criminals. In doing so, it affirmed and widened perceptions of foreigners as polluting and pestilential, and demonstrated the state's commitment to the figurative health and well-being of the nation.

Operation Fiela lit up the public imagination. News outlets broadcast militarised raids on dilapidated buildings, and featured arrests of handcuffed, often confused-looking foreign nationals. Photographs of confiscated firearms flashed on citizens' television sets with excited news anchors describing the loot uncovered by security forces. Over 460 000 people were searched, with approximately 41 000 people arrested, and 329 handguns and other items confiscated. These instances of illegal conduct provided justification to South Africans for their anger; at the same time it illustrated that the government was taking the necessary steps to address their outrage. 'We've concluded that South Africans are not xenophobic,' stated Jeff Radebe, the head of the Inter-Ministerial Committee on Migration.[12] Instead South Africans' concerns about crime and social harm brought on by foreigners illegally flooding the country were valid.

This was particularly true when it came to foreign-owned businesses. The task team indicated to a parliamentary committee probing violence against foreign nationals that foreign traders' business competitiveness was linked to breaking the law. Particular methods allegedly used by foreign groups to discourage competition included 'forming monopolies, evading taxes, avoiding customs and selling illegal and expired goods'.[13] To deal with these alleged activities, the parliamentary committee recommended the continuation of Operation Fiela, better policing of counterfeit goods and closer monitoring of by-laws and business permits.[14] Foreign business competitiveness was no longer attributed to legitimate practices such as price competition. The narrative had shifted to these shops not only breaching a plethora of laws, but selling imitation and substandard products to unsuspecting South African customers.

The operation found a simple way of sifting out foreigners, while leaving many South Africans undisturbed. In particular it disproportionately targeted business districts with high concentrations of foreign nationals. Although officials were authorised to search for a range of contraventions, special emphasis was placed on the policing of immigration laws. A South African informal traders' representative confirmed in an interview with me that the raids at Cape Town station did 'not really' affect South Africans. She explained that most retailers operating on the station deck were foreign. Furthermore, the issue was more about 'if you didn't have your paperwork, as a refugee'. In this way, South African businesses were largely exempt from scrutiny. By using these approaches state actors could rest assured that foreign nationals would feature disproportionately among those arrested and prosecuted.

Operation Fiela was rolled out throughout the country and deployed in numerous towns and cities in different provinces. But despite bold public announcements of arrests and confiscations, Somali inhabitants in Bellville experienced the operation more as a frustrating inconvenience than a serious harm. A refugee rights attorney explained that many of those arrested as undocumented immigrants were later released, often because they did in fact have documentation, just not in their possession at the time. Two Somali activists in Bellville complained that the primary harm caused by these police and army raids was road closures, which prevented parents from being able to fetch their children from school and inhibited some people from being able to attend mosque. Police also ransacked shops, leaving behind a mess; sometimes they confiscated legal items. But, overall, life went on for the most part with little noticeable interruption. After police and soldiers retreated, shops reopened and life returned to the neighbourhood's streets once more. Operation Fiela could not dislodge the status quo. The number of hardened criminals living among foreign nationals was perhaps not as high in proportion as the authorities had anticipated.

By now the foreign shop 'problem' or 'challenge' was acute. Political leaders had inundated public discourse with accusations of foreign shops fostering violent crime, business collusion and rampant illegality. The presence of these businesses allegedly lured South African youth into committing acts of crime. Their resilience – or rather their 'dominance' – was founded on illegal and unsanitary habits, as opposed to legitimate competitive practice. Foreigners were regarded as deviants. As implied by operation 'clean sweep', they were dirt that needed to be swept away. While attempting to quell public pressure political leaders were inadvertently inflaming it.

12 | Infestation and Backlash: The Soweto Cleansing of 2018

Cumming District is a disgusting, rat and rodent infested mess. If [US Representative Elijah Cummings] spent more time in Baltimore, maybe he could help clean up this very dangerous & filthy place.

Donald J. Trump – Twitter post, 27 July 2019

By purportedly sweeping South African cities and towns clean of foreign dirt by means of Operation Fiela, public antagonism towards foreign spaza shops did not abate. If anything, the operation reinforced the perception of these shops as soiled and contaminated. By mid-2018 public distaste and disgust at the alleged unsanitary practices of foreign spaza shopkeepers was evident. Many South Africans had to a large extent internalised the repeated allegations that foreign shops and businesses were unclean and did not comply with laws. This was dramatically illustrated by the catapulting of an isolated incident in a small town to a national-level emergency that year.

On 11 July 2018 in Hartswater, a small rural farming town in the Northern Cape Province, a police investigation uncovered a factory manufacturing counterfeit products. The police discovered a range of goods being produced and packaged on site, including branded spices, baking powder, instant yeast, sanitary towels and shoe polish. Six Chinese nationals were arrested. To raise their awareness of their work, SAPS posted four photographs of the raid on its Twitter feed, with the caption:

> A counterfeit factory worth approximately R77 MIL has been
> closed down by the SAPS #K9Unit in Hartswater during a sting op
> yesterday. 6 Arrested. Household counterfeit goods seized.[1]

No mention was made of the nationality of those arrested, or who
their customers were. There was also no explanation as to how the
police had come to estimate the factory's value at R77m. Photographs
of the premises looked as though the factory was based in someone's
run-down house, with one room containing old curtains and a wooden
wardrobe. Two accused were released on bail of R5 000 and R10 000
respectively.

The brief and seemingly innocuous post immediately ignited intense
reaction. Hundreds of comments containing furious claims and allegations against foreign shopkeepers were posted on the SAPS Twitter feed:

> 'I buy no shit from these people because they contribute nothing to
> the fiscals of our country, worse of all they sell rubbish.'
> 'They must go back to their countries, this animals.'

The post was shared on other media. On 12 July 2018 a woman by the
name of Itumeleng Madumo Setsgedi posted details of the Hartswater
arrests on Facebook.[2] She claimed – incorrectly – that the police had
uncovered a 'R77 Million Somalian Factory which makes various FAKE
GOODS'. She added that 'The black community is being killed silently.
This is just the tip of the iceberg.' She then described an experiment that
she and colleagues had carried out that compared a loaf of bread from a
foreign-owned shop with a loaf from Spar. The 'makula one', she wrote,
decomposed more slowly than the loaf from Spar, allegedly evidenc-
ing that the former had been tampered with. Her post was shared on
Facebook more than 12 000 times.[3]

Throughout August several videos of so-called fake food being
sold by foreign spaza shops spread rampantly across social media. In
one video, a woman left two-week-old bread allegedly sold to her by

a foreign trader in a glass of water for more than two hours, and complained that the texture was similar to a 'sponge'.[4] 'How is this healthy, how is this safe for our families, for our communities, for our children?' she lamented.

Later that month footage of members of Farmers United of South Africa angrily entering a foreign shop and confiscating expired foods went viral.[5] A woman in the video declares that she will dispose of expired products by 'chucking them in a bin', warning 'don't say you didn't know, fuck'. Outrage had widened. Anger was soon related not only to fake food, but also to the sale of goods past their expiration dates.

By the end of August, the National Consumer Commission reacted and appealed to 'communities to not take the law into their own hands' and leave it to the authorities to deal with the allegations 'within the confines of the law'.[6]

Quickly the state stepped in. Health inspectors raided spaza shops in various parts of the country in search of expired, fake and counterfeit items. One such raid took place in Thembisa on 28 August. Online footage shows plain-clothed community members working alongside health inspectors in a foreign-owned shop.[7] A casually dressed woman assisting the inspectors inside the shop shouts aggressively at the shopkeeper: 'Why you pack the expiry stock? From 2017? No, my friend.' Another community member searching shop shelves complains to the shopkeeper: 'My friend, my friend, you think I'm stupid?' When the shopkeeper asks a woman to leave, she replies, 'Hey, don't tell us not to work!' Suspected expired items were tossed onto a collapsed pile of goods simmering in the hot sun in front of a growing crowd.[8]

The following day, the ANC released a statement. The party was 'concerned with the surge of illicit sale of expired and fake consumable goods and potentially harmful food products'. At the same time it repeated the National Consumer Commission's urging for residents not to take the law into their own hands. But it was too little, too late. According to media reports, that same day 23-year-old Banele Qhayiso, a mechanical engineering student, went to a nearby foreign-owned spaza shop to purchase bread. While he was in the shop, angry and likely opportunistic residents stormed the premises. The shop owner opened fire on the crowd, inadvertently killing his young customer. Banele died in his brother's arms outside the shop shortly afterwards.

When news crews arrived at the shop hours later, a crowd had returned and were helping themselves to its contents. Media footage shows police at the scene helping the traders escape by lifting one of the shop's corrugated iron walls so that they could crawl out from underneath. A rescued shopkeeper lies shaking on the ground, weeping into his hands, while police attempt to lift him up by the shoulders. Unrest persisted for two days and resulted in the looting of hundreds of shops and the deaths of four people.

In response to the violence foreign traders closed down their shops, evacuated the area and sought temporary shelter. Shortly thereafter, on 3 September, the country's then minister of health Aaron Motsoaledi held a press conference on the issue of shop safety. The Department of Health had not been passive throughout the crisis; environmental health practitioners had carried out searches on 454 'food premises' across the country. Despite this, no evidence of 'fake food' had surfaced. Many residents had misunderstood the laws governing the sale of food by confusing 'best before' dates with 'use by' dates. '"Best before"', the minister said by way of clarification, 'that's not the expiry date'. These products could be sold and consumed past their dates.

Nevertheless, legal infringements in the food sector were widespread. Of the premises searched (both foreign national and South African), 281 premises were found to be operating without valid health certificates, 100 were issued with notices to stop operations and 292 were found to be 'non-compliant'.[9] Authorities also seized 2 151 foodstuff items. While it is easy to blame small grocery outlets for these transgressions, conditions were also engendered by weak state oversight. Environmental health inspectors in Cape Town explained that shop owners did not as a rule approach the department to apply for health certificates, but inspectors would visit shops and supply owners with the requisite forms. The

National Consumer Commission similarly pinned the crisis on 'municipalities not implementing by-laws or conducting regular inspections'.[10]

But that is beside the point. The hysteria was only in small part about whether shops stocked expired or fake food, or were otherwise 'non-compliant'. Looters protesting the sale of expired food were all too happy to take items home with them, irrespective of their sell-by dates. Many residents, state officials and politicians had already made up their minds about their dislike of these outlets; what they needed was to find convenient reasons to substantiate this. Informal taverns, outdoor township barbecue or braai stands, or youths dealing methamphetamine did not draw the same reproach. Sure, many foreign-owned shops were likely in breach of environmental health standards, but so were many South African-owned township enterprises.

Roadside braai stands and shebeens, however, did not threaten the natural order of things. They did not force communities to confront difference. Residents were genuine about their misgivings over cleanliness but had misdiagnosed the source of their anxiety. Residents I encountered in Cape Town's sprawling townships had long harboured concerns over shop hygiene and they mentioned having purchased expired items, which they would return for a refund. But their more acute revulsion was reserved for the personal hygiene of traders. 'Shops are great,' one youth told me. 'They motivate others'. He also appreciated that they closed late. However, the same youth stated as fact that traders only used 1.5 litre water bottles to wash and 'use a leaf to brush their teeth'. An elderly man seated with some friends on a Philippi roadside said: 'They throw their dirty water in the road. It's bad luck to touch the water. Maybe that's why there's no employment.' Another resident described traders as physically 'filthy', adding: 'They should not deal with food.' A woman in Philippi said Somalis only bathed with a cup inside their shop. 'Early in the morning you can tell that they have not had a bath. They wrap themselves in a dirty cloth.'

Traders I spoke to about this believed that residents mistook their Islamic prayer ablution, which is performed before each prayer of the day, for bathing, and were unfamiliar with the *miswak* (a small tooth-cleaning stick) they used for brushing their teeth. The 'dirty cloth' the Philippi woman described was probably a sarong, called a *macawiis*, a popular form of dress for Somali men, but usually only worn indoors in South Africa. The unfamiliar was viewed as unsanitary and, consequently, the body of the migrant as repugnant.

'Those who are influxing and coming as flies must stop their businesses and leave,' declared a South African shopkeeper at a meeting at Khayelitsha Resource Centre on 20 March 2012. A Somali community leader objected: 'We seem to be discussing two things,' he said. 'We all know the problem of the new shops. However, we must distinguish this from Somalis. We can't refer to Somalis as "flies".' But the declaration – which the claimer was not asked to retract[11] – had exposed a truth. The alleged infestation was only partially about the shops. It was also about the people inside them, and their differing features, smells, beliefs and daily practices.

Complaints over shops' hygiene were not going to root out the perceived harm. Although legal remedies could help to ensure better environmental health standards, they could not eradicate the primary scourge. Goods could be confiscated, and fines and notices issued, but traders remained busily active in their shops. More needed to be done. The penalties were not commensurate with the outrage. No matter how hard state, party and community leaders tried, the fury over shops could not be resolved. Shop standards were only one facet of a larger and more insidious anxiety – that of social hygiene and national cleansing.

O ver time, the perceived foreign shop problem, which began as a series of sporadic and localised headaches, escalated into a national political dilemma. Senior state officials and politicians viewed foreign-owned township grocery stores as economically threatening, a danger to public health, and as contributing to growing crime and illegality. But these concerns, despite being earnestly and repeatedly articulated by those in power, did not seem genuinely held by those who espoused them, even though the desired solution – curtailing shops – certainly was.

One of the earliest, and most common, allegations against foreign-owned spaza shops was that their activities were economically harmful. State officials and members of civil society as early as 2006 in Masiphumelele were of the belief that foreign-owned spaza shops posed a threat to the economic survival of surrounding communities. More recently, the Inter-Ministerial Committee on Migration asserted that the proliferation of foreign traders negatively impacted on unemployed and low-skilled South Africans. But these claims were not convincing. And they disproportionately took into account the interests of competing South African retailers, to the exclusion of all other parties and economic stakeholders. For instance, the views of shop suppliers, deliverers, wholesalers, producers, manufacturers, consumers, landlords and shop employees were not sought or considered by the Inter-Ministerial Committee on Migration. The sole fixation of such claims was pinned on one stakeholder: the South African shopkeeper. Findings of economic harm were thus made in the absence of any real appraisals of local economies, indicating that allegations were weighted by other concerns and considerations.

When it came to claims of fostering rampant crime and illegality, political leaders depicted the role of foreign traders in two ways. Firstly, they portrayed foreigners as undermining laws through their own deviant and unlawful business practices. In September 2019 President Cyril Ramaphosa put it clearly: 'We want foreign nationals here to obey the laws of South Africa. They must obey the laws. They must live in accordance with our protocols, laws and regulations.'[1] Secondly, political leaders branded foreigners as weakening legality through their very existence. By opening shops in townships, foreigners encouraged local youth to rob and murder; they provoked residents to loot and destroy their shops.

But, as with allegations of economic harm, grievances about the illegality and crime were vague and contradictory. While castigating foreign shops for failing to adhere to laws, political leaders made active efforts to prevent retailers from complying with the law. The minister of police, the minister of home affairs, the national police commissioner and others all rushed to the Supreme Court of Appeal vigorously to prevent foreign spaza traders in Limpopo from being allowed to acquire business licences and thereby legalise their operations.[2] Instead of encouraging legality, they attempted to make legal compliance almost impossible for traders in the province.

Many state actors were willing to break the law themselves in order to curtail foreign spaza shops. In Cape Town police fined shops by invoking patently fabricated legislation, such as the infamous – and bizarre – 'Local Authorities Act of 1974', which did not exist. Police and other state officials also condoned discriminatory extra-legal agreements preventing foreigners from opening new spaza shops in most of the city's townships. The legal compliance of informal businesses itself was often cast as a problem, raising doubt about illegality being at the root of the 'problem'. When foreign shopkeepers in Khayelitsha were found to possess permits, a community leader complained that 'they therefore think they have a right for business, but it is not so according to the agreement'.

At the same time, while vocally expressing high alarm about alleged infringements by foreign spaza shops, state authorities and political representatives were usually mute about the legal compliance and standards of competing South African stores. But many of these shops evaded laws too. A study in Port Elizabeth found that foreign spaza retailers were far more tax compliant than their South African counterparts: 74.5 per cent were registered for tax, compared to only 17 per cent of South African shops.[3] In South Africa businesses earning below the tax threshold are still required to register with the Revenue Service. At one meeting in Khayelitsha the chairperson expressed his disappointment with the compliance levels of South African spaza shops, saying that 'Unfortunately, local people are not tending to permits, only Somalis.'

Governance actors often referred in vague terms to alleged laws that were supposedly being breached. Their refrain was usually that shops breached 'by-laws' or did not possess licences. But township zoning schemes allowed for the operation of businesses on residential premises, and spaza shops often did not need permits or licences to operate. Governance actors' stated concern for and investment in legal compliance and conformity therefore lacked sincerity. Their primary interest was in finding ways to limit foreign shops, often weakening the rule of law in the process.

Arguments for the curtailment of foreign-owned spaza shops as a means to reduce crime also did not add up. police attributed increased rates of business robbery to the expansion of migrant spaza shops in the country. In the view of former Western Cape Police commissioner Arno Lamoer, the 'proliferation' of spaza shops had 'resulted in an upsurge in business robberies and attacks' on these same shops.[4] The proposed solution to this cycle of self-induced violence was to reduce the number of spaza shops. In August 2012 police raided hundreds of foreign-owned

shops throughout the North West Province, and closed down and confiscated their goods.[5] A police representative justified the raids as a measure to reduce crime: 'If a R100 is stolen from a spaza shop it becomes
part of house breaking statistics in the province.' He went on to explain
that 'It is for this reason that several operations throughout the province have seen many foreign nationals who operate business illegally
arrested.'[6] Similar raids took place in the Western Cape and Limpopo
over the same period, with hundreds more traders being arrested and
fined by police officials.

Stricter enforcement of laws offers little protection from violent
attackers, however. Whether or not one is tax compliant is not going to
weigh heavily on a robber's mind when identifying his potential victim.
At the same time, an obvious way of ensuring protection – identifying and prosecuting culprits – was not of high priority to many senior
police and political leaders. In other words, focusing on the actual criminals was not a widespread policing priority. This was not only evident
from policy documents, which highlighted the need for greater regulation more than improved investigations or the 'harshest possible punishment';[7] it was also apparent from the experiences of victims of crime
themselves.

That cases in Cape Town seldom ended in convictions is an understatement. Out of 40 Somali victims of crime that I spoke to, most having been robbed and attacked multiple times, I came across only one
conviction. The accused, Lulamele Tshetshe, had been known to and
recognised by many Somali shopkeepers operating in the city's townships since 2009.

During one of my first interviews in November 2010, a shopkeeper
took my photocopied A4 sheet of paper with a map of Philippi on it.
'Philippi East is also known as the "triangle",' he said, indicating how
the N2 highway and the R300 bordering the township converged into
the geometric shape. Using a pen, he circled three intersections along
Stock Road accompanied by the words 'most hijack' to indicate where
Tshetshe habitually accosted his victims. Just down the road a few

hundred metres away stood the bare face-bricked premises of Philippi East police station. 'Why don't the police just send an undercover officer to wait there?' he suggested. 'They will catch Lulamele easily.'

Police did eventually arrest Tshetshe, in December 2010. The court denied bail, and he and three accomplices were kept in custody. These arrests made a significant impact on the day-to-day lives of many traders. 'Since they've been arrested there is no more hijacking now. The Somali vans are driving freely,' an SRA representative informed me happily at the time. He added: 'When government shows its full force and arrests those kind of perpetrators, then it's likely that the number of cases will decrease and then maybe we're headed to a peaceful environment.'

If it looked like police in Philippi East had finally viewed the hijackings in a serious light and taken decisive action, this was not the conclusion of a report documenting the withdrawal of the case the following year, in November 2011.[8] State prosecutors, the report noted, 'have been unable to disguise their frustration at how inadequate the investigation has been'.[9] Prosecutors' enquiries had been left unattended by the station's investigating officer for long periods of time, and investigating officers repeatedly returned dockets without requested information. In the view of one prosecutor, despite there being clear indications that the accused were guilty of repeated crimes, inattentiveness towards the case had rendered the docket almost void of reliable evidence.[10] Tshetshe was eventually convicted, not in 2011, but four years later.

Prioritising investigations would likely yield better results in lowering crime than monitoring the legal compliance levels of businesses. In Kraaifontein, attacks on foreign traders were prioritised by the station in 2010, leading to the arrest of five South African retailers, who were denied bail. Although the case collapsed and all of the accused were eventually released, since then the police officer believed that targeted attacks against foreign traders had ceased. 'Somalis are no longer as afraid of South African shopkeepers because police are harsher than before and the police approach is different,' he explained. In the event that attacks resumed, 'We will go right to the people we arrested before and detain them again. They got such a fright after this. The main guy got so scared of me.'

Although capable of mustering the resources to raid spaza shops throughout the country, the police were unable to give many critical investigations their close attention. Their efforts were far more invested in and focused on curbing businesses than pursuing offenders. In effect their approach punished victims of crime rather than supported them. This made police concerns about escalating crime affecting foreign shops appear secondary to their more urgent preoccupation, which was ousting these businesses from their jurisdictions.

Political leaders and governance actors also raised alarm about shops' perceived role in provoking South Africans into committing violent xenophobic crimes. South African spaza shop traders often threatened to instigate public violence should their foreign competitors not close down. Police and other state officials would call meetings to placate their anger. The 2009 Gugulethu agreement encouraged Somali community leaders to co-operate with mediation efforts 'to avert any ugly situation from happening'.[11] Similarly, when South African traders attempted to close down Somali spaza shops in Khayelitsha in 2012, police and local leaders arranged meetings to reduce tensions. At these meetings South African retailers openly threatened mayhem. At the meeting that I attended at Khayelitsha Resource Centre on 20 March 2012, a participant warned: 'If you say the 2008 agreement is not going to be implemented, you are breeding anarchy.' Along the same vein, SAPS noted in its input to the National Informal Business Upliftment Strategy in 2015 that there was a need to regulate foreign shops 'in order to reduce xenophobia associated with foreign national traders'.[12]

But, as with responses to business robberies and hijackings, it was the shops, more than perpetrators of crime, that were viewed as the problem. South African traders were given open public platforms to threaten Somali shopkeepers with violence. At the same time the police response to mob attacks on Somali shops in Cape Town was weak. Their modus operandi – to rescue shopkeepers, but not their properties – left shops unguarded and at the mercy of looters, who quickly emptied stores, thereby effectively destroying livelihoods. Those arrested were usually released shortly thereafter. Thus, for most political leaders and state officials, protecting foreign shopkeepers from crime and xenophobia did not seem to be of heightened importance. Nor was illegality, or the economy. The stated reasons for clamping down on foreign shops largely rang hollow. The primary concern for those who exercised power was something else.

14 | The Problem as Legitimacy

In 1920 the government of the Union of South Africa, which at the time was a dominion under the British Empire, was confronted with a dilemma. Shopkeepers of mostly Indian descent had made inroads into key business sectors in the Union and had 'become formidable competitors with European traders'.[1] This latter group had turned increasingly agitated by what they saw as an 'Asiatic menace'. Anger was particularly acute in the Transvaal province, where Asiatics had recently returned after having fled the South African War. This posed a particular headache for the British Crown, as the region's large Afrikaner (or 'Dutch', as it was then termed) population was already resentful of British rule. Mobilisations and complaints by European traders, municipal authorities and chambers of commerce had sprung up across the province. In response, the governor-general of the Union, British aristocrat Viscount Sydney Buxton, established a commission of inquiry into laws regulating Asiatic trade in the country.[2]

The objections against Asiatics, especially 'Bombay Mahomedans',[3] were diverse. They are set out in a worn-out copy of the commission's report held by the University of California's Southern Regional Library Facility (SRLF). Witnesses in the Transvaal testified that Asiatics sent their money out of the country and were a 'source of danger to the public health owing to their unclean habits'.[4] Their trading methods also differed from those of Europeans. They resided on business premises, kept their shops open for longer, habitually sold 'short weight and adulterate foodstuffs', and formed '"rings" to keep out European competitors'. Importantly, by operating businesses, Asiatics were believed to 'close avenues of employment which should be open to Europeans'.

The Asiatic menace was not an isolated phenomenon. During the 1950s and 1960s studies theorising the phenomenon of 'middleman minority' emerged in the United States. Middleman minority groups, they highlighted, are particularly prone to hostility from host populations. Examples of these groups include Jews in pre-war Europe, Indians in East Africa, Chinese in Southeast Asia, and Koreans in North America. Middleman minorities play an intermediary role in host societies.[5] They are usually immigrants or descended from immigrants and bridge what some theorists have termed the 'status gap' between ruling elites and subordinate groups in certain polarised and unequal societies. This entails moving into and offering services in areas that have been neglected and avoided by a country's ruling classes.[6]

Despite their usefulness as intermediaries in distributing goods and services between large commercial interests and downtrodden populations, middleman minority groups often encounter hostility from host societies. Edna Bonacich views these hostilities as stemming from two factors, namely, 'economic matters' and 'solidarity'.[7] She believes that middleman minority groups' economic activities often draw resentment from clientele, competing businesses and labourers. At the same time their group solidarity leads host societies to perceive them as 'clannish, alien, and unassimilable' and ultimately unpatriotic and economically parasitic.[8] Bonacich finds that negative sentiments are made more extreme by the host society's inability to dislodge middleman minorities due to their economic and organisational power. Karen Douglas and Rogelio Saenz argue that cultural features of middleman minorities, such as their sojourner status and in-group ties, give them a competitive edge, which in turn garners hostility from surrounding communities.[9]

What stands out from the above explanations, as well as from previous and recent agitations against immigrant shopkeepers in South Africa, is that hostilities against traders are viewed primarily as a result of traders' own actions. These groups – be they Mahomedans, Barakas, or 'Somalians' – are viewed as attracting hostility through their behaviours, ranging from trade practices, perceived solidarity, their breaching of relevant laws, and allegations of poor hygiene, strange habits and sociocultural differences.

This analysis would hold fast if all societies shared similar levels of resentment and anger towards foreign or minority group traders in their midst. But, despite middleman minorities existing in many countries, not all populations respond to them in the same way. For example, Somali shops in Nairobi, although far more numerous, have not fallen victim to the same levels of violent xenophobia as those in South Africa. This suggests that broader sociopolitical contexts also shape host societies' attitudes towards foreign shops. Levels of animosity are therefore not solely an outcome of the actions and behaviours of foreign traders alone.

Authors such as Frantz Fanon and Mahmood Mamdani bypass engaging with detailed lists of grievances used to explain resentments towards foreign traders and shopkeepers. Instead, they view campaigns against immigrant businesses in newly independent African countries through the lens of postcolonial politics. Both authors believe that hostilities are rooted not so much in foreign shops' trade practices, social inwardness or degrees of legal compliance, but rather in citizens' perceptions of rights. In many post-independence countries in Africa, notions of rights and entitlements in effect were not grounded on formal citizenship or residency but were vested in indigeneity.[10] Those who were not indigenous to a country or region enjoyed secondary citizenship at best, and at worst were perceived as wholly invasive and parasitic.

Fanon describes post-independence nationalist violence as one of the 'pitfalls of national consciousness'.[11] This occurs when calls for democracy transform into claims for 'nationhood'. He sets out how the 'working class of the towns, the masses of unemployed, the small artisans and craftsmen' join the footsteps of the country's bourgeoisie by adopting a 'nationalist attitude'. The outcome, he argues, is that whole societies rise up against 'non-national Africans' and in the process wreck and burn their shops, stalls and businesses. Like Fanon, Mamdani sets out how postcolonial populations attempt to grasp entitlements by attacking and expelling 'nonindigenous immigrants', who are concentrated in middleman occupations.

To a degree, agitations against foreign traders in South Africa reflected these assertions. Notions of rights, whether articulated by the state president or at meeting halls in Khayelitsha, were associated with being black African and 'local'. Speaking at a noisy Cape Town rally in February 2016, former president Jacob Zuma declared: 'We need to change the economy of this country radically. We the blacks who are a majority, but they have very little to do with the economy. And that is the task of the ANC.'[12]

In 2014 Zuma established a new ministry, Small Business Development, whose minister, Lindiwe Zulu, maintained a few months later that the 'participation of black people in the country's economy still leaves much to be desired'.[13] To address this state of affairs she stressed that the country's economy should 'reflect the active and meaningful participation of Africans in particular, and black people, in general'.[14] But 'African' and 'black' in this context have a particular meaning. They do not include those originating from the northern side of the silted, winding Limpopo River.

Calls for black South African economic empowerment are justifiable. The crimes of colonialism and apartheid persist and run deep in modern democratic South Africa. This was patently clear each time I climbed out of my car in the Cape Town's neglected satellite townships. It is also especially evident in the country's high level of economic inequality (the highest in the world, according to the World Bank) that cuts largely along racial lines. But demands for rights grounded on previous disenfranchisement, if not framed carefully, can generate heightened antagonism towards perceived economic rivals. Foreign traders have come to be viewed as interrupting and undermining the promised economic upliftment of previously disadvantaged indigenous citizens.

Figure 14.1: Community meeting at Lookout Hill, Khayelitsha, attended by the then incumbent minister of police Nathi Mthethwa, and the then incumbent Western Cape commissioner of police Arno Lamoer (2012). Photograph by Vanya Gastrow.

At a follow-up meeting at Khayelitsha Resource Centre in March 2012, one South African shopkeeper claimed: 'It is not true that we have xenophobia. We just want to benefit from the fruits of our revolution.' Another likened the arrival of Somali spaza shopkeepers to colonial settlers: 'They come here rich, they find us poor and take advantage of us. It's the same as when Jan van Riebeeck came here – it's exploitation.' These beliefs also exist latently in day-to-day passive assumptions about rights and privileges in local neighbourhoods.

But assertions of indigeneity amongst township residents were not as all-encompassing as the popular 'demonstrations' and 'hostile manifestations' depicted by Fanon and Mamdani. Neither were such sentiments alone powerful enough to drive large numbers of citizens to the streets. The notion of whole societies rising up against foreign traders – propelled by their sense of indigenous entitlement – does not ring true in the South African context if one looks closely at how political dynamics have unfolded in Cape Town's urban outskirts.

'Foreign spaza shopkeepers have nothing but respect for residents,' a tall broad-shouldered woman in her mid-40s tells me on a Kraaifontein sidewalk. She looks at me directly, squinting slightly in the bright morning sun. 'They keep their premises very clean, take out dirt bins and clean the street. They give a lot of credit because they know what struggling is about.'

Her sentiments were not uncommon. 'Somali traders will still sell if I'm 10 cents short, but not Xhosas. This is why I like Somali shops,' a woman seated inside her makeshift house in Philippi told me. She took care to assure me that 'when they came they didn't take anyone's shop. They never actively closed down anyone's shop.' Two youth sitting on a nearby street corner felt similarly. 'If it were up to me,' said one, 'I'd make bigger facilities for foreigners to thrive because as business people they create avenues for growth and the community benefits a lot.' His friend said, 'I cannot agree more. We need to further strengthen their security so that they don't feel threatened.' The son of a Gugulethu spaza shop owner did not visit shops 'to buy, just for small talk'. Somalis, he said, were 'the right people to have because they are trying to make a living for themselves. I would like to see everyone welcome Somalis because they are not doing anything wrong.' A pensioner in Gugulethu pleaded, 'Let's not blame Somalis for our misfortune. Me, myself, I'm suffering...' Then she added: 'I don't have money to buy Xhosa bread.'

Other residents had mixed feelings about the presence of foreign shops in their streets and neighbourhoods. 'It's 50-50,' said a Philippi youth. 'They are cheap, and the people are poor.' On the other hand, he said, 'Local people can't have self-initiated businesses because foreigners took over the market.' Along the same lines a resident in Better Life, Philippi East, stated: 'I have no problem with Somalis, but they should not have 20 shops in Better Life alone because it cancels the chances of local South Africans.' A Khayelitsha resident saw foreign shops' long operating hours and low prices as benefiting her, but also held the view that they 'take away opportunities'. Some residents appreciated foreign shop prices and services but had concerns over hygiene. They described shopkeepers and their premises as unclean, and recalled having purchased certain items that had expired.

A few residents harboured venomous anger, but they were in the minority. 'Shops are no good,' an elderly unemployed woman seated in a garage with some friends in Gugulethu complained. Her face was ashen and furrowed with deep lines. 'They come like a snake. When you come in the morning you see a snake.' 'Mama buys from Somalis,' her friend put in, 'but she doesn't even want to see them.' A group of men sitting in a yard in Lower Crossroads, Philippi East, did not mince their words. 'Foreign shops should fuck off,' said one. 'They are here to destroy local initiatives.' Another in the group opined: 'They are so conniving. They open one shop, then another and another. Then you have five shops owned by one family.'

Despite varying views on the matter, what the great majority of residents held in common was that the topic of foreign spaza shops was not of immediate concern to them. None had ever raised complaints about foreign spaza shops at street committee meetings. They all agreed that the primary actors actively mobilising against foreign businesses were competing South African shopkeepers. A group of residents sitting on a street corner in Better Life, Philippi, held varied opinions about foreign retailers. One suggested, 'We should organise trucks to ship them out of South Africa and back to their own countries.' Another disagreed. 'Shopkeepers should stay because they don't have criminal intentions.' But irrespective of their differing views, none of them had personally mobilised against shops. 'If the community did not want them to be here, they would be chased long ago,' said one resident meaningfully. A Kraaifontein resident echoed this sentiment: 'Somalis are not going anywhere. The group of people with a problem are business.'

It was not the violent everyday hatred of people on the street that elevated the shop 'problem' to a critical country-wide governance dilemma. Even though degrees of animosity were widespread, they did not propel residents to organise protests against shops. Rather, the shop threat was elevated to a national fixation by the political machinations of a key stakeholder in the spaza market – South African shopkeepers. This group has been able successfully to pursue its agendas and drive change through its ability to wield one of the most base of political tools: the threat of mob violence.

The phenomenon of xenophobic mob violence in South Africa has been analysed in detail.[15] Jean Pierre Misago, for example, has long claimed that, despite appearances, such violence is for the most part not a spontaneous eruption of popular zeal. Instead, it is planned and led by specific individuals, usually in pursuit of their own private interests.[16] The spaza shop sector is no exception. The mob that surrounded Mohamed's shop on the winter's evening of August 2006 was not a spontaneous gathering. The attack was planned by South African retailers, whose calls for foreigners to close their shops had not been heeded. After their letters were ignored, and community meetings proved unfruitful, they intentionally sent 'their dogs' to attack foreign shops. South African retailers are not alone in orchestrating attacks on foreign retailers. Shops are often ransacked during the course of strikes, service delivery protests and other seemingly unrelated demonstrations.

Although mob attacks were for the most part a planned and led phenomenon, group participation was largely spontaneous. Many residents described how looters often joined in on the spur of the moment: 'Just one person says "Let's go and do this" – then they all go there.' A man sitting in his yard in Philippi explained the recent looting in the area as being incited by South African retailers: 'Local shopkeepers must have bought certain individuals to fuel the situation so the rest would join in.' Another said, 'When there is something untoward happening in a typical township, it catches the attention of the community, like paraffin being poured on a flame.' People participated without even knowing what the protest was about.

Mob participants were fuelled by a variety of often overlapping motivations. While acute fear or hatred of foreigners may have motivated some, others felt little overt animosity towards their victims. Most, irrespective of their levels of hostility, were prompted by the clear awareness that on some level they had nothing to fear. For many, looting and rioting was a way of taking advantage of an opportunity to grab free items, motivated by the logic that 'at the end of the day we cannot stop these looters, so let's take something for ourselves as well'. Some residents described violent protest as a means to vent pent-up social frustration. 'Most people living in an informal settlement have an anger issue. They're always frustrated,' one Khayelitsha resident maintained. 'And then you find lots of people are sitting there doing nothing. So now you come there and say "Let's go to that shop."'

Attacking or threatening foreign shops can also serve another purpose, especially for local-level instigators. Looting and destroying foreign-owned spaza shops is an effective means of drawing attention to economic and social grievances. A Khayelitsha resident summed it up. 'People are angry with the government and by committing xenophobia they think that maybe government will pay attention and meet their needs.' Many Somali shopkeepers also viewed their repeated targeting as a means of attracting 'attention' from the state.

Shops' effectiveness in drawing political attention lies in their symbolic power. They represent a form of economic mobility that continues to elude many residents, whose lives remain marked by unemployment, lack of mobility and economic stagnation. 'South Africa has a huge problem,' a Philippi resident seated on a Coca-Cola crate outside her cramped RDP house told me. 'We claim to be free, but freedom only benefits foreigners.' This concern is also evident in residents' anxieties over foreign shops' perceived take-over of business 'chances' and 'opportunities'. When poor and seemingly desperate protesters turn on visible beacons of foreign economic mobility, they draw attention to their own socio-economic malaise, the implication and message being that leaders have abandoned their 'own' people. Those in power come across as permitting foreign nationals to thrive while failing their own citizens.

Violent mob attacks on foreign shops therefore put state actors in an uncomfortable position. When police officials attempt to intervene to protect shops, they are viewed as siding with foreigners. Government representatives who did not clearly align with South African retailers at meetings in Khayelitsha were similarly put on a severe back foot. At a meeting there one afternoon South African retailers castigated a law enforcement representative for stating that his department could not evict foreign shopkeepers. One retailer expressed his views forcefully to the official: 'I am shocked because if you work for this government, which says "batho pele, people first". Now you want to leave. It shows you don't put people first. I will follow this up with your bosses.' More outbursts against the official followed. 'If you say Khayelitsha is not regulated, you are trying to systematically oppress the black people,' complained an aggrieved participant; another accused the official of 'trying to oppress the black people in this province as much as he can' and compared him to an apartheid functionary: 'We just received our revolution in our country, but those who used us still have the system to oppress us again.'

Although xenophobic threats or attacks against foreign-owned spaza shops are often localised, their potential political impact is not. Local, national and global media reporting of hostile meetings, nervous press conferences or shambolic attacks amplify the political stakes of mobilisations. Small-scale conflicts and sporadic protests have the potential to be elevated to national-level consciousness. This places even greater pressure on political leaders seeking to maintain and grow their political constituencies.

By positioning state actors in this way, threats or acts of mob violence touch on the very legitimacy of political establishments. Inciting violence against foreign-owned shops is therefore an effective protest strategy, if instigators can stomach the potential harm this entails. Political leaders and state authorities – not wanting to appear as having betrayed their electorate – respond by trying to reassure citizens that their economic interests come first. As Lindiwe Zulu asserted in the aftermath of the 2015 xenophobic attacks, 'foreigners need to understand that they are here as a courtesy and our priority is to the people of this country first and foremost.'[17]

As a result, when threatening chaos, South African retailers' associations find a ready audience of state officials and political leaders. Invitees at meetings in Cape Town included the national minister of police, the provincial police commissioner, representatives from the City's mayoral council, as well as law enforcement and disaster management departments. Officials would usually accede to South African retailers' demands rather than confront them. The acute legitimacy crisis that arises whenever foreign shops enter public debate – the high stakes to politicians' reputations as popular leaders – is the real and underlying threat posed by the presence and expansion of foreign-owned businesses.

In response to mobilisations and attacks on foreign shops, political leaders and state actors hurriedly seek ways of urgently pacifying flare-ups, not strictly out of concern for the victims, but for their own political survival. They do this by calling for the regulation and containment of foreign shops. This reassures populations that political leaders and state officials do indeed have the people's interests at heart, while also pacifying South African retailers. Calls for increased restrictions on foreign-run businesses also tacitly attribute responsibility for local economic stagnation to the proliferation of foreign enterprises, rather than the state's own policies.

The Buxton Commission established by the Union of South Africa a century ago acknowledged the political force of mobilisations against foreign retailers. It argued that 'the only remedy' for alleged dishonest and unlawful trading practices by Asiatics was not discriminatory laws, but rather 'greater vigilance on the part of the authorities in prosecuting offenders'. Yet, at the same time the commission chose not to contest the Transvaal government's discriminatory policies on Asiatic traders, recognising 'public opinion' on the matter.[18] In spite of its recommendation, the commission permitted the Transvaal government to establish separate areas for Asiatic trade and prohibit 'Asiatics' from settling in the province.

Instead of highlighting their fear of threatened legitimacy, political leaders and state actors problematise shops with an array of misinformed or partial reasons in order to constrict them. Shops are portrayed as economically harmful, illegal and unhygienic, and chronic crime affecting them is attributed to their presence, not to the assailants who attack them. Mob violence against foreign shops in this sense is not indicative of an entire people rising up in protest against a foreign menace to claim their national entitlements. It is an uneven and complex display of multiple sentiments, including hatred, prejudice, greed, opportunism, fearlessness and raging disappointment. These feelings and discontents are directed against foreign shops by those seeking to negotiate with an anxious state. In this sense, the perceived foreign spaza shop threat or problem is an outcome of unstable political establishments seeking to retain legitimacy among an impatient populace by showing where their loyalties lie. But how to act on these pronouncements and combat this espoused threat presents altogether other challenges.

15 | Regulating Trade: Informality and Segregation by Agreement

The shop is painted glowing red, making it hard not to notice. Large white curved letters spelling Coca-Cola stretch across its walls, accompanied by giant silhouettes of the soft-drink company's iconic glass bottle. The message 'All pre-paid airtime' is written next to one of the Coca-Cola signs in a similar font. 'That's one of their shops,' a Kraaifontein police officer points out to me. He slows down his patrol car next to the shop and I take a quick photograph with my camera.

A police sector manager in Philippi East is also eager to point out businesses owned by local 'big bosses' in the area. One is a liquor store containing an ATM with large shiny billboards outside advertising Castle Lager, Windhoek Draught and Hunters. He then drives me past a butchery and a neatly painted spaza shop around the corner. These are the businesses belonging to local ringleaders, he informs me.

A few days earlier, while seated in his dimly lit small office at Philippi East police station, he had given me the rundown on crime affecting foreign traders in the area. The informal and densely populated settlements of Pola Park and Never Never had never experienced attacks. 'They do not have any foreign shops,' he said. He described the Philippi neighbourhood of Marcus Garvey, originally established as a Rastafarian commune, as 'mixed race' with 'coloureds, blacks, whites and Rastas', which made the area 'more accepting'. But in Lower Crossroads crime was 'worse because there are big bosses'. He went on to explain: 'There

Figure 15.1: A Burundian-owned spaza shop in Kraaifontein (2011). Photograph by Vanya Gastrow.

are big shops in Lower Crossroads. Some people own one, two or five shops, such as bottle stores and taverns.' When conflicts arose 'they organise the little shops'. This took me by surprise. I had until then assumed that the instigators were small and rudimentary business owners buckling under the competition new foreign entrants posed.

Demands for the removal of foreign-owned spaza shops in Philippi East were primarily being voiced by larger businesses, a police detective told me. 'The bigger spazas are the ones most angry because it's easier for them to determine if they are losing customers.' Smaller shopkeepers in the area had for the most part rented out their premises to foreigners because 'if you rent out you get more'. A Kraaifontein police investigator's narrative was the same. 'The businessmen we arrested were big business. Businessmen with more than one business place. The little guys don't worry about other people.'

The situation in Khayelitsha was more ambiguous. Harare police did not know of any 'big bosses', only supermarkets, and a Somali community representative assured me that the South Africans that he knew operated small enterprises. But a local community activist who had investigated shopkeeper conflicts in the area in 2010 differed. Most of the shopkeepers mobilising against Somalis in Harare at the time were 'big shop owners', she commented, who owned 'at least three shops'. When I asked her why smaller traders were not equally hostile, she gave the same response as many others. The majority of smaller spaza shop owners in Khayelitsha had 'rendered their shops to the Somalis' in return for rent. By renting out their premises, these shopkeepers could earn 'triple the amount' they were making before.

The return of foreign spaza traders from their temporary exile following the 2008 xenophobic attacks was clearly a source of opportunity for some and misfortune for others. They were joined by large numbers of 'Somalians' – the lost, scattered and barely literate youth of Mogadishu fleeing Ethiopia's US-backed invasion of Somalia in December 2006 and its aftermath. Mohamed described it as 'all-out war'. 'Al-Shabaab bring problems but not like the Ethiopian invasion. The whole environment was overrun. They used heavy weapons, not just AKs. There was shelling and tanks.' Before the invasion, fighting was concentrated in certain parts of the city. 'For example, Somalis would arm themselves in Mowbray and Rondebosch, but not in Milnerton,' he said, referring to Cape Town suburbs to help me understand. 'When Ethiopians came, the war spread to every part of Mogadishu.'

A 2007 Human Rights Watch report mirrored Mohamed's account. It found that Ethiopian forces 'routinely and repeatedly fired rockets, mortars, and artillery in a manner that did not discriminate between civilian and military objectives or that caused civilian loss that exceeded the expected military gain'. Their actions, the organisation asserted, showed 'evidence of criminal intent necessary to demonstrate the commission of war crimes'.[1]

The youth of Mogadishu did not leave Somalia immediately. Initially, many thought they would wait it out in the hope that Somali fighters would come out victorious. But this did not happen. The Islamic Courts Union quickly succumbed to Ethiopian bombardments and the radical Islamist militant group al-Shabaab became the largest insurgent force. 'The earliest of them arrived in February and March 2007,' recalled a representative of the SRA, with numbers increasing in late 2007 up until 2009. Mohamed described how hundreds of new arrivals would queue daily at the Department of Home Affairs, leading him and others to volunteer support.

These youth were accompanied by another entrant to the spaza market. Formal supermarket chains had long shunned the township grocery market, but this changed in the early 2000s. They began rapidly to expand into this previously neglected sector, setting up both large supermarkets and smaller retail outlets. Shoprite developed U-Save and Boxer launched Punch, which is now owned by the country's second-largest supermarket chain, Pick n Pay. By situating their outlets in township areas, these large formal enterprises could capitalise on the same key competitive advantage as traditional South African spaza traders: the simple convenience of shopping where one lives. This particular 'influx', though, differed from that of the foreign one in the sense that it was never termed an 'influx' and was not of heightened concern to South African spaza retailers. New corporate entrants remained mostly invisible to political actors, despite their stores' modern aesthetic that jarred loudly with the surrounding impoverished areas.

In response to the increase in foreign-owned spaza shops, South African township traders, especially those with prominent businesses, demanded action from the state. But immediate legal remedies were not available. Recognised refugees or asylum seekers were permitted to work in the country, and there were no laws prohibiting them from opening businesses. Laws governing township trade were also of general application and did not empower state actors selectively to target specific groups. South Africa also has a progressive constitution that protects the rights to equality and dignity. Most foreign entrants in the market were furthermore protected by international law such as the 1951 Refugee Convention. This meant that when South African 'big bosses' congregated angrily at the offices of local councillors or police station commanders, there were no clear legal remedies available to anxious and bewildered officials. As a result, from the outset the foreign shop dilemma was characterised by a degree of legal and strategic creativity by governance actors.

Local leaders and state officials confronting growing hostility from South African spaza retailers initially did not need to look far for a unique path out of their regulatory quandary. When South African retailers threatened chaos, the first port of call for relief was right at hand. The deadly power of local community structures, and their ability to regulate the intimate affairs of township life, created an avenue of possibility where formal legal routes appeared to offer none. These informal regulatory structures could bypass laws and oversee the spaza market on local levels. They could authorise or prohibit new shops, close down errant ones and mediate disputes. In Cape Town, SANCO was seen as the appropriate party to get on board in this regard. But in supporting this route, state leaders and officials implicitly accepted that the principle of rule of law was pliant and optional. It could be discarded when confronted with political pressure and when the rights at issue were those of marginal groups who held little political sway.

SANCO was quick to assist. There were differing reasons for this. In Kraaifontein and Philippi many prominent South African retailers were among its ranks. A Kraaifontein police investigator said that 'big bosses want to be members of SANCO and use political power' to reduce foreign competition. Notices distributed to foreign traders in the township in 2010 mentioned that SANCO had decided along with South African retailers that foreign traders should 'pack and go'. Similarly, letters sent out by South African retailers instructing Somali traders to leave Philippi township in July 2011 were written on SANCO letterheads.

SANCO in Khayelitsha also participated in the informal regulation of spaza shops, but seemingly for different reasons. South African retailers did not occupy key positions in the organisation, but SANCO members still vigorously intervened. A local community activist believed that SANCO members in all likelihood were being bribed. She said that there was only one South African shopkeeper involved in mobilisations in Harare in 2010, who happened to be a taxi owner and 'a powerful guy'. The rest of the participants were all SANCO members. This led her to conclude that local SANCO leaders must have been 'promised something' because 'at the end of the day if you are a community leader or a SANCO member you do not get paid, but you get paid in some way'.

The emergence of informal regulatory arrangements followed a common pattern. They were usually precipitated by South African retailers' associations sending out threatening notices to foreign shops. In August 2008 in Khayelitsha, the ZRA, representing South African traders, delivered A4 notices to foreign spaza shopkeepers in the township. The notices instructed traders to close down their businesses for a three-week period, during which time retailers would discuss the future of their shops. Unlike in Masiphumelele, where police had adopted a wait-and-see approach towards those inciting violence, police in Khayelitsha intervened quickly and charged at least two ZRA members with intimidation. The xenophobic attacks of May 2008 were still fresh in their minds, and officials were determined to avoid similar mayhem. The members later received suspended sentences after agreeing to enter into talks with Somali retailers.

The talks in Khayelitsha followed roughly the same model as those set up in Masiphumelele. Police established a multi-party crisis committee, chaired by local community leader Reverend Mbekwa, to find a solution to the ZRA's grievances. The SRA, which had been recently formed, was invited to participate, and talks between the two organisations were overseen by SANCO, along with the police.

Initially, discussions appeared to go nowhere. Somali retailers, still recovering from the shock and trauma of the violent destruction and evacuations in May that year, were outraged by the demands that they leave the township. 'Our only way to survive is to create our own livelihoods,' one Somali community leader complained to the media.[2] Somalis refused to budge on the ZRA's demands, even in the face of potential death. 'If they must kill us, they must kill us, but we will not close our shops,' another trader told a journalist, adding: 'I will sell here till I die.'[3]

But as talks progressed, traders gradually began to see eye to eye on certain issues. Both groups shared a common business challenge: that of new shops. An SRA representative, speaking in 2011, felt that 'new arrivals' were also a threat to their own members: 'This is even a problem to everybody, to the foreigners themselves, not even to the local shop owners,' he said. 'The moment you have got your shop and you are just making some sort of a living, then another person puts up some kind of shop just in front of you.' Not all of his Somali colleagues shared his view. Another member of the SRA argued that 'the areas are different. You may have one street with 10 shops, and you may have the other one with nothing. So that's the difference.'

After lengthy deliberations, an agreed outcome was reached, albeit under duress. On 28 October 2008, the SRA issued a written declaration requesting Somali shopkeepers who had opened new businesses since the beginning of October to close down. It concluded by stating: 'There is no new shop which can be opened by members of our community' without the association's approval. The following month the SRA signed a trade agreement with the ZRA, dated 27 November 2008.[4] It provided that all new spaza shops in Khayelitsha, whether South African or Somali, must first be approved by both associations before opening. The agreement appealed to 'all stakeholders, such as KDF [the Khayelitsha Development Forum], local leaders, ward councillors, law enforcement agencies, religious leaders, SANCO and all other stakeholders to assist us to enforce these agreement'.

No matter the wording of the agreement, its intent was to stem foreign shops. Somalis protested that they would never attempt to close down new South African shops. Police in Harare said: 'The agreement in Harare says no foreign shops.' In contrast, 'South Africans can open shops anytime.' Asked why the SRA had agreed to these terms, its representative said: 'We signed the agreement in Khayelitsha out of pressure from local people.' He explained further: 'People will ask, why are Somalis signing these agreements? That is probably the answer then. You have to say "yes, yes" – otherwise, you know, someone can even shoot you.'

By the following year further agreements had been entered into in the Strand, Mbekweni, near Paarl, and Gugulethu. The Gugulethu agreement was mediated by the UNHCR and an NGO called the Anti-Eviction Campaign in June and July 2009. It obliged Somali traders to curtail their business activities in three ways. First, they were required to cease opening new shops; second, to fix their prices to those of South African retailers; and third, to ensure that their outlets were not less than 100 metres distant from South African shops.

The Somali Association of South Africa initially attended meetings with South African retailers at Gugulethu police station – 'For the safety of our members we had to attend and say we are going to be in line with you and have a dialogue,' a representative said – but eventually the association withdrew. 'The meetings were becoming more and more dangerous,' the same representative recalled tensely. 'You do not even know if they are going to shoot you.' This potentiality was not merely imagined. One evening, three hours after leaving a meeting, a Somali colleague of his on the negotiation committee was shot and killed in his shop. On the association's decision to withdraw, he said: 'Police were coming one day and not the next. They were risking our lives.' Their decision was made spontaneously one evening. During a particularly heated meeting, both association members excused themselves under the guise of needing the restroom. But instead of making their way there, they walked swiftly to their dilapidated sedan parked outside, started the engine and left.

The Gugulethu agreement notes the murder of the Somali negotiating committee member. It states that the then provincial minister of community safety, Lennit Max, 'promised the Somalis that the police will do all it can to bring the killer of the Somali trader to justice'. Several years later I asked one of the victim's colleagues about the eventual outcome of the investigation. He looked surprised that I had bothered to ask. 'No, nothing. The police never contacted us about it.'

In August 2009 the Anti-Eviction Campaign and the UNHCR announced that Somali representatives had signed an agreement in Gugulethu. The UNHCR hailed it as a victory, their senior liaison officer Lawrence Mgbangson revealing that 'for communities it could be used as a blueprint, but only if implementation is correct'.[5] There was little political or institutional opposition to the agreement. A spokesperson for the Competition Commission stated to the media that not all such agreements fell foul of competition laws. Police announced that their policy was to remain 'neutral' and leave parties to decide on regulatory outcomes. But the Somali Association was less optimistic. 'No, there is no agreement that has been signed actually. I never signed up. I was part of the team and I never signed up myself,' their representative told me.

These informal arrangements soon became the norm in Cape Town's township spaza markets. In 2011 Somali retailers' representatives in Kraaifontein and Philippi agreed to prohibit new Somali shops in the townships, although the word 'agreed' is clearly misleading. A Somali community worker in Philippi described how 'three businessmen organised themselves' to remove Somali traders from Philippi, Philippi East, Nyanga and Gugulethu. One of them, the president of the Cape Peninsula Business Forum, operated two shops in Nyanga and one in Delft, which he rented out to a Somali retailer. The forum reached out to other South African shopkeepers and sent out letters instructing South African landlords to evict their Somali tenants. A few days after the letters were distributed, three Somali shopkeepers in Philippi were shot and killed in separate incidents. The community worker believed at the time that 'there are three or four men behind it. At the last meeting they came to the meeting.'

After the deadline for the closure of Somali shops had passed, South African retailers proceeded forcibly to shut down foreign shops in person. After eight shops had been closed down in Lower Crossroads in Philippi East, police officials intervened and called a meeting. 'It was pure crime. They were supposed to be arrested,' the Somali representative complained. At these meetings, South African retailers unashamedly threatened violence. A Somali representative recalled how at one meeting, South African retailers had warned that if no agreement was reached 'then you going to see what's going to happen to you in December'. In his view such statements amounted to 'a straight threat, which they are not hiding from nobody'. Due to the pressure exerted on them, Somali representatives could not speak their minds at meetings, he said. 'We couldn't feel free. All we could say was okay, here's a problem. What can we say? We could only listen.'

Although a police officer in Philippi East stated that all parties had agreed to prohibit new Somali shops, the Somali representative disputed this. 'I was the person who was involved for the Somali Retailers and I told them straight in the meeting that I won't be able to stop people from opening their shops. But if the police themselves are going to remove them, it's their own decision.'

Agreements regulating Somali trade even existed as far afield as the Eastern Cape, with Somali shop numbers being informally capped in Nompumelelo township in East London in 2010, and in Motherwell outside Port Elizabeth in 2011. In Nompumelelo the local ward councillor endorsed the local agreement, stating to a journalist that 'citizens had agreed' that 'there should be no more Somali spaza shops because of the xenophobic attacks'. When complaints over the opening of a new Somali spaza shop arose in 2012, Major General Ernest Sigobe advised that the police would investigate Somali traders accused of bribing residents to let them open new shops. At the same time municipal law enforcement officials fined a landlord of a new Somali shop R1 000 for renting out a shop that was operating without a licence.

The matter in Nompumelelo escalated to the office of the then Eastern Cape premier Noxolo Kiviet. Her office acknowledged that she had received 'a letter of complaint from Somali national Abdullah Ali Mohamed alleging that he had been refused permission to open a spaza shop in the township by the councillor'.[6] Local Government and Traditional Affairs MEC Mlibo Qoboshiyane then led a delegation of councillors, government officials and law enforcement officers to discuss the matter with the community. The eventual outcome of these consultations did not prove fruitful for Abdullah Ali Mohamed. Instead of upholding his formal legal entitlements, the MEC found that the local arrangement barring new foreign shops from opening in the township was justified and should be enforced.

Somalis themselves were not always opposed to informal curtailments, many viewing them as a means of establishing peace as well as prohibiting new competition. A Somali trader in Nompumelelo was quoted in the media recommending that a new Somali shop be shut down 'in order to avoid xenophobia'. A Somali shopkeeper in Mbekweni outside Paarl likewise protested against the establishment of a new Somali shop in the township, because the owner 'didn't get permission to be there'.

Agreements limiting Somali township spaza trade amounted to a form of regulation, but not in the sense that they created official legal obligations. They were rules that emerged from social and political pressure, rather than legislative processes. Having bypassed official law-making mechanisms, they stood drastically apart from the country's formal laws. They selectively targeted groups based on their national and ethnic origin, and prohibited them from opening new businesses. In most cases, newcomers, by their very nature, were not there when agreements were negotiated and finalised. In effect, then, agreements bound many new traders to terms they had had no role in creating. These local rules also subverted competition laws. By delegating new economic opportunities in numerous urban neighbourhoods solely to 'locals', traders allocated markets on the basis of nationality. Demands for price conformity in Gugulethu were also legally questionable. The overall impact of interventions was that foreign newcomers who resided lawfully in the country and enjoyed the right to work were told to stay out – albeit informally. These arrangements were made in the full view of multiple state actors.

Throughout the Western Cape Province and beyond, forms of segregation arose, not by law but by compelled agreement. Somali representatives agreed that their countrymen would no longer enter black township markets to start up shops. Where new traders were meant to establish their businesses was not clear. Official as these agreements might have appeared, they were not, however, legally binding. The state was not entirely free to act as it pleased. At the same time, local power and opinion, so vital to the enforcement of informal regulation, was not as homogenous and uniform as parties had envisioned.

16 | When Agreements Fall Apart

'That time when Zanokhanyo stopped the things ... was when one boy in Town Two stood there and say he's going to kill someone if they do not stop.'

Khayelitsha resident, interview, 2015

Masiphumelele is located off a quiet scenic road that meanders down to the small seaside suburb of Kommetjie. It is framed by the picturesque mountains of the coastal peninsula. Large swaying eucalyptus trees greet you at the township's entrance, their leaves rustling in the gentle breeze. The area feels markedly different from the expansive parched townships of Cape Town's Cape Flats. It comes across more like a rural town than a mass urban satellite.

Mohamed and I walk into a spaza shop in one of the township's busy thoroughfares. Maryam is expecting us and greets us warmly from behind her shop counter. Her daughter Zamzam is sitting on a stool in the corner of the shop, her face bright and alert. While Mohamed and I speak with Maryam, Zamzam works behind the counter, accepting faded notes from customers and returning coins for change. As with many interviews, this one begins with logistical deliberations. Maryam would prefer to be interviewed at her home across the road, but her husband is away collecting stock and cannot watch the shop. Zamzam chips in animatedly, saying her father will probably be away for a while because he's in Bellville and reminding her mother that they will need to fetch her brother and cousins from crèche.

Maryam eventually agrees for the interview to go ahead in her shop, but it quickly descends into an awkward experience. She is noticeably upset about life in Masiphumelele. 'I was stabbed two months ago,' she says, flustered, showing me a dark scar on her wrist. But before she can carry on, a customer waiting to be served in front of us comes within earshot and we quickly stop talking. Maryam fidgets and looks around while I check my phone for messages. 'My uncle has a phone like that,' Zamzam remarks. She speaks with a 'Model C' accent typical of Cape Town's more affluent public schools. When we are able to talk comfortably again, I ask Maryam about rules governing the spaza market. In December 2011, she says, the 'chief' informed Somalis that they could not open new shops or purchase houses. Just then another customer approaches the till. Sensing her discomfort, and realising that we are not going to be able to maintain a consistent thread of conversation, I end the interview early.

My interview with Abdifatah further up the road is much easier. He and Mohamed excitedly greet each other and share memories of Mohamed's time in the township. We seat ourselves in a quiet bedroom at the back of Abdifatah's home. The front street-facing rooms have been converted into a small shop, where his wife is busily arranging products and assisting the occasional customer. He remembers the August 2006 riots in Masiphumelele very well. A South African business association had ordered South African landlords to evict their Somali tenants. Like Mohamed, the lead-up to events is still etched clearly in his mind. He describes how landlords refused to evict their tenants 'because we need money' and how the South African retailers' response was: 'We will send out dogs to them.' Mohamed looks on, nodding. That was how he remembered it too. After the 2006 violence subsided a few traders returned to the area. In Abdifatah's view the outcome of the 2006 and 2007 peace interventions in Masiphumelele was very effective. South African and Somali traders got to understand each other and know 'who is who'. 'We would greet in the street,' he says.

Despite the limits imposed on new foreign shops, the South African traders gradually left the market. 'South African business owners quit,' Abdifatah says. 'They now run shebeens, are landlords, and do deliveries.' A nearby Somali shopkeeper describes the same scenario. 'There are no more black-owned shops,' he tells me. 'Black shop owners now run shebeens and deliver stock for Somalis. Some rent shops for Somalis and create jobs for themselves.' Restrictions on opening new spaza shops remain in place all the same. 'You can't open a shop in Masiphumelele. We've tried, but it doesn't work. You can only buy an existing shop,' Abdifatah says. This time it is Somalis who are enforcing the agreement, and most of those trying to open new shops are not Somali nationals, but Ethiopians. Referring to the informal prohibition, Abdifatah adds: 'It's not supported by the police and the government.'

Somali traders in Masiphumelele unsuccessfully attempted to use the 2006 agreement to prevent new foreign national arrivals from opening businesses in the area. 'The government says that you can't stop landlords from renting,' says Abdifatah. 'The landlord will say I'm hungry and I want to rent.' Unlike previous South African retailers, Somalis did not garner much state sympathy towards their efforts to close down competing shops. 'If Somalis and Somalis or Somalis and Ethiopians fight, police will arrest one of those,' he says frustratedly. 'People run to the police and then the police come and arrest that person.' The agreement therefore amounted to very little. Whenever conflict arose over its implementation 'one person ends up going to jail for nothing,' he concludes.

'We are faced with an internal problem. The problem is with the people of Khayelitsha,' General Molo tells the audience. Molo comes across like a veteran leader. Unlike Reverend Mbekwa, there is no malice in his tone. He seems more like a parent-figure giving the audience a pep talk. I am at a follow-up meeting at Lookout Hill in Khayelitsha. It is April 2012, and the weather has cooled slightly from the previous month. The light shining through the venue's large airy windows is whiter, less golden. It is the fourth meeting that I have attended in Khayelitsha. The hall feels grey and empty. Just a few people are seated at the front, in a venue that can easily seat a few hundred. Unlike the first tense meeting that I attended, where emotions were raw and explosive, participants now seem fatigued and slightly bored, as though they had to drag themselves to attend. Instead of fraught introductions with darting eyes, the meeting had started with people milling about the hall and engaging in friendly small talk. General Molo continues: 'The people of Khayelitsha are giving land to foreigners and hire containers to foreigners. That is the problem.'

In Molo's view the increase in foreign shops is not due to any 'influx'. 'When we talk about influx we are lying,' he acknowledges. The problem is simple. 'It is the business people hiring to foreigners. We need to leave foreigners alone and talk amongst ourselves. That is the problem that we need to deal with.'

South African landlords – many of whom had previously been shopkeepers – posed a serious stumbling block to the enforcement of the township's informal trade agreement. They were the ones who enabled foreign traders, by giving them access to their emptied garages, gravelled front yards or RDP houses in return for a livelihood. Were it not for these South Africans, Somalis would, for practical purposes, not exist in Cape Town's almost exclusively 'Xhosa' townships.

But General Molo's identification of the problem was not quite accurate. The problem was not only that South African retailers were renting out their properties, but *also* that these traders-turned-landlords were prepared to fight back. Whenever South African shopkeepers in the township mobilised, many landlords would now counter-mobilise in return. One resident recounted how, in 2010, in Town Two a landlord's son had intervened to stop looting by threatening that 'he's going to kill someone if they do not stop'. As a result, the looters, many of whom were his friends, 'changed their minds'.

Because of these individuals, the envisioned backing from SANCO in Khayelitsha was not consistent. 'You can go in one area and find two chairpersons,' a community activist told me. A South African shopkeeper complained to a meeting audience, saying, 'On the one side SANCO says the shops must close, but the other side says the shops must not close,' to which a SANCO chairperson at the meeting retorted: 'The problem is that if I keep the agreement and try to implement it, I am seen as going against the landlords.'

This lack of clear and unanimous local political support made enforcing the agreement very difficult. This was especially the case given that the agreement was not legally enforceable. 'The agreement itself could not be implemented because of the fact that there was no government support of the agreement; it was just an agreement between two business organisations,' a representative of the SRA explained. 'You know, people have got rights of private property. You cannot tell people what they can do with their private property.'

This was correct. The city's informal trading by-law only regulated trade taking place on public land. There were also no formal prohibitions against Somalis opening new shops in townships. If anything, formal laws were generous to township informal economies, permitting the establishment of 'house shops' without the need for re-zoning. Somali retailers' representatives also did not possess a legal mandate to enter into trade contracts on behalf of all Somali nationals, especially those yet to enter the township. Although the agreement had police support in spirit, police had no legal authority to shut down shops themselves. 'The police tell you they can only work to a certain level,' one SRA representative told me. A police officer had advised him that the police service's 'power is limited. Somewhere we cannot cross a border.'

As a result of police hesitance, members of the SRA attempted to shut down shops themselves. But these efforts also fell short. A Somali representative explained that individual Somali shopkeepers wishing to open new businesses brought in lawyers, which 'complicated the whole thing'. 'We would be telling the people to "Stop man, don't open any more shops, this is enough,"' but new traders would argue that 'I wasn't there when you were doing this agreement so I want to do my own thing. The government told me to go and seek work and employment.' The association found that new traders were often further emboldened by the support of a range of local community members – from landlords to SANCO to neighbours.

The 2009 agreement in Gugulethu proved even harder to enforce than the one in Khayelitsha. 'It never worked. It never worked for long,' said a member of the Somali negotiating team. What weakened the agreement, he believed, was the unreasonable nature of the terms. Moving Somali shops 100 metres away from South African shops was highly impractical. Price fixing was also unfeasible. 'You cannot fix the price because me and you and somebody else we are not buying the groceries at the same place,' he pointed out. 'There are different wholesalers in Cape Town with different prices. There are different manufacturers with different prices.' Traders also obtained different prices based on the quantities they purchased. 'Even the wholesalers cannot give the same price for bulk buyers and single buyers.' He had told the negotiating team that the issue of fixing prices was not possible. 'But they were insisting that thing to be there.' As in Khayelitsha, new Somali spaza traders in Gugulethu also ignored requests to close shop – 'because this person is looking for a living'.

Another member of the Somali negotiating team in Gugulethu gave a different reason for the failure of the agreement to hold. 'A shopping mall opened,' he said. Gugulethu Square, a large shopping centre containing a Shoprite and a Spar supermarket, opened its automatic glass doors in the centre of the township in January 2010, just a few months after the agreement was entered into. Given the proximity of the mall, traders in the surrounding vicinity could not charge inflated prices.

These obstacles and challenges meant that the Gugulethu agreement 'was just some few months and it just ended, like that,' one Somali negotiator stated. He added reflectively, 'I think everybody got tired of it. You know, some things they will just start and then after some time they will just perish by themselves.'

The agreement in Lower Crossroads in Philippi suffered from the same affliction as the one in Khayelitsha: that of SANCO being divided.

Although South African retailers sent out threatening letters under the banner of SANCO in June 2011, it soon became clear that these mobilisations did not have the organisation's unanimous support. 'Local shops are not united because some close down and open to rent to foreign shops,' an elderly SANCO member in Lower Crossroads said, and some of these shopkeepers-turned-landlords were also members of SANCO.

Most of the South African landlords I met seemed not to carry very much political sway or be of economic importance. Sometimes they were single mothers trying to cope with unruly toddlers or lingering teenagers. There was also the odd pensioner or unemployed resident. But there were exceptions to this state of affairs. As with South African retailers, some landlords could also be classified as 'big bosses'. They were able to expand their township business footprint by renting out shop premises to foreigners, thereby freeing up their time to invest in new ventures, be these shebeens, taxis or new spaza shops. These former shopkeepers also wielded influence in local political affairs and governance. The owner of a formal licensed shebeen in Philippi had attended meetings at Philippi East police station to block South African retailers' efforts to close down Somali spaza shops. He had previously operated a spaza shop in Philippi himself, but rented out the business to Somali traders so that he could start up a shebeen. He relied on his tenants to operate the shop as he could not manage both businesses alone.

Informal trade agreements were therefore very difficult to enforce. They lacked clear local popular and political support, and police could only assist to a degree. But this did not mean that they were completely obsolete. By far the majority of the Somali shopkeepers I interviewed from Khayelitsha between late 2010 and 2011 had opened their businesses before 2008. Philippi, by contrast, was full of newcomers, some only having opened shop a few months prior. It seemed to me that the 2008 agreement in Khayelitsha had played a role in this: new Somali traders were bypassing that township and opening shops in adjacent Philippi.

Somalis were aware of the inability of the state to intervene in curbing their businesses. Standing in a dusty township parking lot, a community leader explained his strategy to me. 'When I call upon the government to take action against new shops, I don't really want it to go and remove new Somali businesses,' he said. His statement seemed nonsensical at first, but then he elaborated. 'I know that the government can't do anything.' His calls on the state were instead intended to draw out conflicts and frustrate South African retailers, while at the same time demonstrate solidarity with them. Eventually, disillusioned and exhausted South African traders would abandon their efforts and life would go back to 'normal'. He was right, but only in the short term.

17 | Legal Imaginaries: Trading without a Licence

'Do you feel as though the police make things worse rather than better?' a police sector manager asks me. I am accompanying him while he is patrolling the streets of Philippi East. I awkwardly laugh off his question to deflect having to answer. We continue driving for a short distance, and I mull over what he'd said.

'Why did you ask me that?' I finally ask, curious to hear the answer.

'Oh, I was thinking about the fining that you were asking about,' he says. 'I don't think it's helping the situation.'

Later, when he drops me off at Philippi East police station, I ask him whether he knows who ordered the fining operation.

'The orders came from above,' he replies vaguely. I decide not to press the issue any further, and thank him for his time.

A couple of weeks earlier, in November 2011, I had met Omar, a Somali community activist, to find out more about mobilisations against Somali spaza shops in Philippi earlier that year. We had arranged to meet at Nando's in Tyger Valley, the fast-food restaurant being more anonymous than Little Mogadishu in Bellville. Conveniently, too, it serves halal food. It is not that Omar wishes to meet with me discreetly; this was my suggestion. I sometimes find the stark visibility of being a white female researcher in Bellville something of a weight. Sometimes I prefer to meet in the more diverse and familiar interior of the popular South African chicken takeout franchise. We find a table and I switch on my voice recorder. The restaurant is busy and so, unfortunately, loud chatter reverberates over the bad saxophone music coming out of the restaurant's speakers; together they almost drown our voices.

Omar speaks animatedly about recent meetings with South African retailers in Philippi. But then the conversation takes a surprising twist. 'Yesterday's meeting,' he says, 'in the beginning it was okay, but then it seems like the government departments are involved. They have been using some of the Metro Police friends.' The Metro Police serve the City of Cape Town's law enforcement department. They are responsible for enforcing the city's by-laws and traffic regulations. 'Some of the Metro Police officers went to Somali shops in Gugulethu and Nyanga, where they issued fines against Somalis of R1 000 or R1 500.' By this stage Omar is speaking more hurriedly and the sense of anxiety at the table is not helped by a baby crying loudly in the background. 'They said, "You don't have business licence then you should close your shop,"' he explained. The same operations had occurred in Khayelitsha the previous month. 'They are not going to check the South Africans and they are not going to the other nationals. They are using the Local Authorities Act of 1974, which we cannot find in the library.'

By this stage I had little idea what he was talking about, having heard only the word 'library' over all the noise. Omar probably noticed my confusion because he went straight to the point. He riffled through some papers in his file and passed me a crumpled fine. It cited in clear letters: 'Local Authorities Act 19 of 1974 sect 8 sub sect 1(a) Trading without a licence'. 'We have consulted already with UCT law clinic,' he added. 'This Act you cannot get.'

The notion that legislation that did not exist could be cited on fines seemed impossible to me, so later that evening I decided to research the legislation myself. Traders would need to know which law they were breaching if they were to remedy the situation. I would succeed, I thought to myself, where UCT's Refugee Rights Clinic had failed. But when I googled 'Local Authorities Act' the only South African legislation that appeared on my screen was the Black Local Authorities Act of 1982.

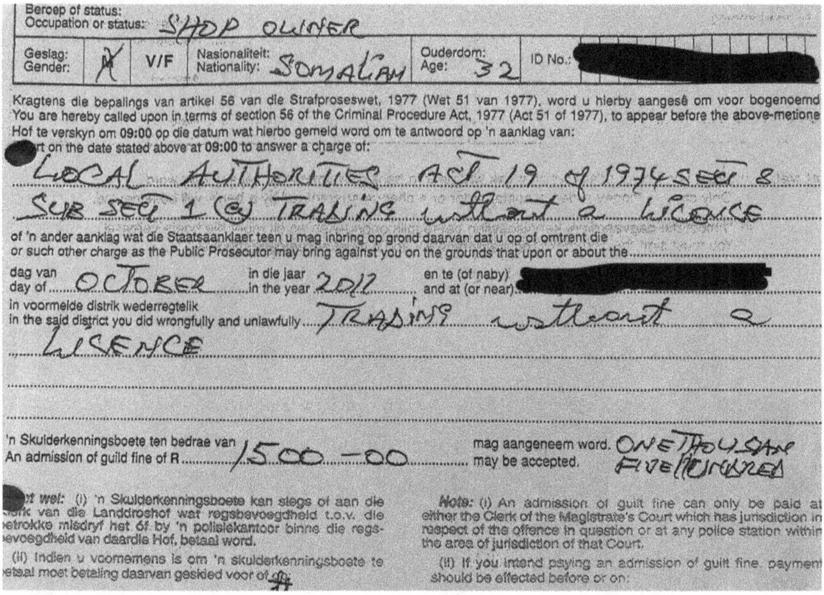

Figure 17.1: A portion of a fine citing the 'Local Authorities Act'. The recipient's identifying information has been blacked out by the author (2012). Photograph by Vanya Gastrow.

This Act gave black South Africans a degree of authority over local governance issues in the dying days of the apartheid regime. Although an interesting piece of historical knowledge, the Act was repealed in 1994 and bore no relation to trading without a licence.

I tried again. This time I typed 'Act 19 of 1974' into the search box. On my screen appeared the 'Subdivision of Agricultural Land Amendment Act 19 of 1974'. Again, the legislation had been repealed. It also had nothing to do with shop licences. I tried various other permutations of the above, but nothing came up.

Shortly thereafter more Somali shopkeepers started raising the issue of fines during interviews. One trader brought along his paid receipt for admission of guilt in the sum of R1 000. They came from all corners of the city: Gugulethu, Elsies Rivier, Khayelitsha, Philippi, Kraaifontein and Observatory. National police – not only municipal law enforcement officials – were also engaged in fining operations. The legislation on fines came in slightly different variants such as 'Act 19/1974 Section 8(1)(a)' or 'L/A Act 19/1974 8(I)(A)', but ultimately they all pointed to the same non-existent law.

Somali traders and activists believed that authorities were unfairly targeting foreign nationals, but they only had anecdotal illustrations to support their claims. A Somali activist asked eight South African shop-keepers purchasing stock at a wholesaler about these fining operations. They said they had received warnings, but no fines. Somalis arrested in Cravenby said that the police vehicle that had picked them up had only Somalis inside it. Most revealing on this issue, however, was the com-plete silence from South African spaza shopkeepers about fining oper-ations. It seemed that no South African shopkeepers were being fined on this score and no complaints were aired either in the media or at meetings. More than likely this suggests that fining operations did not acutely affect South Africans.

The apparent motives behind the fining operations varied, but the failure of informal agreements to keep foreign shops in check was pos-sibly one of them. A Kraaifontein police officer told me frankly that fining operations were intended to 'restrict foreign people from doing business in South Africa'. When I asked who was carrying out the fin-ing he stated: 'The Metro Police are involved. SAPS only deals with sec-ond-hand goods.' A police officer at the same station informed me that when foreign shops opened in breach of an informal agreement bar-ring new foreign shops in the area, the police would contact the Metro Police to 'do the necessary'. Possibly a similar state of affairs existed in Khayelitsha, where, during one meeting, Reverend Mbekwa acknowl-edged: 'We tried to use law enforcement to limit the influx.' A South African participant at that meeting urged that 'Police must make sure that when they fine they must close the shops.'

A group of five Somali traders from Elsies Rivier believed they were being penalised for a different reason. Fining operations in their neigh-bourhood – carried out by police officers in 2011 and 2012 – occurred at night. Nuur, with his thinning grey hair, was noticeably older than the other four shopkeepers. He was short, small-framed and slightly hunched. He came across as someone who had lived a life of bare survival and subsistence. Describing how police arrested him at his shop at 9 pm, he said: 'They were shouting and threatening, "Come, come, come."' They informed him that they were arresting him because his shop was open late, but when he arrived at Ravensmead police station he was told that his fine of R1 000 'was about business licences'. 'Why don't they come at midday if it's about licences?' he complained.

Somali spaza traders in Cravenby argued that closing their shops early was not feasible. 'Shoprite gets customers during the day; we get customers at night,' one of them pointed out. Another trader agreed, confirming the inconvenience of police closing down shops at between 6 pm and 8 pm. 'Most people come at that time, after work,' he said. 'Other groceries they get from Shoprite or Pick n Pay during the day.'

The night after Nuur's arrest, police returned to his shop. This time Nuur resisted letting them in, protesting that he could not leave his shop unattended. 'My car was there, my TV was there,' he told me. Nevertheless, the police forced open his shop door, and 'kicked and slapped me'. A female customer who shouted at the police was arrested and fined along with him. When he asked the police if he could call someone to keep an eye on his shop, their response was 'Fuck you. This is not your country.' At the station he was issued with another fine, this time in the sum of R2 000. Traders in Cravenby were often kept at the police station for several hours without assistance, he said, and sometimes were only released in the early hours of the morning.

Somali shopkeepers in Cape Town were confused. To their relief, courts rejected their fines. But shopkeepers were hesitant to take action against the state's legal breaches. Their fear was that the raids might persist, but next time with correct legislation. I understood the logic. Maybe shops do need a licence, and the police are just citing the wrong legislation, I thought to myself at the time. Rather than protest against the unlawful police action, traders went along with the act. They accepted their fines, and then presented themselves in court and had them withdrawn. The harassment, they believed, would not come to an end by highlighting the abuse of a non-existent law, but rather by ascertaining what exact permissions they actually needed to operate their shops.

But ascertaining what the law said was not easy. Some traders claimed that they had received 'permits' to operate their shops from the Fezeka municipal office in Gugulethu in exchange for a fee: 'You pay R150 for three months or R600 for a whole year.' This seemed odd to me and required closer examination. The city's informal trading by-law required businesses operating on demarcated trading bays on public land to apply for permits. This did not apply to spaza shops; they did not need permits. But shopkeepers kept applying for them all the same.

On 7 February 2012 Nuur and I waited together at Goodwood Magistrate's Court to find out about his court cases. His face was gaunt. I checked the court roll for the day and when I did not see his case, I approached a prosecutor in Courtroom C to ask about Nuur's matter. Glancing irritably at the fine, he told me the fines were 'rubbish', adding that they should not be heard in court but dealt with by other administrative bodies. He referred us to the case manager downstairs. A plump Afrikaans-speaking woman listened to our query and responded abruptly. 'These people pay nothing to the government,' she said. 'I pay my taxes and these people must therefore pay their taxes too and get a licence.' She did not appear to be aware that the fine itself was invalid. When I asked about Nuur's case, she said all fines had been withdrawn and taken off the roll because they were 'de minimus'. In other words, too small for the court to bother about.

Later I sat and drank a can of Coca-Cola at Nuur's shop, which was located in a converted garage in the coloured Afrikaans neighbourhood of Cravenby. He showed me his living quarters behind the store. There was a simple bed and a closet. The room opened up onto a shower and bathroom. He was still worried about police harassment, but there was also reason for optimism: he had received a permit to operate his shop.

'But you don't need a permit,' I told him, to which he replied, 'It's better than nothing.'

I looked into other laws regulating the spaza market. Zoning schemes allowed the operation of spaza shops in the city's townships. A law enforcement representative stated at a meeting in Khayelitsha in March 2012 that 'All former disadvantaged areas, that is, black areas, are exempted from the Land Use Planning Ordinance. Therefore no re-zoning is needed for business.' To make it clear for everyone, he added, 'So any business can run from a property, RDP or container, and people do not need to apply for re-zoning.' Although helpful, his statement still did not clarify whether shops still required permission – and if so what type?

I looked into the issue of business licences. It seemed to me that spaza shops might require a licence in terms of the Business Act of 1991. The Act provides that businesses engaged in the 'sale or supply of meals or perishable foodstuffs' require a business licence. In Cape Town, these licences are issued by the City's environmental health department. In my view, the Act could cover spaza shops because they sold perishable foodstuffs such as milk, meat, fruit and vegetables.

But many traders struggled to obtain business licences from the environmental health department. 'They said I don't need a licence,' one shopkeeper told me. The Parow municipal office published a notice that was circulated among shopkeepers indicating categories of businesses that needed licences. These included 'Accommodation establishment (providing meals)', 'baker', 'café keeper', and 'place of entertainment'. To my surprise, grocery shops, general dealers and spaza shops were not included. The City's environmental health website also appeared to exclude spaza shops from needing to apply for business licences. Its licensing web page stated that businesses requiring a licence comprised those involved in the 'sale and supply of meals', 'health and entertainment' (such as massage parlours and night clubs), and 'hawking in meals'. No provision was made for grocery shops or spaza shops on the website or application forms.

Eventually I spoke to environmental health officials directly. An official explained: 'All people who are trading in food must have a certificate of acceptability.' Spaza shops did not need a business licence because they did not prepare meals on site, but rather sold 'pre-packed' foods. In other words, whether a business requires a business licence 'depends on whether you prepare food. If you prepare food, then you need a business licence.'

Environmental health officials admitted that they did know of instances where law enforcement officers had fined spaza shops for trading without business licences, even though they didn't need one in order legitimately to operate. 'I've known places where they've gone and written fines for business licences,' one official told me. In these instances, the department tried to assist traders. 'We give them an extract of the legislation and say take it to court to contest it.' The officials believed the fining was a result of legal error, perhaps 'because they don't always know the finer technicalities of what constitutes a meal and what doesn't constitute a meal'.

The coin dropped. Township spaza shops in Cape Town did not require a permit, they did not need a licence, and they did not require re-zoning. They simply needed to apply for a certificate of acceptability, which was free of charge and did not come with the penalty of a fine. 'We're trying to create business opportunities and employment,' the health official explained.

Shops might have been informal and unregulated, but they nevertheless operated, for the most part, within the confines of the law. For many in political leadership in Cape Town, this was an undesirable situation. After attempts at informal regulation via trade agreements proved difficult, their next port of call was to apply state laws, albeit imaginary ones. For them the law was not a rigid system but a flexible social tool to engineer society to their will. This was especially the case when targets were tentative pariahs with little social, economic and political power. Somali shopkeepers relied on legal advice from under-resourced NGOs. In addition, many of them were not proficient in English let alone had the benefit of higher education. For them, navigating the city's legal system – replete with misinformation, corruption and inaccessible and contradictory jargon – was often beyond their grasp. Luckily for them, however, the reaches of legal manipulation and invention were limited. Certain officials along the chain of enforcement either did not understand the programme at play or did not wish to co-operate. Political leaders attempting to intervene in the spaza market found their efforts largely thwarted. Something fundamental about the country's formal legal system needed to change for them to see their efforts through.

18 | Turning to Formality, 2012

In 1998, when South Africa's refugee framework was in its infancy, asylum seeker applications in the country were a barely noticeable phenomenon. Department of Home Affairs records show that in total 11 135 applications were made across the country that year – a matter of little significance in a country with a population of tens of millions. By 2009, the picture was very different. Applications had grown to an alarming 223 324 and overwhelmed the country's refugee reception offices. But, as with most phenomena related to migration, the crisis was not permanent. Over the following years the number of applicants dropped steadily, never to reverse. By 2018, South Africa, a country with a population of almost 60 million people, received only 18 354 asylum applications, hardly a deluge of catastrophic proportion.[1]

Trends in Somali migration have been slightly different. Somali asylum applications to South Africa peaked in 2011. According to UNHCR data, 9 986 Somali nationals applied for asylum in the country that year. Their arrival alarmed political leaders. This was the year that Helen Zille, in her capacity as premier of the Western Cape, reportedly bemoaned the high numbers of Somalis arriving in the city every week.[2] She warned that foreign retailers threatened local business interests. These new arrivals, she declared, opened spaza shops that drove South Africans out of business. Furthermore, foreign retailers were economic migrants competing over scarce resources; they were not genuine refugees. This claim did not correspond with UNHCR records. Somalis – who made up the large majority of foreign township traders in the city – had an 84.47 per cent refugee recognition rate in the country that year.[3] Zille pressed on, complaining that foreign-run businesses paid negligible amounts of tax and did not use banks. Laws governing migration, she argued, needed to change.

The following month, October, national police commissioner Bheki Cele demonstrated more or less the same alarm at a breakfast meeting of police officers in Khayelitsha: 'Our people have been economically displaced,' a media article quotes him as saying.[4] 'All these spaza shops are not run by locals.' While he was speaking, an audience member shouted: 'They're not banking!' To which Cele replied, 'One has to ask, what happens to the money?' The situation, in his view, was untenable and needed addressing. 'One day, our people will revolt,' he said, 'and we've appealed to DTI [Department of Trade and Industry] to do something about it.'

Zille's and Cele's remarks signposted that the foreign shop challenge was no longer a local political matter for weary police station commanders, local government officials and, at times, opportunistic NGOs and community leaders to deal with. By bringing it to national attention in this way, they were elevating the issue to formal policy level, suggesting that new legislative frameworks and strategies be reconsidered by political parties on all spectrums.

The following year, the spike in Somali migration subsided dramatically. New Somali asylum applications in 2012 nosedived to a mere 3 453 applications in the country.[5] That year signalled a change in political direction for Somalis in South Africa and abroad. Al-Shabaab had been defeated in Mogadishu in late 2011 and the Federal Government of Somalia was established in August 2012 – the first effort towards having a central government in the capital since the fall of the Somali Democratic Republic in 1991. Somali asylum applications in South Africa continued to drop each year thereafter. By 2018, South Africa received only a trickle of Somali applicants, 672 across the entire country.[6] Over the same period many Somalis left the country, raising the possibility of a national outflux rather than an influx.

But these trends did not see any change in political alarm and momentum. While asylum seeker applications – in general, not just Somalis – declined year on year, political paranoia about migration and the activities of migrants only grew. In 2012 the first new formal proposals to stem Somali and foreign national trade in the country were explicitly considered by key political actors.

'Over 95 percent' of asylum seekers in South Africa are 'not genuine asylum seekers but rather looking for work or business opportunities,' an ANC policy document announced in March 2012.[7] It went on to claim that one of the ways that these mostly fake asylum seekers earned a living was 'to rent or manage retail outlets such as "Spaza" shops'. The policy document, titled 'Peace and Security', was published in anticipation of the ANC's June 2012 policy conference in Midrand. Despite the many challenges relating to peace and security in South Africa at the time, half the document was dedicated to matters of migration. The document portrayed asylum seekers' businesses not as social or economic assets, but as contributing to social uncertainty and disorder. Concerted state intervention, therefore, was required.

While the document recommended the strengthening and better enforcement of municipal by-laws in order to 'control and regulate' asylum seekers' business activities, this did not go far enough.[8] Laws required rehauling altogether. In the view of the ruling party, the involvement of asylum seekers in informal trading 'should not be legal under the Refugees Act'.[9] More specifically, 'Non-South Africans should not be allowed to buy or run Spaza shops or larger businesses without having to comply with certain legislated prescripts.' The document asked: 'Should by-laws apply equally to both asylum seekers and citizens?'

The ANC in the Western Cape lauded the policy document. The party's provincial secretary, Songezo Mjongile, claimed that township branches were concerned about the high number of foreign-owned shops and that South Africans were 'losing out'. The 'number of foreign-owned spaza shops has to be cut,' it concluded.[10]

The shop problem was no longer confined to meeting halls in Khayelitsha, Masiphumelele or Gugulethu. Now it was the highest channels within the governing party that were heading the calls for foreign spaza shops to be reduced and limited. When the time arrived to discuss the party's policy document at its June conference, however, the ANC backtracked on its calls. Leaders were hesitant to draft laws specifically discriminating against asylum seekers and refugees. Rather than targeting shopkeepers, the strategy turned towards acting against general illegality. At a breakfast session Minister of Trade and Industry Rob Davies stated: 'We have too many illegal activities and businesses going on in South Africa that are restricting the space for South African businesses to succeed. We must clamp down on these illegal businesses.' Laws would be tightened to help monitor the alleged unlawful practices of foreign traders rather than restrict their rights in the country.

Political leaders did not waste any time. Soon after the policy conference, clampdowns occurred as promised. On 26 July 2012, Limpopo's police commissioner launched Operation Hardstick, and instructed police to raid unlicensed spaza shops and informal taverns, closing down of hundreds of foreign-owned spaza shops in the province. Simultaneously, they set about drafting new legislation. In March 2013 the Department of Trade and Industry published a Licensing of Businesses Bill. The Bill required all people carrying on businesses in South Africa to possess business licences. In doing this, the government hoped to better monitor and control foreign shops operating in informal sectors and 'eliminate unfair competition from illegally operating businesses'.[11] The Bill also proposed to empower local officials to revoke the licences of businesses targeted or threatened by public violence or riots. But the intervention was a flop. It was met with protest from a range of business sectors, who believed that its provisions were too drastic and would undermine economic growth in the country. The department held public consultations around the country, after which it seemed to reconsider its intervention. The Bill was scrapped.

The Department of Trade and Industry was not completely done, however. It mooted a draft Business Registration Bill to combat alleged illegality. In April 2013 Davies, speaking to a crowd of South African business owners in Orange Farm, Gauteng, explained how this would work: 'If we convict you of trading in illegal goods, employing illegal immigrants, trading in counterfeit goods, or doing other things of that sort, don't come back. You're off the register.' He assured the audience that this approach would prevent unfair competition by foreigners. 'A number of these shops,' Davies said, 'they have networks. Networks that bring in the goods cheaply. That's what it is, isn't it?' Buoyed by the crowd's 'Yes' in unison, Davies asked, 'Which goods?' and imme-diately answered his rhetorical question: 'Goods that are imported, probably illegally. Bad productivity. Are not made in South Africa. That are not proudly South African.' Wagging his finger as if scold-ing a hypothetical foreign shopkeeper, he declared, 'We say if you do that – out!'

Davies' earnest fanfare notwithstanding, nothing came of the Business Registration Bill either. Like the Licensing of Businesses Bill, it was criticised as too draconian towards the country's informal sectors and pronounced generally unfeasible.[12]

Police raids on foreign shops, initially so effective, also proved legally disappointing for the state. The success of raids in Limpopo had been underpinned by the municipality's withholding of businesses licences to foreign nationals, but all of this changed when the matter reached the Supreme Court of Appeal. In the *Somali Association of South Africa* case[13] the court affirmed asylum seekers' right to human dignity. Although this did not mean that they could enter vocations of their choice, the state's policies could not 'condemn the appellants to a life of humiliation and degradation'.[14] The court found that denying licences and closing down asylum seekers' shops could potentially leave them indigent. This was especially the case given that South Africa, unlike other countries, did not provide financial support to asylum seekers and refugees. It ordered that asylum seekers and refugees were entitled to apply for new business or trading licences and declared the closures of asylum seeker and refugee businesses invalid and unlawful.

In making its ruling the court relied on its previous ruling in the *Watchenuka* case,[15] which had similarly found that a general prohibition against asylum seekers from working was an unlawful infringement on the right to dignity.[16] But the *Somali Association of South Africa* and *Watchenuka* cases did not mean that the right to dignity accorded asylum seekers a positive right to work. Their right to work could be limited, but not to the extent that they possessed 'no alternative but to turn to crime, or to begging, or to foraging'.[17]

Political leaders must have been bitterly disappointed by the judgment. After many years of failed attempts at informal regulation, their efforts at using formal state apparatuses and laws to curtail shops had also come to very little. It was by now clear that simply targeting illegal business behaviour would not work to curtail foreign shops. But all was not lost. By the time that the *Somali Association of South Africa* judgment was read out in the ornate wood-panelled Supreme Court of Appeal in Bloemfontein, winds of change had already swept through the meeting rooms and offices of state departments. As early as 2013 a new approach to formal regulation had emerged, one that reverted back to the initial vision set out in the ANC's strategy document.

19 | Formalising Exclusion as the African Way

'... that thought that someone may be excluded becomes mediated into our lives. The thought that somebody can be stigmatised, that someone may be alienated. And that's how it is done, step by step, slowly, people begin to see that this is something normal.'

> Marian Turski – former prisoner of the
> Auschwitz-Birkenau concentration camp,
> speech at 75th anniversary of the camp's liberation

On 10 October 2013, in the quaint holiday town of White River in Mpumalanga, Deputy Trade and Industry Minister Elizabeth Thabethe did not mince her words. 'The scourge of South Africans in townships selling and renting their businesses to foreigners unfortunately does not assist us as government in our efforts to support and grow these informal businesses,' she informed an audience at a national small, medium and micro enterprises (SMMEs) summit.[1] She continued: 'You still find many spaza shops with African names, but when you go in to buy you find your Mohammeds and most of them are not even registered.' But all was not lost, she assured them. 'To step in, the DTI has proposed the development of the informal business strategy which is envisaged to go a long way in advancing possible intervention programmes to assist these businesses.'

The DTI presented its informal business strategy to cabinet early the following year. The document politely and cautiously entered the muddied waters of legislated exclusion. 'International experience,' it emphasised in a tone of scholarly neutrality, 'has shown that countries like Ghana have experienced similar challenges, particularly in dealing with foreign businesses.'[2] As a result, the document goes on to state, Ghana passed the Ghana Investment Promotion Centre Act of 2013, which reserves wholly owned enterprises for Ghanaians only, and restricts petty trading and hawking to citizens only.

The DTI had been thrown a life vest. By identifying restrictions in Ghana, its proposals to legislate against foreign businesses in South Africa could be presented to the public as 'pro-African' rather than anti-African. In showing deference to the continent, their policy could be presented in a different light, one that did not reveal traces of xenophobia. As the current minister of small business development Khumbudzo Ntshavheni highlighted, 'Countries within the continent are regulating this way. Why should it be xenophobic when it is applied in South Africa?'[3] The discovery of Ghanaian legislation emboldened policymakers in the face of increasing African scrutiny of anti-foreigner sentiment in the country, and gave them tools to re-brand and normalise exclusionary proposals as the 'African' way. Those not in agreement could be inferred to be naive or not familiar with the workings of the continent.

Soon 'Africa' was the popular catchphrase in governance circles. On the eve of Human Rights Day in March 2016, the ANC's secretary general Gwede Mantashe tried to justify calls by the North West premier to expel and prohibit foreigners from operating spaza shops in the province's townships and villages. He explained that 'in the past there are quite a number of countries in Africa which say small businesses must be the preserve of that nation'.[4]

The DTI was correct. Ghanaian legislation does strictly prohibit foreigners from engaging in the country's informal retail sector. But the country's policy primarily affects traders from neighbouring Nigeria, who are not for the most part refugees or asylum seekers, but immigrants living legally in the country under the auspices of the free movement provisions of the Economic Community of West African States (ECOWAS). Moreover, although enacted in 2013, the Ghana Investment Promotion Centre Act has rarely been implemented, and all indications are that its provisions will likely be withdrawn. Although initially enjoying the full support of the Ghana Union of Traders Association, which praised the Act's potential to 'sanitise the retail industry',[5] the few efforts made to enforce the Act quickly backfired.[6] State attempts to close down Nigerian businesses in 2020 gave rise to conflicts between traders, protests by Ghanaian employees of Nigerian businesses, and the straining of diplomatic relations with Nigeria. It also jeopardised the livelihoods of hundreds of thousands of Ghanaians living within Nigeria's borders, the vast majority of whom lacked any documentation.[7] The Nigerian high commissioner in Ghana issued a warning in 2019: 'There are several Ghanaians living in Nigeria and the Nigeria Immigration Service has never deported any of them, because of a sense of brotherliness between our two countries.'[8]

Mantashe was also accurate when he pointed out that a number of African countries had curtailed small foreign-owned businesses in the past. Ghana's 2013 legislated prohibitions were not entirely new. They can be traced back, not to Africa, but to the government of King George VI of England, which, in 1947, first barred 'Aliens' from starting or expanding their businesses in the country.[9] The foreign retailers affected at the time were mainly Lebanese, Syrian and Indian traders whose activities were viewed as unproductive and 'detrimental to the economic development of the inhabitants of the Gold Coast'.[10]

In 1969 and 1970, a decade after independence, Ghana found itself grappling with the challenges of nation building, economic decline and political instability.[11] Against this post-independence backdrop, on 18 November 1969 Prime Minister Kofi Busia issued the 'Aliens Compliance Order' and instructed undocumented foreigners to leave the country within a period of two weeks.[12] At the time, paperwork in West Africa was largely absent, much as it still is today. People had moved throughout the region for centuries unencumbered by colonially imposed borders.[13] But abruptly, and with little warning, hundreds of thousands of West African immigrants were forced to pack their wares and flee Ghana's territory, abandoning their homes and businesses. At least half of these evacuees were Nigerians concentrated in trade and small enterprise sectors.[14]

The Aliens Compliance Order was accompanied by the Ghanaian Business Promotion Act of 1970. The Act prohibited 'Aliens' from operating in the country's small and medium business sectors, and in wholesale trade.[15] It targeted both medium-scale businesses operated primarily by Lebanese, Syrian and Indian nationals, as well as small businesses carried on by nationals from other African countries, particularly Nigerians. Large European businesses were for the most part unaffected. It was believed that expelling foreigners would advance economic opportunities for Ghanaian citizens, who could take over and occupy vacated businesses and professions.[16]

However, the expulsions resulted in few of the claimed economic benefits. Lynne Brydon notes that those who fled the country took capital with them, and Ghanaians struggled to take over and reconstruct businesses that had been abandoned.[17] In the aftermath of the expulsions, the government implemented retrenchments and wage restraints, cut army and civil service benefits, and ordered a devaluation of the currency.[18] By January 1972, Busia's government had been overthrown in a coup d'état, one of the reasons for his downfall being that he had completely failed to rescue the county's deteriorating economy.[19]

It wasn't long before Nigeria reciprocated. By the early 1980s the oil boom in Nigeria was over and the country was buckling from an economic downturn. At the same time attitudes towards foreigners within its borders became increasingly hostile. On 17 January 1983, Nigeria's leader Shehu Shagari ordered the expulsion of approximately two million West African immigrants, half of whom were Ghanaians. The deadline given to leave was 31 January, with the president declaring, 'Illegal immigrants, under normal circumstances, should not be given any notice whatsoever.'[20] The move had major humanitarian consequences, with large crowds of evacuees stranded at border points without food, water and shelter, and others trampled in stampedes or drowned as a result of overcrowded boats.[21] The expulsion led to harsh diplomatic fallings-out between governments and deeply held misgivings between the inhabitants of the neighbouring countries, which have lasted for generations. Trauma and bitterness still exist on both sides of the border.

Legislated curtailments, deportations and expulsions of foreign national businesses were not limited to Ghana and Nigeria. They characterised many post-independence states in Africa. Frantz Fanon describes how Africa's post-independence working classes and small artisans followed the nationalist ambitions of the continent's new elites by agitating against non-national Africans – especially those engaged in petty trade.[22] Taking up the calls of their leaders, these groups turned against Africans from other countries, whom they saw as their competition. He states that 'On the Ivory Coast these competitors are the Dahomans; in Ghana they are the Nigerians; in Senegal, they are the Soudanese.'[23]

The most well known African example of curbing foreign traders is that of President Idi Amin in Uganda, whose government passed the Trade Licensing Act in 1969. In doing so it followed the lead of Kenya's Trade Licensing Act of 1967, which had fuelled an exodus of much of Kenya's Indian population in the late 1960s and early 1970s. The Ugandan legislation reserved designated trading spaces in the majority of the country's major towns for citizens only, thereby excluding many Ugandan Asian retailers who possessed British nationality as a legacy of colonialism. The justification for this was that 'the spirit of the Africanisation policy was that priority should be given to citizens of African origin'.[24] However, this intervention was not enough, and in 1972, 60 000 British 'Asians' in Uganda were given 90 days to leave the country. Idi Amin put it bluntly: 'I want to see that the whole Kampala Street is not full of Indians. It must be proper black and administration in those shops is run by the Ugandans ... They must go to their country.'[25]

Despite many African precedents being notably worrisome, the South African government pushed ahead with its plans. On 16 June 2016, the Department of Home Affairs published a Green Paper on International Migration, followed by a White Paper in July 2017. Both papers called for an overhaul of the country's refugee system. In particular they argued that asylum seekers should not be entitled to work while awaiting the finalisation of their claims. Rather they should be housed in asylum seeker 'processing centres' tucked away near the country's northern borders. These centres would, so the documents claimed, cater for the basic needs of asylum seekers. 'Low risk' asylum seekers would be permitted to leave facilities on condition that they could support themselves or access welfare assistance without having to work. By introducing a policy of incarceration and detention, the state believed that it would reduce 'the incentive for abuse by economic migrants'.[26]

The establishment of processing centres could arguably enable the state to circumvent the *Watchenuka* case judgment, which held that policies that rendered asylum seekers destitute were unconstitutional. The White Paper proposed that asylum seekers would have their basic needs met by the state in these centres, in conjunction with international bodies such as the UNHCR and the International Red Cross.

It might have sounded like a feasible plan at the time. Some policy-makers perhaps envisioned well-run centres offering food, education and medical care to relatively content and compliant detainees. Others may not have really cared one way or another, so long as asylum seekers were not operating businesses and selling bread and vegetables to suspicious citizens in key political constituencies. But the plan struck a hurdle early on, when the UNHCR rejected it outright. As far back as 2015, the UNHCR had been clear that it would not fund asylum seeker shelters in the country; its focus was on helping refugees, not those seeking asylum.[27]

In December 2017 the government passed the Refugees Amendment Act of 2017, omitting any explicit reference to camps or shelters. But the state was still determined somehow to remove asylum seekers from key workforces. The Act sets out elaborate tests and conditions for endorsing asylum seekers' visas with the right to work, which ultimately prevents them from engaging in self-employment.[28] Its regulations also empower the state to prohibit asylum seekers from working in certain economic sectors. Shelters or processing centres were, however, still on the agenda. The Act requires asylum seekers to report to a refugee status determination officer at any refugee reception office 'or at any other place' designated by the director-general.

By the close of 2017, after years of unsuccessful attempts to dislodge foreign traders, the state had finally taken a legislative step to remove asylum seekers from the country's small business markets. The law would only permit recognised refugees to engage in self-employment. These changes, however, would only be implemented once regulations had been passed. As a result, rather than immediate spectacle and aggressive upheaval, the opposite occurred. In the aftermath of the Act's passing there fell a quiet hum. Bureaucratic processes and day-to-day life continued as usual, the status quo maintained for the time being.

But political events in South Africa did not follow the same pattern. On a sunny afternoon in central Johannesburg on 1 August 2019, metro law enforcement officers and South African police officials were taken by alarm. An operation aimed at clamping down on the sale of illegal and counterfeit goods in the city's fashion district had gone haywire and culminated in angry shopkeepers chasing down officers with stones and glass bottles. Footage showed a police armoured vehicle gearing quickly into reverse, spewing black fumes into the air and then driving hurriedly away. It soon turned out that many in the crowd were foreign nationals, causing a public outcry. It is unclear what triggered the protest. One trader complained that routine police harassment had eventually led to eruption of violence: 'They treat us as if we are aliens, it's an everyday thing.'[29] Along the same lines, David Bruce and Tanya Zack interpret the actions by traders as a response to frequent heavy-handed police raids, extortion and corruption.[30]

Politicians were quick to capitalise on the events. Gauteng Premier David Makhura took to Twitter that evening, blaming 'foreign nationals' for the attack on police, which he described as a 'despicable crime against our state'.[31] Gauteng Community Safety MEC Faith Mazibuko asserted that 'We can't co-govern with criminals, especially foreign nationals who want to turn our country into a lawless Banana Republic.' She added: 'We will assert our authority and show ungovernable foreign nationals that there are laws in South Africa and they must be respected.'[32]

A week after the riots, a mob gathered in the vicinity of the Noord Street taxi tank in the Johannesburg CBD. Its members were not foreign traders, but South Africans wielding knives, hammers, scissors and other makeshift weapons.[33] As they made their way through the city, they smashed shop and car windows and looted stores.[34] Police conducting raids in the area reacted and dispersed the crowd with rubber bullets. But violence did not dissipate altogether. Three weeks later more xenophobic attacks broke out, this time in Pretoria, allegedly fuelled by the death of a taxi driver at the hands of a foreign national. This was followed by further riots in Johannesburg the following week.[35]

Although the 'Johannesburg riots', as the violence later came to be called, seemed quite typical of the usual collective ritual involved in xenophobic attacks in South Africa, this time the backlash against the havoc was unusually acute. This was not because the country's citizens had expressed greater alarm at the looting and hatred; the source of the fallout came from further afield. On 3 September, thousands of kilometres north-west of South Africa, a man with thick-rimmed glasses and wearing a traditional *fulani aboki* hat decided to take action on the matter. The man was President Muhammadu Buhari of Nigeria, leader of the continent's largest economy. Buhari's special adviser released a statement that day noting the president's 'deep concern' about reported attacks on Nigerians in the country and 'Nigeria's displeasure over the treatment of her citizens'.[36] The statement announced that Buhari had summoned South Africa's high commissioner to Nigeria to brief him, and had dispatched a special envoy to meet with President Cyril Ramaphosa. That afternoon, Ramaphosa, who up until then had been silent about the violent destruction, quickly condemned the attacks against foreign nationals in the country in a recorded statement as 'something totally unacceptable, something that we cannot allow to happen in South Africa'.[37] His envoy Jeff Radebe boarded a flight to Nigeria two weeks later to apologise for the country's misdeeds, much like a remorseful lover.

Buhari's intervention was popularly supported at home. Nigerian musicians boycotted a music festival in Johannesburg, and major South African companies, Shoprite and MTN, were forced to shut their doors in the West African country. So did the South African consulate and high commission in Lagos and Abuja. It turned out that South Africa's perceived anti-Africanism was a useful means of generating patriotism and nationalism in Nigeria. The country boycotted the World Economic Forum in Africa, which was held in Cape Town, alongside Rwanda, DR Congo and Malawi. A local Nigerian airline, Air Peace, also stepped into the fray, offering to evacuate Nigerians from South Africa at no cost. The first flight arrived in Lagos on the night of 11 September 2019 with much fanfare. International media shared images and recordings of passengers cheering on arrival, hugging and embracing the airline company's emotional CEO.

The xenophobic attacks in South Africa were a political win for governments across the continent, but a critical embarrassment for the host state. The humiliation entailed having to send emissaries across the continent to communicate condolences, being booed at public events and having to attend tense and awkward press conferences abroad. This generated renewed urgency among South African officials to finalise the country's new asylum seeker framework.

At a joint sitting of parliament on 18 September 2019, Ramaphosa prepared some groundwork for introducing the new altered refugee system in the country. He once more highlighted that in doing so the country was simply mimicking its African neighbours. 'We should consider, as many other countries have,' he said, 'the regulation of how foreign nationals can own and participate in certain types of businesses within the small and medium enterprise sector.'[38] A few days later, Small Business Development Minister Khumbudzo Ntshavheni elaborated further in a radio interview: 'In countries like Nigeria, Zimbabwe, Ethiopia, Tanzania, Ghana, Bangladesh, Pakistan they have regulations that specify the sectors where foreign nationals are not allowed to participate,' she stated.[39] The list of examples had grown. Instances of discriminatory laws could be found throughout the global South. In these countries, she explained, foreign nationals were excluded from various sectors 'including in the micro businesses, in the retail sector, in the pharmaceutical sector'. The government was keen to follow suit as small business sectors 'contribute to the alleviation of poverty, survival of our people, and the ability of our people to create jobs for themselves'.

The minister did not present any evidence to illustrate the harmful impact of foreign businesses on the South African economy, many of which paid rent to South African landlords, purchased goods from South African suppliers, and encouraged economic circulation and access to markets in low-income areas. The accuracy of the minister's list of examples is also doubtful. Nigeria does bar investment into certain economic sectors, but these prohibitions – contained in the Nigerian Investment Promotion Commission Act – apply to 'both foreign and Nigerian investors'.[40] In other words, the Act does not reserve any economic sectors exclusively to citizens. Prohibited sectors in the Act's 'negative list' include the production of arms and ammunition, the production of and dealing in narcotic drugs, and the production of military ware – sectors that are commonly illegal to private actors in other countries. Moreover, Nigeria does not prohibit foreigners in any way from engaging in its small and medium retail markets. Other countries appear less than enthusiastic about their legislated exclusions. For example, in August 2019 Zimbabwe announced its intention to repeal its Indigenisation and Economic Empowerment Act of 2008, and the longevity of Ghana's legislation is also in question.[41]

In calling for curtailments on foreign businesses, the state continued cautiously and carefully to emphasise African precedent. Although the pariah in South Africa lacked the political leverage enjoyed by the elite and the common people, the government was aware that Africa's most populous country and largest economy could summon its own masses and political and economic strength. By reasoning that such policies were prolific across the continent, the state was intentionally normalising an ideology of exclusion, which would otherwise have widely come across as abnormal and abhorrent.

The promised regulations were eventually passed in late December 2019, and the Refugees Amendment Act came into effect on 1 January 2020. Camps were still off the table, but not necessarily in the long term. When explaining the new refugee regime, Minister of Home Affairs Aaron Motsoaledi depicted refugee camps in other countries as sites of plenty and places that those seeking refuge should envy. 'You are taken care of by the United Nations High Commissioner for Refugees, NGOs, they give you money, they treat you when you are sick, they even give you education,' he enthused.[42] In contrast, in South Africa, he said, 'we don't have anything like that. They stay in communities.' His comparison left the impression that asylum seekers and refugees would be happier and more fulfilled in camps than in seeking out a living among hostile neighbours. Camps were places where they would be better off.

Asylum seekers themselves did not describe camps in such admiring terms. One day I asked a Somali community activist what he had heard of camps elsewhere on the continent. He knew of some individuals who had stayed in camps in Malawi. A camp was like being in a prison: 'They're not allowed to freely move, they're not allowed to trade, they're not allowed to do anything.' Inmates simply survived, living off substandard food, which they 'only eat because they are hungry'. Services were poor and often unavailable: 'They just wait for the UNHCR to come and give them what they need, but they don't get what they need,' a former Malawi camp inmate recalled. 'Actually, if I think about camping in Malawi, whatever will happen to me in South Africa I will tolerate it because I don't want to be in a camp.' Camps were places where people went to rot. 'You become a useless person,' one asylum seeker described. 'There's no future,' concluded another. South Africa already had experience in running camps in the aftermath of the 2008 xenophobic attacks. An asylum seeker who had lived in Soetwater camp near Cape Town recalled the experience: 'You never lived in a place like this. There's no hygiene, nothing. Children get sick.' Reports of Lindela Repatriation Centre in North West Province are similarly littered with infringements and abuses.[43]

The plan was first and foremost to exclude asylum seekers from certain economic sectors. Because no camps had been established in South Africa yet – albeit not for any lack of trying – Motsoaledi explained in a radio interview on 6 January 2020 that 'these people must be allowed to work'.[44] The right to work precluded the state from taking extreme measures to curtail asylum seekers' economic activities, but allowed for conditions. The Standing Committee on Refugee Affairs, he informed the radio host, would set conditions regarding 'what kind of work are you allowed to do, in what areas of studies should you be allowed, where should they be restricted'.[45] Strangely, the statement did not in any way elicit alarm or concern from the radio host, whose response was matter-of-factly to seek clarification: 'And that would be physical areas as well, which then speaks to limitations. Right?'

The sudden advent of the Covid-19 pandemic in 2020 did not inhibit the state from continuing its attempts to curtail foreign shops. In March 2020, when the country entered its first national Covid-19 lockdown, the minister of small business development assured the public that spaza shops would remain open to provide essential supplies to local customers. However, this allowance was subject to one condition: 'We must indicate,' the minister emphasised, 'that those spaza shops that will be open are strictly those that are owned by South Africans, managed and run by South Africans.'[46] By implication all other spazas – irrespective of whether they were operated by refugees, asylum seekers or permanent residents – would be required to shut down.

This condition, however, never materialised in state policy, probably because the minister's opportunistic reliance on a catastrophic national health disaster to shut down foreign businesses was too repugnant for its time. Instead, the department, in agreement with Nedbank, more meekly limited its spaza support scheme to those stores 'which are 100% owned by South Africans'.[47]

When discussing its legislative manoeuvrings, the state has conveniently ignored the *Somali Association of South Africa* case, which had found that barring asylum seekers and refugees from the spaza market could render them destitute and undermine their right to dignity. As a result of the judgment, the one sector from which asylum seekers could likely not be excluded was the one the state most desperately wanted altered.

In enacting new legislation, the state was cautiously venturing into the realm of formally regulating the pariah, purportedly the African way. What started in 2006 in the aftermath of the dogs being sent out in Masiphumelele had materialised into national legislation. Protectionism, prejudice and fear had overrun the values of plurality, dignity and freedom that underpinned South Africa's early democratic political dispensation. The regulation of difference, previously confined to small township meeting halls across the Western Cape and beyond, had turned mainstream. Presidents and ministers spoke confidently of it without retort, and the state passed legislation with minimal fanfare. The roots of legislated fear and pariahdom run far and deep, and emerge after many years of gradual accustomisation. South African leaders, allegedly inspired by Ghana and other real and imaginary policies across the continent, were finally intent to follow the many notorious and largely tragic postcolonial examples of nation building. But they had to tread lightly. African states were watching from the sidelines, waiting to exploit xenophobia in South Africa to drum up nationalism at home – the pitfall of when competing nationalisms collide.

Part III
The Politics of Pariahdom

20 | Pariahdom and Bare Life

It was all predictable, I think to myself as I read up on Irwin Rinder's concept of the 'status gap' one evening.[1] A status gap exists in societies when a significant social and economic chasm exists between a society's ruling elite and its masses. Such gaps were common in feudal Europe and colonial states.[2] In societies where large status gaps exist, the ruling elite are reluctant to deal directly with the lower classes in business dealings, viewing such engagements as below their social status and dignity. The status gap therefore often impedes the flow and distribution of goods between the ruling classes and the rest of society. This in turn produces, in Rinder's words, 'an economic gap which persists until filled by a third party'.[3]

To say that a status gap existed during apartheid South Africa is an understatement. Prior to democratic rule, the country's economy was mostly in white South African hands, and populations lived in divided and racially homogenous neighbourhoods. The same patterns of racialised inequality and geographical settlement still persist today. These conditions impacted on the way that economic markets operated and developed, the grocery sector being no exception. South African supermarket chains neglected township markets for decades. For white South Africans who owned and managed multibillion rand conglomerates, townships were alien and distant social and economic satellites. They were looked down upon as poor, turbulent and unfamiliar spaces to be avoided.

Status gaps usually do not serve economies and citizens very well. In South Africa millions of black township residents across the country were to a large extent cut off from formalised large-scale grocery distribution chains, reliant on mostly rudimentary spaza shops for many of their household items. While these shops were a source of employment for some residents, they often did not adequately meet broad customer needs. Residents that I spoke to in 2010 and 2011 complained that spaza shops that were South African owned were generally expensive and poorly managed. They had small product ranges, were often out of stock, had shorter operating hours, and frequently did not possess the right quantities of change. At the dawn of democracy it could be safe to say that a status gap opened up a corresponding gap for foreign retailers in South Africa's grocery market.

By the time the earliest asylum seekers and refugees began filtering into South Africa in the mid to late 1990s, it should have been clear where many would eventually end up working. Somalis quickly identified opportunities as middlemen between formal distributors of goods and South Africa's poor and working classes, whether this involved hawking clothes outside welfare offices, selling chips and sweets at taxi ranks, or opening spaza shops in townships. In doing so they filled a gap in the market that white corporate South Africa had shown little interest in closing. In this sense the Somali trader in South Africa's townships is both a symptom and signifier of a highly unequal and divided nation.

For many, this arrangement was mutually beneficial. Large numbers of South African spaza shopkeepers happily leased out their shops to Somalis and other foreign nationals, and customers reported improved service and easier access to household goods. At the same time suppliers and manufacturers courted the new distribution channels emerging in the market. But some South African retailers, particularly those with larger enterprises, saw this as unwelcome competition, and in carrying out campaigns against their economic rivals, they found many willing participants among the poor and downtrodden. Their followers were motivated by a myriad of post-apartheid grievances, and fuelled by the knowledge that they had little to fear.

In Cape Town, governance actors initially tried to allay threats of violence against foreign spaza retailers through local regulatory interventions. The solution – informally prohibiting foreigners from opening new shops – ultimately could not be strictly enforced. As one Khayelitsha police officer explained to a Somali community representative: 'Somewhere we cannot cross a border.' But this did not make informal regulation and containment insignificant or of short duration. The informal was a testing ground for the formal. Principles and beliefs that emerged as dominant were condoned, nurtured and normalised. The permissible use of violent threats and discriminatory curtailments, backed by senior politicians and community leaders, served to entrench the notion that the law could mete out different rights and laws for different classes of people. These beliefs become consolidated through local rules and agreements, and finally filtered up political and formal legislative channels, where they materialised into nation-wide legal constraints and sanctions. It was at this point that Somali and other foreign retailers in South Africa transformed from being mere middleman minorities into a national pariah. The former category is characterised more by traders' economic roles and locations, and the latter by their political condition as social, political and legal outcasts.

But hostile interventions against the pariah are not only underscored by status gaps and inequalities in South Africa. They also spring from emerging political trends. The post-apartheid dispensation has been characterised by the political elevation of citizens' economic interests over political rights, values and concerns. This was evident early on by the scrapping of corruption charges against former president Jacob Zuma in 2009, vigorously supported by popular left-leaning organisations such as the country's Communist Party and trade unions. The move – highly detrimental to the state's independent institutions – facilitated Zuma's rise to power under the auspices of finally delivering economic salvation to the country's poor. But this process was also evident in the experiences of Somali shopkeepers at the country's grassroots. Here, local economic grievances were violently raised with little concern for constitutional principles. Residents often looked the other way when xenophobic looting occurred, unless their own economic interests were at stake, and threats and bigotry went unpunished by those in power.

What does this say about the nature of rights and perceptions of freedom? Mohamed recalls how, as a high school student living under totalitarianism in Ethiopia, those around him yearned for political freedom. Irrespective of the conditions that they were languishing under, they understood implicitly 'that you have a right to live freely, to think freely and nobody can actually impose their thoughts against you'.

But in South Africa, understandings of rights and freedoms have come to depart from such notions. Despite having one of the world's most progressive constitutions, rights in South Africa have largely become linked to economic interest and mobility. For township residents, liberation was often equated to an escape from the degradation and poverty of satellite neighbourhoods. For the middle and upper classes, it related more to the ability to engage in conspicuous and unstoppable consumerism. In post-apartheid South Africa, these values gradually rose to prominence over early democratic political emphases on inclusivity, equality and dignity.

These developments echo theories put forward by Hannah Arendt, Michel Foucault and Giorgio Agamben. For them, the political preoccupation with economic matters – termed the rise of the 'social' or 'biopolitics' – is part of a broad global phenomenon and characterises government in the modern age.[4]

The rise of the social results in the transformation of the political sphere from being a space of plurality where differing views and opinions are exchanged and debated (to 'live freely, to think freely,' as Mohamed put it), to a bureaucratic realm that caters for a giant 'super-human family'.[5] Public discourse and machinery becomes primarily focused on servicing society's physical needs, whether relating to housing, employment or health. The arrival of the Covid-19 pandemic in South Africa made this process even more all-encompassing.

In the South African context, however, the social does not only manifest in state departments and their cobwebbed and opaque bureaucracies. It is also evident among local township political structures that enjoy a high degree of devolved power. Here the social sphere includes diverse organisational structures set up by ordinary residents. But to see this phenomenon as epitomising local democratic power and engagement would be misleading. Township leadership structures in Cape Town were frequently entangled in patronage streams and bribery and extortion operations. Their alignment to political parties and widespread meting out of violent punishments meant that genuine and free political deliberation at these localities was constrained. This was all too apparent at the meetings I attended in Khayelitsha, where dissenting voices were stifled, and lives were threatened with impunity. While it is not possible to separate the ancient Greek distinction between the private sphere of life and the public realm of politics, the extreme elevation of private concerns over political values in the public sphere risks reducing spaces for free political thought, engagement and action.

But the rise of the social has further repercussions. In his account of biopolitics, Foucault examines how the political preoccupation with economic concerns results in power attempting to control, foster and regulate individuals' bodies and collective populations. The flipside of this process is that it encourages a form of racial thinking where certain non-conforming groups become perceived as biological threats to the nation. As a result, in spite of its apparent economic goal of fostering life, Foucault argues that biopolitics can be deadly.

Foucault views racism as not only running along the lines of ethnicity or skin colour, but having the ability to encompass biological or evolutionist thinking towards various categories of people, be they the mentally ill, criminals, class enemies or political adversaries. These racially threatening or inferior lives and bodies become the target of the state and politics.[6] But unlike common perceptions of murder as active and forceful, Foucault views the biopolitical killing as mostly passive. It entails the 'power to *foster* life or *disallow* it to the point of death'.[7] The latter includes 'indirect murder' through 'exposing someone to death, increasing the risk of death for some people, or, quite simply, political death, expulsion, rejection, and so on'.[8] Such an attitude was observed in the *Somali Association of South Africa* case, where the court noted: 'When, during argument before us, we enquired of counsel what was to happen to destitute asylum seekers and refugees, no answer was forthcoming. There appeared to be some suggestion that, regrettably, some persons might be left to their destitution.'[9]

Forms of racial exclusion were evident in state and township policies aimed at sweeping urban neighbourhoods clean of deviant and polluting groups – be they immigrants or 'skollies'. While the former are often targeted by state search operations and xenophobic mobs, the latter are frequently murdered through violent community punishments. In South Africa, it could be said that biopolitical efforts to disallow life – both passive and active – have intensified over the years. New formal legislative efforts to inhibit foreign nationals from working have the potential effect of forcing many to live below the breadline.

Agamben builds on Foucault's account of the social sphere by depicting how biopolitical murder is facilitated by the expulsion of perceived threatening groups from political communities. This causes individuals to be stripped of rights and relegated to a state of exception where they live under the condition 'bare life' and 'mere existence'. The suspension of legal protections in a state of exception enables the biopolitical state to kill with impunity. Agamben argues that expulsion has been part and parcel of politics and the establishment of political boundaries for millennia, but has become more aggressive in modern times. With the rise of the social, citizens' natural lives have become the object of politics and bearers of rights. As a result the exclusion of what he terms '*homo sacer*' – the sacred man who possesses only bare life – today plays a key role in defining the boundaries of who is entitled to the biological protection and nurture of the nation state.

The biopolitical process of expelling threatening groups for the sake of national health relies on certain mechanisms. Agamben argues that the instrument used to rid the nation of tainted groups and individuals is the 'camp'. The camp amounts to a state of exception, where inhabitants enjoy no political or juridical rights and possess only bare life. Camps come in numerous forms, ranging from concentration camps established by totalitarian regimes to spaces such as Guantanamo Bay, certain city outskirts, and zones *d'attentes*. The camp need not even have a physical location, as Agamben argues that it has become the 'hidden paradigm of the political space of modernity'.[10]

The rise of the social globally has seen the rise of camps throughout the world. South Africa is no exception. The state relies on prisons to separate out 'skollies' and makeshift hospital tents for Covid-19 sufferers. In the case of the Somali asylum seeker, there is now the potential of the 'processing centre'. Through these acts the South African state perceives itself as nurturing its citizens by protecting them from infectious or unhygienic bodies and thwarting those that parasitically usurp resources. But this also entails the creation of a class of largely rightless people – pushed behind bars or near or beyond state borders.

In relation to the Somali shopkeeper, the path to this state of affairs was not only prepared by political leaders. The country's courts decided as early as 2003 that asylum seekers' constitutional right to dignity in relation to work extended only so far as to ensure the sustenance of their bare lives.[11] Dignity entitled them to work, but solely so that they did not starve. The right did not extend to allowing meaningful occupation, choice of vocation or the basic fulfilment that comes with being a productive member of society.[12] In the state's view, these judgments meant that asylum seekers may as well then just exist in camps. In these spaces it would ensure that asylum seekers would receive everything they were seemingly entitled to – bare life and little more.

The pariah is often one of the first to be expelled or disallowed from nation states and their political and juridical orders. But falling into a state of exception is a risk faced by all. Agamben believes that this is because notions of 'the people' are always evolving and uncertain, leaving all citizens prone to being rendered to bare life. Social and political identity is fluid and can change with time.

In my view, this vulnerability is linked to the inherent utilitarian ethic of the social sphere. When economic interest becomes the highest value of the political sphere, then people's political relevance to the nation begins to hang on their economic utility. This can be either in the form of what they contribute materially to the state and economy, or what they can potentially undermine or destroy. In South Africa, those wielding economic power could risk being excluded should they lose their economic indispensability to the nation. At the same time, the country's poor face slipping into states of exception should they become politically passive and fail to keep the state on constant edge through threats or demonstrations of unrest. This dynamic puts all citizens on edge.

While the political focus on economic matters may appear to bode potentially well for national economies, it could in actuality comprise a significant threat to a nation's economic interests. When the highest purpose of the political sphere becomes the advancement of economic concerns – unanchored by political rights' values – then there is little to prevent *individual* economic interests from entering the political arena. Once this occurs, what becomes at stake is not only the economic interests of a delineated group of citizens, but also the private concerns of political actors. Individuals begin to rely on group membership to further their own personal economic interests, rather than selflessly enter politics to advance the welfare of the 'people', whomever they happen to be. This causes the political sphere to focus on increasingly narrowly defined beneficiaries, until in effect the 'nation' purportedly being advanced comprises small nepotistic circles that cut out large segments of the population.

As a result, biopolitical policies, although ostensibly driven by the economic interests of the nation, become less about growing and developing national economies or advancing general health and welfare.

Politics instead becomes engaged with delineating those whose lives are useful to a small political elite working under the guise of 'the nation' and those whose lives are not. The outcome is that policies often undermine general economic growth and upliftment. This can be illustrated by South Africa's efforts to dismantle the foreign spaza sector to service a vocal political constituency, irrespective of the high likelihood that such policies could prove very detrimental to vast numbers of the country's poor.

The social spheres portrayed by Arendt, Foucault and Agamben therefore do not bode well for the citizen or the pariah. But there is scope for intervention. No social sphere is static. Political communities evolve and can be challenged. The nature of politics is processual and multiple rather than fixed and singular.

While those included in political communities enjoy greater rights and state protections, this does not mean that the excluded are entirely politically powerless and irrelevant. This is evident in Arendt's depiction of the role of town-hall meetings, district assemblies and popular clubs and societies as the keystones of political power during the course of revolutions.[13] These platforms can serve as alternate sources of political power and springboards for political change.

The notion that politics need not be limited to formal state institutions is also emphasised by Jacques Rancière, who stresses that political action is not confined to the comfortable parameters of political communities, but also arises from without.[14] Politics is in the first place, he argues, a form of dissensus aimed at disputing the border between the world of the citizen and the world of the outcast.[15] He asserts that: 'The point is, precisely, where do you draw the line separating one life from the other? Politics is about that border. It is the activity that brings it back into question.'[16] In Rancière's view, challenging social, political and legal boundaries is the very substance of politics. As a result, politics is primarily waged by those who lack rights, rather than those wielding them. This makes *homo sacer* not a marginal political figure but a central one.

Fundamental economic and structural change is much needed in the contemporary world. But such transformation should be linked to political principles relating to the creation of a free, inclusive and humane society rather than to plain citizenship or indigeneity – that is, one or other form of grand-scale family. The rise of the social realm and its concomitant desire to control, purify and, by implication, rid life has the potential to reduce the foreign shopkeeper as pariah to 'mere existence'. Yet this phenomenon is not complete and total. The pariah simultaneously possesses the potential to question and rebel against this status. But this undertaking is not seamless. The pursuit of pariah justice, the pariah's search for security, freedom and self-realisation, or, more modestly, the enjoyment of a plain, simple life, brings to the fore the political predicament of the outcast.

21 | Pariah Justice

The room is quiet and dimly lit. I take a sip of warm bottled water and stare at the PowerPoint presentation in front of me. It is 2018, and I am attending a university workshop in Cape Town on the informal food sector. The presenter, a tall tense-looking man with fine light-brown hair, is discussing informal enterprises in Philippi East. The projector makes a quiet humming sound which makes me drowsy.

I am shaken out of my peaceful state by the presenter announcing with a sense of certainty and authority: 'Many of the spaza shops we looked at are essentially agents of wholesalers …' I force myself to pay attention. 'They are not autonomous entities,' he goes on. 'They are simply providing an outlet for the very same products that are being sold in supermarkets.' I sit up in my seat, now fully awake and attentive, expecting further elaboration, but the presenter has moved on. That informal sector businesses stock similar food items to those sold at supermarkets, he says, shows that the two sectors are 'very closely linked'. Both formal and informal sectors operate 'within a corporate controlled food system, with the vast majority of profits going to corporate entities'. None of these remarks sheds any light on his conclusion that spaza shops are acting as agents of larger enterprises.

Several minutes later the presentation comes to an end and neon lights are switched on. The workshop facilitator, with hair tied up in wispy bun and a more relaxed and mellow air about him, introduces two respondents to provide comments. The first, a South African woman who works with informal workers, begins by thanking the presenter but does not go on to address the presentation itself or the points it made. Instead, she proudly highlights the work of her organisation and laments the general plight of South African informal workers in the country. 'We want a hand up and not a hand out,' she declares, before ending her contribution with a call for closer relationships between informal and formal sectors, and the government.

The second respondent, a Somali community leader with a serious demeanour, is next. His response differs markedly from hers. 'Mine is in fact not a presentation,' he states firmly. 'It is questions that I would like to get clarity on.' He looks down at his jotted notes. His first question relates to whether the data presented on spaza shops comes from shopkeepers or from their customers. 'That's my first question. I hope that you are noting my questions,' he emphasises, making explicit a desire for his queries to be addressed properly.

He goes on to raise more questions – seven in total – relating to the research findings. 'You stated that spaza shops are agents of supermarkets, and there's a corporate controlled food system, and the corporate world is actually benefiting,' he says. 'I would like to get the facts and the data you are using to make that kind of statement.' He ends by thanking the audience and hands back the microphone.

I, too, am keen to hear the presenter's response. To my surprise it's the workshop facilitator who speaks. 'May I just respond briefly to that,' he states nervously. 'I think it is difficult for the presenter to respond to all of your points.' He feels that the Somali community leader's questions go beyond the scope of the case study presented and that it is not 'fair' to expect detailed explanations of data to be forthcoming on this platform when the research findings are still to be written up. 'I also want us to try and maintain a way of engaging that is unconfrontational,' he adds. He then recommends that the conversation be redirected: to the subject of spatial planning, which was a key concern of the presentation. Believing the matter to be resolved, he invites more questions from the audience. This time it is the presenter who intervenes. 'I'd just like to make a general response,' he states defensively, but his 'general response' does not speak to any of the Somali man's questions. Instead, he takes the opportunity to commend his own research, saying how 'immensely proud' he is of his and his team's work, which involved a census, household survey and qualitative interviews relating to the informal food sector. He assures the audience that once the findings have been written up he will welcome 'the kind of detailed comments that we have received'.

With that, the session continues smoothly, this time without any undesired confrontation. Follow-up questions – asked mainly by white men in attendance – are politely taken up by the facilitator. Their queries range from the nature of brand loyalty to the role of upstream suppliers. 'Let's see if we can get some responses?' the facilitator eagerly suggests, now much more at ease. The presenter answers each question in detail. 'Are you happy with that?' he courteously asks one participant.

With the round of questions completed, the facilitator glances across the room again. He notices a raised hand and acknowledges the Somali community leader. 'My question is actually to you, the facilitator. I have asked so many questions, but you did not allow even one of my questions to be answered, and I think that's not fair. You have been taking other questions and allowing those questions to be answered.'

The facilitator attempts cautiously to explain. 'My main concern was, well, twofold,' he says. 'The one was the tone, the second was that it was a barrage. It was maybe six or seven questions, which makes it very difficult.' Also, the facilitator tells him, some questions were based on other studies and were not even relevant. The presenter then intervenes with a compromise offer: the Somali community leader may ask him one question. When the community leader protests, the facilitator permits him to ask two.

The Somali community leader begins: 'I still want an answer on the one that he said that spaza shops are agents.' In his view, the presenter's use of the term 'agent' is misguided: 'If I am your agent, then I'm working for you.' In his experience as a former spaza shopkeeper, the only relationship between spaza shops and wholesalers 'is I buy from you, and you are selling a product in wholesale. That's it. So I don't know where the agent aspect comes in.' He would like an answer to this not merely out of research interest, but more urgently because such statements are 'a very big concern for us and our community'.

The interaction was cringeworthy. Watching a participant who had been specifically invited to respond to a piece of research be muzzled on a public platform left me uneasy. The topic of discussion – the informal food sector – was highly pertinent to the community of which this Somali man was an integral part, yet his queries were made out as if they were the least relevant in the room. Whether or not traders were 'agents' became less of interest to me. The discussion had instead provoked in me a curiosity about the nature and predicaments of pariah resistance.

In retrospect, it is clear that the Somali community leader's questions were on point. The presenter's claim that shops were 'agents' was derived from the case study that he had presented, not some other body of work, as alleged by the facilitator. The Somali community leader's request for more clarity regarding evidence was relevant. It turned out that the presenter's case study had involved only six interviews with spaza shopkeepers in one township section, none of whom were foreign nationals. This was an important detail, given that most spaza shops in the city and province are presumed to be foreign run. The study's participants were thus not reflective of general understandings of spaza shop demographics.

It also became apparent that the presenter's data was anecdotal and circumstantial at best. The finding that 'many of the spaza shops' surveyed were 'essentially agents of wholesalers' was based on the fact that three spaza shops in the study were in possession of one-page advertising pamphlets printed by nearby wholesalers. These pamphlets advertised hampers (bulk combinations of goods) and a few specials (between three and six discounted items) to shop customers. But hampers made up only a small share of shops' turnover; the presenter highlighted that 'hampers are not the key product for spaza shops' and that he 'was quite surprised at how few hampers the spaza shops are actually selling'. At the same time, all three shops were found to procure stock from a range of other suppliers, suggesting independent choice in procurement.

It struck me that the pariah was not only frequently shunned by the common people, but equally, if not more so, by many of the elite. Admission was possible, but on certain terms. Signs of anger or protest were not to be tolerated. The tools used by members of the elite to keep the pariah in his or her place were a combination of patronising censure and rendering the pariah invisible.

For some pariahs the solution to this predicament is to play the game. Hannah Arendt – drawing on the work of Bernard Lazare – identifies the *parvenu* as the pariah who is happy to play the role required for admission into society. The *parvenu* joins those elements of society that are hostile to the pariah, acting as their 'lackey' in return for special privileges.[1] The *parvenu* is assimilated into mainstream society, but does not necessarily try completely to blend in. Rather *parvenus* continuously draw on tropes and stereotypes of the pariah to distinguish themselves and make themselves seem unique or exotic to those around them. Arendt illustrates this through an examination of the British prime minister Benjamin Disraeli, who readily played the 'exception Jew' while at the same time orientalising himself to draw curiosity towards himself in elite aristocratic circles.[2]

But this role does not serve pariah justice. Arendt argues that *parvenus* tend to undermine the pariah groups from whom they trace their origins, albeit often unintentionally. *Parvenus'* lack of real contact with pariah communities results in them drawing on and play-acting stereotypes of the pariah in their attempts to garner appeal. This, in turn, reinforces and feeds dangerous and harmful prejudices. Arendt illustrates how Disraeli's use of romantic illusions about Jewish money and power in his pursuit of social recognition were not only completely out of sync with the actual conditions of most Jews in Europe at the time, but they also contributed to the growth of anti-Semitic superstitions and conspiracy theories that wreaked havoc on Jewish communities the following century.

But in Cape Town the role of *parvenu* was not an option for Somali retailers and community representatives. Most Somalis had arrived too recently in the country to mingle comfortably in elite South African circles and understand its codes and modes of operation. Even if they had wanted to assimilate, too many obstacles to assimilation – religious, cultural and linguistic – stood in their way. Rather, the meagre role prescribed to them by many members of the elite, as well as the common people, was not the exotic vice epitomised by the *parvenu*, but that of the acquiescent servant. Somali traders and their leadership were frequently invited to township meetings, government consultations and university seminar rooms, but more because they politely accepted conclusions and, when requested, complied with instructions – whether these came from politicians, community leaders or academics.

In township community meetings, Somalis who did not toe the line were often accused of being 'arrogant' and equated to colonial settlers or apartheid oppressors seeking to take advantage of unassuming nationals. In air-conditioned seminar rooms, politicians, policy-makers and researchers were given free range to espouse all forms of extreme theories pertaining to foreign communities and their enterprises. Yet when these radical attacks were queried by affected groups, these groups' points were regularly struck down as insensitive and confrontational. A particular disdain was shown by researchers for Somali traders who refused to participate in their studies, as though traders were under an obligation to co-operate. 'We encountered terrible hostility from the Somali traders in that site who didn't want to be part of the research,' the presenter complained to the audience that morning.

Within these constraints how should the pariah mobilise politically to advance justice? This pursuit is not aimed at achieving strict formal legal equality, as there will always be some legal discrepancies between groups, whether these are based on race, religion, gender, age, nationality or levels of income. Rather, pariah justice entails being considered more generally as an equal and valued human being. It is only when discriminatory laws lack such a regard that they become dangerous and problematic.

The first option for those Somali traders who felt hopeless, disillusioned or fearful for their lives was simply to depart. Closing shop and starting over was a continual narrative in the lives of most retailers. While some managed to escape high levels of crime through these efforts, relocation in itself did not enable most of them to overturn their marginal and subservient social status. Even those who managed to restart their lives in wealthy societies in the West had no guarantee that they would not be met with further social prejudice and hostility. Many Somalis escaping to Europe or America risked falling further down the perceived social ladder, with those remaining in South Africa depicting their options abroad as being limited to becoming 'a blue-collar worker' carrying out the West's most menial and unrewarded tasks. Flight and relocation, therefore, could improve one's sense of security but was no guarantee of a fruitful and dignified future.

One way for pariahs to address their dilemma is to become conscious of the roles imposed on them and actively rebel against them. Writing in the late nineteenth and early twentieth century, Zionist writer Bernard Lazare articulated the need for Jewish national liberation. At the time, emancipated Jews in Western Europe were facing social prejudice and pressures to assimilate. Further afield the Jews of Eastern Europe were living under extreme poverty, hostility and oppression. In Lazare's view this meant that neither Jews in the West nor those in the East could be said to be truly free. But for Lazare, the means of achieving this desired national liberation was not pinned on the founding of a nation state in Palestine. Nor could it be realised through assimilation, 'a disguised slavery'. Lazare believed that freedom rested on Jews reformulating their national identity by adopting the stance of the 'conscious pariah'.

For Lazare, freedom means being able to be oneself. He states that 'every human creature must know how to resist oppression and preserve his right to total development, his freedom to be and *to be himself*.[3] In his view this form of freedom demands that Jews become conscious of their servile and outcast condition, and actively rebel against it.[4] Pariahs need to cease viewing themselves unconsciously through the lens of gentile society and its prejudices. Lazare declares: 'Henceforth I am a pariah, and I know not out of what elements to rebuild myself a dignity and a personality. I must learn who I am and why I am hated, and that which I can be.'[5] He criticises those who cower to society by presenting themselves as humble subjects to win 'forgiveness and a little table'.[6] This, he believes, would do little to counter anti-Semitism. Instead, it will keep Jewish populations languishing under conditions of secondary citizenship at best and violent oppression at worst.

Seventy years later, in apartheid South Africa, student leader Steve Biko appealed to black South Africans to similarly free themselves from 'spiritual poverty' through Black Consciousness. In Biko's view, the attainment of political freedom required a change in black self-perception and the development of a 'free self'.[7] He argued that black South Africans had become a shell of their former selves by accepting the status quo: 'In the privacy of his toilet his face twists in silent condemnation of white society but brightens up in sheepish obedience as he comes out hurrying in response to his master's impatient call.'[8]

Biko's Black Consciousness entails both internal reflection into how black South Africans have allowed themselves to become used as props in the apartheid system, as well as developing a renewed pride in being black. By defining themselves as black (and not 'non-whites'), black South Africans consciously affirm who they are, rather than try to escape their identities or define themselves in relation to whites.

Like Lazare, Biko is sceptical about assimilation. Black South Africans cannot escape their predicament through attempting to assimilate into white society and blindly accept its norms and social codes. In order to realise substantive political and social change, black South Africans need to engage with white society freely and on their own terms.

Both Lazare and Biko believe that a key step for achieving liberation on their own terms is for oppressed and marginalised groups to establish and develop their own grassroots organisations. Lazare warns: 'So do not insist on entering a house where you will be insulted, on sitting down at a table whence you will be driven away. Learn how to build your own house, a house where you will welcome all men ...'[9] Both are also aware of the need to build broader unity and solidarity with other oppressed groups, Biko interpreting 'black' broadly as a 'reflection of a mental attitude' rather than a specific race or ethnic group. Lazare calls for Jews likewise to work with other oppressed groups, suspecting their oppression to be part of a broader moral collapse across the world.[10]

Somali communities across South Africa have largely succeeded at self-organisation. They tend to avoid occupations that make them reliant on South Africans for a living. They have developed their own institutions, including mosques, crèches and community centres. Individuals invest in personal development. This can be seen not just through entrepreneurism, but also through aspirations towards tertiary education. This self-sufficiency is an important part of building resilience. Community members develop an awareness that to a great extent they can survive and even flourish irrespective of the hostile environments that surround them. It also reduces dependence on South African civil society or the state. Somali community organisations are frequently approached and relied on by South African political and civil society leadership when attempting to carry out policies and programmes. But too much inward focus can leave Somalis vulnerable. Internal cohesion and self-sufficiency cannot on their own grapple with the problems of violent crime and xenophobic anguish. At some point, circumstances dictate that pariah groups engage directly with dominant societies.

When advocating for political mobilisation, both Lazare and Biko call on outcast and oppressed groups to come out of the shadows and engage honestly on their own terms with dominant groups. Biko calls on black South Africans not to reform, but rather to 'completely transform' the apartheid system.[11]

Somali traders in township settings were not in a position to 'completely transform' their reality. Raising complaints or making demands at meetings could put individuals' lives in peril. A Somali community leader explained to me that 'the most difficult thing' about township politics was the levels of intimidation. 'You won't be able to say some of the things because you might be attacked,' he said, recalling how his efforts to speak his mind at a meeting in Khayelitsha had backfired – 'we were threatened in Khayelitsha by a guy claiming to be a businessman' – and how the incident had left an indelible impression on him. 'He was pointing a stick to us and saying, "You guys are not meant to be here."' The memory of the event was all too familiar to me from many of the interviews I had conducted, although my recollection was from the safe perspective of a silent spectator. But there was more to that interaction. 'One of the persons from government was the adviser to the minister of police, who at the time was Nathi Mthethwa. His adviser was the guest of honour.' But this had little impact on the level of threats of violence: 'There was also police presence there, but nobody told him "You cannot do that."'

In township settings it was particularly difficult to shrug off the role of the meek subordinate, let alone advance a transformation of the social and political order. 'It was not safe in Khayelitsha to challenge the local community directly,' Mohamed told me over a WhatsApp call. In the midst of the Covid-19 lockdown, it feels as though Mohamed, who now lives in Birmingham, might as well be my neighbour. It makes little difference anymore whether he lives in England or in Bellville. Family, colleagues and old friends are equally only available to me via my internet service.

Breaking with the code of servile agreeability could invite backlash, but most stifling was the continual underlying threat of death. Speaking out also risked inciting broader violence and unrest against traders and their livelihoods. On several occasions meetings that went sour were followed by the quick and silent murder of nearby shopkeepers. Traders' ability to serve pariah justice was limited by their own sense of mortality and that of others.

Another strategy that was mostly out of bounds for Somali retailers when it came to township politics was legal intervention. Despite many glaring breaches of law that came to light at township meetings, traders had little appetite for advancing pariah justice through the courts. 'Courts drag out the issues for years,' Mohamed complained when I asked him about the country's formal justice system. Furthermore, if traders 'make a case against the local community there will be more trouble,' he said, aware of the fact that traders lacked both popular support and political clout. The relevance of a court judgment was also questionable in a context where, as Hassan had put it, 'there is no law'.

Laws were more effectively used in civil litigation against state actors. Judges at high courts and the Supreme Court of Appeal heard many matters over the years relating to the Somali community with the state acting as respondent or defendant. Community leaders took matters to court when efforts at lobbying the state had failed and matters potentially impacted on large numbers of people. 'The kind of case you can take to court is an issue that affects a lot of people,' one Somali community leader maintained. He gave the example of the closure of the refugee reception offices in Cape Town and Port Elizabeth. 'The elderly, women and children had to go to renew documents in Pretoria. If it's too much for people and people are struggling, then we go to court.' Cases taken to court related to asylum applications, police brutality and accessing trading licences.

These matters were usually won. Judgments such as the *Somali Association of South Africa* case upheld foreign traders' rights to apply for business licences in Limpopo, enabling many traders to continue to work and secure their livelihoods. But at the same time the formal justice system did not entirely empower traders to shirk their pariah status. Like township meetings, court hearings were not typically places where Somalis could speak their minds and participate as equals. Their role was usually to sit silently and observe lawyers argue on their behalf, often with little comprehension of what was being said and why.

While the condition of plaintiffs and complainants did improve as an outcome of court proceedings against the state, it was not without problems. For instance, the *Somali Association of South Africa* case, while allowing traders to access licences, had an eerily disturbing justification. Traders, the court ruled, were entitled to licences because their inability to work could force them into conditions of degradation and threaten their dignity. This basic human right did not extend very far. When it came to a choice of vocation or entitlement to meaningful work, their rights were restricted. Asylum seekers and refugees could enjoy some dignity, but not much beyond.

While courts were strategically important and at times essential to secure basic rights to survival, they were not as effective in enabling Somali retailers fully to shed their outcast and denigrated status. Sometimes sophisticated and elite court systems only officialised the pariahs' subordinate predicament, even as they advanced their livelihoods and interests at the same time.

Advancing justice entails more than reliance on formal courts and laws. But at local township levels vocal mobilisation – the honest confrontations urged by Lazare and Biko – was effectively ruled out. Faced with these constraints, traders pursued justice less through legal action or grandiose speeches at tense public forums, and more in the streets and shadows of everyday township life. This way they avoided the scrutiny of the public sphere and its volatile and sometimes deadly sentiments. Traders negotiated rental agreements with landlords and engaged with community leaders in their homes, keeping out of sight of hostile audiences and anxious state power. Others curried favour with surrounding residents by donating blankets to flood victims or handing out food parcels to the hungry. They tidied streets, chatted with youth sitting on street corners, and were courteous to customers. Their passive and repeated presence at contentious meetings sapped the energy of competing South African retailers. Over time, plans for follow-up meetings never materialised, and threats subsided. Often Somali shopkeepers emerged from fraught engagements as comfortable acquaintances with South African ringleaders and acquired the contact details of key police officials. It was these efforts, more than the eloquent delivery of political arguments, that enabled traders to establish and protect their footholds within township areas. Customers arrived with crumpled banknotes in their pockets, asking few, if any, questions. Business continued as usual irrespective of deals concocted in contentious meeting rooms. As pariahs, they knew how to circumvent challenges when direct confrontation was not possible. In Khayelitsha South African traders could not close down new shops because, when it came down to it, they did not enjoy sufficient local political and popular support.

But these largely invisible gestures could not upend traders' continued condition of precariousness. Such politics can only achieve a tenuous grasp of basic rights. Traders remained largely isolated from neighbouring residents and vulnerable to crime. 'We're heading to the kind of integration where a Somali guy can walk through the streets without getting stabbed,' one Somali retailer told me in relation to the Somali community's outreach efforts in Khayelitsha. This did not amount to a full realisation of justice in the sense of being considered wholly equal, however. Traders could not escape their social stigma and marginalisation through tacit material offerings and discreet informal relationships.

Reaching out to local leaders and residents can help to forward individuals' interests and make their lives more secure, but it cannot contribute to fundamental change. By not speaking out at critical times, and rather opting for backroom local-level diplomacy, Somali traders witnessed the sprouting of informal agreements across Cape Town's townships barring new Somali businesses. In doing so, community representatives exchanged ideal notions of justice and equality in return for the tenuous lives and livelihoods of their community members. Gradually, these agreements and understandings established norms and standards that took root. It became broadly understood that irrespective of the law, foreign traders were outsiders with few to no entitlements to trade in townships. These perceptions were ramped up at provincial and national levels to become mainstream discourse and policy.

Despite their many efforts and interventions, foreign traders' formal rights in South Africa have become constricted, sporadic xenophobic attacks and deadly robberies continue, and political discourse has only become more extreme. Currently the state is on the verge of passing policies to militarise its borders. The possibility of the erection of processing centres remains on the table. Laws also oblige asylum seekers to renew their documents every few months and live as tenuous guests in the country for many years, with little hope of naturalisation. Many asylum seekers, refugees and other immigrants accordingly enjoy little certainty regarding their futures, with their right to work being increasingly threatened and curtailed.

Thus, more is required from the pariah than shadow politics. Quiet gestures and behind-the-scenes arrangements can only be a starting point for broader political inclusion. Shadow politics can help to establish protection and build solidarities, but it cannot transform the system. On their own, subtle and anonymous acts will not release the pariahs from their secondary and outcast status, and ultimately from political and social stigmatisation. While at local street levels traders may live under the illusion that they have found acceptance, their conditions of social and political insecurity persist. If a better deal comes along, traders may well find themselves cast out and evicted. They remain under the condition of a pariah, living on 'tenterhooks'.[12]

In addition to local mobilisation, the pariah therefore also needs to engage the elite, as fraught as the process can be. Elite platforms are less tense and deadly than local township ones. South Africa's middle and upper classes are far removed from the socio-economic discontentment and anxieties that underscore township politics and its propensity for bloodshed. The elite have recourse to many means of political sway, such as access to information, the courts and connections to political leaders and mass media. In this way the pariahs might find venues and spaces where they can participate relatively freely without intimidation.

This may not be at Khayelitsha Resource Centre, but may be in parliament, on radio, at civil society workshops. These efforts may eventually alter the persuasions of amenable groups at grassroots levels. But seeking alliances with elite actors, whether state officials, civil society or other professionals, comes with other challenges. There is the possibility of being simply ignored and disregarded, one's presence simply being a box-ticking exercise. Alternatively, overzealous enthusiasts could trample local shadow arrangements and fragile coalitions, thereby undermining traders' security and livelihoods.

To avoid such fates, the pariahs must turn to Biko and Lazare and consciously discard the roles cut out for them, and sometimes forced upon them, when navigating political terrains. In the case of Somali retailers, this does not mean dispensing with Somali cultural norms of generosity and polite etiquette, but perhaps with some of the caution. The pariahs should consciously voice their opinion openly at key moments and become a visible political participant as opposed to a simple caricature. At the same time the pariahs need to identify, confront and, if necessary, shun those platforms where real participation is obstructed. By resisting the role of humble servant who takes instructions or sits in the back seat, they can begin to challenge those norms and principles that set them up as barely human. Efforts to dislodge and expel the pariah will become more difficult when the pariah becomes a discernible and at times disobedient person. Only through such interventions and appearances can the pariah escape being an afterthought to political leaders at best, or the subject of deliberate targeting and disposal at worst. These principles are not only relevant to the Somali shopkeeper. In our increasingly polarised world, individuals may find themselves falling outside constricting elite circles and at the mercy of heightened popular frustration. The social and political outcast may become more the norm than an exception. In this respect it may be wise to consider the experiences of a pariah community on Cape Town's urban outskirts.

This is not to say that pursuing justice through more diverse avenues will be successful. It is more about improving chances of disputing borders and generating change than of guaranteeing the realisation of full recognition. The state of affairs confronting the pariah is symptomatic of whole societies having gone astray, which will require a concerted effort from diverse sectors to alter. Failure introduces the risk of being swept up in a politics of control, cleansing and order. But that does not mean there is no significant part for the pariah, whose increasing exclusion both exposes society's fault lines and presents opportunities for action and regeneration. What I witnessed at the seminar on a quiet unassuming morning in Cape Town revealed not only the predicament of the pariah, but also how pariahs transcend their condition by not accepting delegated roles, and crossing the boundaries into a new political community on their own terms.

Notes

Preface

1   Quinton Mtyala, 'Somalis Refuse to Sign "One-Sided" Deal for Spaza Owners', *Cape Times*, 17 August 2009.

2   Petra Krusche and Vanya Gastrow, 'Somali Traders Could Pay the Price for Authorities' Failure to Uphold Basic Rights', *Cape Times*, 31 August 2009.

3   Vanya Gastrow with Roni Amit, *Elusive Justice: Somali Traders, Access to Formal and Informal Justice Mechanisms in the Western* Cape (Johannesburg: African Centre for Migration & Society, 2012). Vanya Gastrow with Roni Amit, *Somalinomics: A Case Study on the Economic Dimensions of Somali Informal Trade in the Western Cape* (Johannesburg: African Centre for Migration & Society, 2013). Vanya Gastrow with Roni Amit, *Lawless Regulation: Government and Civil Society Attempts at Regulating Somali Informal Trade in Cape Town* (Johannesburg: African Centre for Migration & Society, 2015).

4   These studies were published in the following reports: Vanya Gastrow, 'Problematizing the Foreign Shop: Justifications for Restricting the Migrant Spaza Sector in South Africa', *SAMP Migration Policy Series* no. 80 (Waterloo, Ontario: Southern African Migration Programme and International Migration Research Centre, 2018). Jonathan Crush, Caroline Skinner and Manal Stulgaitis, 'Rendering South Africa Undesirable: A Critique of Refugee and Informal Sector Policy', *SAMP Migration Policy Series* no. 79 (Waterloo, Ontario: Southern African Migration Programme and International Migration Research Centre, 2017). Jonathan Crush, Godfrey Tawodzera, Cameron McCordic and Sujata Ramachandran, 'Refugee Entrepreneurial Economies in Urban South Africa', *SAMP Migration Policy Series* no. 76 (Waterloo, Ontario: Southern African Migration Programme and International Migration Research Centre, 2017). Godfrey Tawodzera, Abel Chikanda, Jonathan Crush, and Robertson Tengeh, 'International Migrants

and Refugees in Cape Town's Informal Economy', *SAMP Migration Policy Series* no. 70 (Waterloo, Ontario: Southern African Migration Programme and International Migration Research Centre, 2015). Mulugeta F. Dinbabo, Yanga Zembe, Sharon Penderis, Sergio Carciotto, Chris Nshimbi, Vanya Gastrow, Michael Nguatem Belebema, Jonas Nzabamwita, Kenny Chiwarawara, Maryan A. Ahmed, Murus Gidey Alemu and Leon Tshimpaka Mwamba, *Refugee and Asylum Seeking Representative Structures and Their Communities in South Africa* (Cape Town: Institute for Social Development and the Scalabrini Institute for Human Mobility in Africa, 2017). Sergio Carciotto, Vanya Gastrow and Corey Johnson, *Manufacturing Illegality: The Impact of Curtailing Asylum Seekers' Right to Work in South Africa* (Cape Town: Scalabrini Institute for Human Mobility in Africa, 2018).

Chapter 1: Introduction

1   For example, Cape Town's Municipal Planning By-Law 2015 distinguishes between single residential 1 and 2 zones. Areas that are zoned single residential 2 (mostly townships) include 'house shops' as additional use rights subject to conditions around shop size, operating hours and building layout (s 26).

2   Max Weber, Guenther Roth and Claus Wittich, *Economy and Society: An Outline of Interpretive Sociology* (Berkeley: University of California Press, 1978), 933.

3   The Refugees Act 1998 (South Africa) s 27(f) grants refugees the right to seek employment in the country. The Supreme Court of Appeal has upheld asylum seekers' right to work, linking it to the constitutional right to dignity (*Minister of Home Affairs and Others v Watchenuka and Others* [2004] (1) All SA 21 (SCA) (28 November 2003).

4   Roni Amit, *Queue Here for Corruption: Measuring Irregularities in South Africa's Asylum System* (Johannesburg: Lawyers for Human Rights and the African Centre for Migration & Society, July 2015). Theresa Alfaro-Velcamp, Robert H. McLaughlin, Gahlia Brogneri, Matthew Skade, and Mark Shaw, 'Getting "Angry with Honest People": The Illicit Economy in Immigrant Documents in Cape Town', *Migration Studies* 5, no. 2 (July 2017): 216–236. Theresa Alfaro-Velcamp and Mark Shaw, '"Please GO HOME and BUILD Africa": Criminalising Immigrants in South Africa', *Journal of Southern African Studies* 42, no. 5 (September 2016): 983–998.

5   Hannah Arendt, *The Jew as Pariah: Jewish Identity and Politics in the Modern Age*, ed. Ron Feldman (New York: Grove Press, 1978), 290.

6   Arendt, *The Jew as Pariah*, 293.

Chapter 2: Getting Started

1   This was stated to me by both police and residents in the township areas covered by the study (Khayelitsha, Philippi and Kraaifontein). It is also illustrated by a 2011 Philippi East police station audit of spaza shops, which found that most foreign-operated shops in the station's jurisdiction were Somali owned. In particular the audit showed that South Africans owned 90 shops out of 172 spaza shops in the station's jurisdiction, and foreigners owned the remaining 82 shops. Somalis operated 57 of the 82 foreign-owned shops (69.5 per cent). Other foreign nationals in the Philippi East spaza market were Burundians (nine shops), Ethiopians (seven shops), Bangladeshis (three shops), Pakistanis (one shop) and Malawians (one shop).

Chapter 3: The Unwelcome Guest

1   Roger Southall, 'African Capitalism in Contemporary South Africa', *Journal of Southern African Studies* 7, no. 1 (1980): 38.

2   Southall, 'African Capitalism'. Roger Southall, 'The ANC & Black Capitalism in South Africa', *Review of African Political Economy* 31, no. 100 (2004): 313.

3   Andrew Spiegel, 'Refracting an Elusive South African Urban Citizenship: Problems with Tracking Spaza', in *Limits to Liberation After Apartheid: Citizenship, Governance & Culture*, ed. Steven L. Robins (Oxford: James Currey, 2005), 195–205.

4   Spiegel, 'Refracting', 195.

5   Lynette Johns, 'Myriad Laws on Foreigners "Must Change"', *Cape Argus*, 22 September 2011.

6   Ad Hoc Joint Committee on Probing Violence against Foreign Nationals, *Report of the Ad Hoc Joint Committee on Probing Violence against Foreign Nationals*, 19 November 2015, 19–20, http://pmg-assets.s3-website-eu-west-1.amazonaws.com/151119Final_Report.pdf.

7   Andrew Plastow, 'Spaza Shops, Xenophobia and Their Impact on the South African Consumer', *Daily Maverick*, 22 June 2015, https://www.dailymaverick.co.za/opinionista/2015-04-20-spaza-shops-xenophobia-and-their-impact-on-the-south-african-consumer/.

8   Abdullahi Ali Hassan, 'Enterprising Somali Refugees in Cape Town: Beyond Informality, Beyond the Spaza Shop' (Master's thesis, University of Cape Town, 2019), https://open.uct.ac.za/bitstream/handle/11427/31811/thesis_sci_2019_hassan_abdullahi_ali.pdf?sequence=1&isAllowed=y.

9   Refugees Amendment Act 2017 (South Africa) s 18.

Chapter 4: Crime and the Fluid Migrant

1   See quotes by police minister Nathi Mthethwa in Tara Polzer and Kathryn Takabvira, '"Just Crime"? Violence, Xenophobia and Crime: Discourse and Practice', *SA Crime Quarterly* no. 33 (September 2010): 3 and 4, https://www.ajol.info/index.php/sacq/article/view/101463.

2   Heribert Adam and Kogila Moodley, *Imagined Liberation: Xenophobia, Citizenship, and Identity in South Africa, Germany, and Canada* (Stellenbosch: SUN PRESS, 2013), 35. Jean Pierre Misago, 'Disorder in a Changing Society: Authority and the Micro-Politics of Violence', in *Exorcising the Demons Within*, ed. Loren B. Landau (Tokyo, New York, Paris: United Nations University Press, April 2012), 89. Noor Nieftagodien, 'Xenophobia's Local Genesis: Historical Constructions of Insiders and the Politics of Exclusion in Alexandra Township', in Landau, *Exorcising the Demons Within*, 109. Jonny Steinberg, 'South Africa's Xenophobic Eruption', *ISS Paper* no. 169 (November 2008): 1–13. Jonathan Crush, 'The Perfect Storm: The Realities of Xenophobia in Contemporary South Africa', *SAMP Migration Policy Series* no. 50 (Cape Town: Idasa, 2000).

3   Sapa, 'The Body Count ...', *IOL News*, 12 June 2008, https://www.iol.co.za/news/south-africa/the-body-count-404220, date accessed 6 March 2021.

4   South African Police Service, *SAPS Western Cape Annual Report 2012/2013*, 2013, 38, https://www.wcpp.gov.za/sites/default/files/SAPS_Ann_Rep_2012_2013[1].pdf.

5   South African Police Service, 'SAPS Crimestats', accessed 8 September 2020, https://www.saps.gov.za/services/crimestats.php.

Chapter 5: A Window on Statistics Opens Up

1   South African Police Service, 'SAPS Crimestats', accessed 15 May 2012, http://www.saps.gov.za/statistics/reports/crimestats/2011/crime_stats.htm.

2   Peter Gastrow, *Lifting the Veil on Extortion in Cape Town* (Geneva: Global Initiative Against Transnational Organized Crime, 2021), 18.

3   Natasha Prince, 'Men Left Trail of Death and Destruction', *IOL News*, 5 March 2014, https://www.iol.co.za/news/men-left-trail-of-death-and-destruction-1656532.

4   South African Police Service, *Annual Crime Report 2015/2016: Addendum to the SAPS Annual Report*, 2016, 45, https://www.saferspaces.org.za/resources/entry/annual-crime-report-2015-2016-addendum-to-the-saps-annual-report.

5   Sintha Chiumia, 'FACTSHEET: How Many International Migrants Are There in SA?', *Africa Check*, 14 August 2016, https://africacheck.org/factsheets/data-migrants-numbers/.

6   Not all victims report crime. South African and foreign national victims of business robbery could have different rates of reporting crime, which could in turn influence official statistics on victim profiles. According to STATS SA, 60 per cent of households in South Africa that experienced *home* robberies reported them to the police (Statistics South Africa,, *Governance, Public Safety and Justice Survey: 2018/19 (Pretoria: STATS SA*, 2019), 27). The year earlier, STATS SA's *Victims of Crime Survey 2017/18* (Pretoria: STATS SA, 11 October 2018), 31, found that 58 per cent of 'Black African' households reported the incidents to the police. A study conducted in 2012 shows that approximately 60 per cent of crimes in Khayelitsha were reported to the police (Khayelitsha Commission of Inquiry, *Towards a Safer Khayelitsha: The Report of the Commission of Inquiry into Allegations of Police Inefficiency and a Breakdown in Relations between SAPS and the Community in Khayelitsha*, August 2014, 131). There is no data specifically on business robbery reporting rates in South Africa or Khayelitsha, nor has any research been carried out on reporting rates among foreign nationals. Should national reporting rates of business robberies be similar to those of home robberies, then even a 100 per cent reporting rate among foreign nationals could not in isolation explain why foreign nationals fall victim to 47.6 per cent of business robbery cases in the country.

Chapter 6: Fortress South Africa

1   The Khayelitsha Commission of Inquiry (*Towards a Safer Khayelitsha*, 193, and 214–218) states that police identified 78 dockets of vigilante crimes (referred to as 'Bundu courts') between 1 April 2011 and 30 June 2012 in the Khayelitsha cluster. Almost all of these dockets involved cases of murder. However, on closer analysis, five dockets were duplicates, and seven murder dockets were not provided to the commission so could not be analysed. Of the 66 dockets that were examined, 63 related to murder and three related to attempted murder. Three dockets did not involve vigilantism, two comprised double murders, and two comprised triple murders. Thus, there were between 66 and 73 vigilante killings in Khayelitsha over the period. Police statistics for the Khayelitsha cluster show that 359 murders were reported between 1 April 2011 and 31 March 2012.

Chapter 7: Elusive Justice and Xenophobic Crime

1   South African Police Service, *SAPS Western Cape Annual Report 2013/2014*, 29.

2   South African Police Service, *SAPS Western Cape Annual Report 2013/2014*, 29.

3   Gastrow, *Lifting the Veil*, 18.

4   Xenowatch, 'About Us', accessed 29 May 2020, http://www.xenowatch.ac.za/about-xenowatch/.

5   Jonathan Crush and Sujata Ramachandran, 'Xenophobic Violence in South Africa: Denialism, Minimalism, Realism', *SAMP Migration Policy Series* no. 66 (Cape Town and Waterloo, Ontario: Southern African Migration Programme and International Migration Research Centre, 2014), 7.

6   Loren B. Landau, 'Loving the Alien? Citizenship, Law and the Future in South Africa's Demonic Society', *African Affairs* 109, no. 435 (April 2010): 213.

7   Belinda Dodson, 'Locating Xenophobia: Debate, Discourse, and Everyday Experience in Cape Town, South Africa', *Africa Today* 56, no. 3 (Spring 2010): 3.

8   Tendayi Achiume, 'Beyond Prejudice: Structural Xenophobic Discrimination Against Refugees', *Georgetown Journal of International Law* 45, no. 2 (2014): 337.

Chapter 8: An Ordinary Crime

1   Azad Essa, 'South Africa's Soweto Tense after "Xenophobic" Attacks', *Al Jazeera*, 23 January 2015, https://www.aljazeera.com/news/africa/2015/01/south-africa-soweto-tense-xenophobic-attacks-150123044841532.html.

2   Khadija Patel, Xolani Mbanjwa, Zinhle Mapumulo, Abram Mashego and Sipho Masondo, 'Soweto Unrest: "Cops Told Us to Loot"', *City Press*, 25 January 2015, https://www.news24.com/SouthAfrica/News/Soweto-unrest-Cops-told-us-to-loot-20150125.

3   Rapula Moatshe, 'Zuma: Marches Were Anti-Crime, Not Xenophobic', *Pretoria News*, 25 February 2017, https://www.iol.co.za/news/politics/zuma-marches-were-anti-crime-not-xenophobic-7923422.

4   Jacob Zuma, speaking after the launch of Operation Phakisa, Johannesburg, 24 February 2017, https://www.news24.com/Video/SouthAfrica/News/watch-south-africans-arent-xenophobic-jacob-zuma-20170224.

5   Thabo Mbeki, 'National Tribute in Remembrance of Xenophobic Attacks Victims'. Speech, Tshwane, Gauteng, 3 July 2008. https://www.polity.org.za/article/sa-mbeki-national-tribute-in-remembrance-of-xenophobic-attacks-victims-03072008-2008-07-03.

6   Police minister Nathi Mthethwa, quoted in *IOL News*, 'Minister Tackles Xenophobic Attacks', 12 July 2010, https://www.iol.co.za/news/south-africa/

minister-tackles-xenophobic-attacks-489525. See Crush and Ramachandran, 'Xenophobic Violence in South Africa', 8–9.

7   South African Police Service, *SAPS Western Cape Annual Report 2013/ 2014*, 29.

8   South African Police Service, *Annual Crime Report 2015/2016: Addendum*, 41.

9   Wyndham Hartley, 'Illegal Foreign Business Owners "A Soft Target for Criminals"', *Business Day*, 9 February 2012. South African Police Service, *An Analysis of the National Crime Statistics: Addendum to the Annual Report 2011/2012*, 2012, 36, https://www.saps.gov.za/about/stratframework/annual_report/ 2011_2012/saps_crime_stats_report_%202011-12.pdf.

10   South African Police Service, *Provincial Policing Needs and Priorities Report (PNP): Report for the Blue Downs Police Cluster 2016/17: 1–2 July 2016*, 2016, 39, https:// www.westerncape.gov.za/assets/departments/community-safety/ policing_needs_and_priorities_report_blue_downs_cluster_16-17.pdf.

Chapter 9: The Masiphumelele Shop Threat, 2006

1   The first Somali spaza shop to open in Masiphumelele was called Baraka Cash Store, which then became a colloquial term for Somalis in the neighbourhood. See Craig Timberg, 'Not So Welcome in South Africa', *Washington Post*, 1 October 2006, http://www.washingtonpost.com/wp-dyn/content/ article/2006/09/30/AR2006093000982.html.

2   Western Cape Provincial Government, *Documenting and Evaluation Report: Masiphumelele Conflict Intervention August 2006 – March 2007*, undated, https:// www.westerncape.gov.za/text/2009/3/masiphumelele_conflict_interven- tion_report.pdf, accessed 10 April 2021.

3   Western Cape Provincial Government, *Documenting and Evaluation Report*, 48.

4   Western Cape Provincial Government, *Documenting and Evaluation Report*, 16.

5   Western Cape Provincial Government, *Documenting and Evaluation Report*, 47.

6   Western Cape Provincial Government, *Documenting and Evaluation Report*, 42.

7   Ciska Verster, 'Four Somali Shops Held Up in Past Week', *False Bay People's Post*, undated, http://www.compcom.co.za/wp-content/uploads/2016/09/ Vanya-Gastrow-Submission.pdf, accessed 4 March 2017. Western Cape Provincial Government, *Documenting and Evaluation Report*, 43.

Chapter 10: In the Shadow of Masiphumelele

1   South African Police Service, 'SAPS Crimestats', http://www.saps.gov.za/ statistics/reports/crimestats/2011/crime_stats.htm, accessed 15 May 2012.

2   South African Police Service, *Annual Report 2007/2008*, 29 August 2008, 13, https://www.gov.za/sites/default/files/gcis_document/201409/saps-an-rep-complete.pdf.

3   South African Police Service, *Annual Report 2007/2008*, 12.

4   Sydwell Citwa, chairperson of Zanokhanyo Retailers, quoted in Pearlie Joubert, 'Nafcoc Calls for Somali Purge', *Mail & Guardian*, 5 September 2008, http://www.mg.co.za/article/2008-09-05-nafcoc-calls-for-somali-purge.

5   South African Police Service, *Annual Report 2008/2009*, 21 July 2009, 18, https://www.gov.za/sites/default/files/gcis_document/201409/sapsan-rep-0809.pdf.

6   South African Police Service, *Addendum to the Annual Report 2011/2012*.

7   South African Police Service, *Addendum to the Annual Report 2011/2012*, 36.

8   South African Police Service, *An Analysis of the National Crime Statistics 2012/2013: Addendum to the Annual Report 2012/2013*, 31 August 2013, 13, https://www.arrivealive.co.za/ckfinder/userfiles/files/national%20crime%20situation.pdf.

9   South African Police Service, *Addendum to the Annual Report 2012/2013*, 33.

Chapter 11: The Shifting Problem and Changing Narratives

1   Western Cape Provincial Government, *Documenting and Evaluation Report*, 5.

2   Unsigned agreement titled 'Draft Mutual Agreement Between Local and Somali Traders in Gugulethu and Other Communities in Western Cape Province, 6 August 2009'. The document was given to me by a member of the Anti-Eviction Campaign in Cape Town who stated that it comprised the trade agreement concluded between Somali and South African spaza shop-keepers in Gugulethu in 2009.

3   Rob Davies, 'Minister Rob Davies Urges Orange Farm Small Businesses to Take Advantage of Economic Opportunities Provided by Government', speech, Orange Farm, Gauteng, 9 April 2013, https://www.youtube.com/watch?v=BGTvJWlTSFg.

4   Lebogang Seale, 'Groups Do Rounds Closing Down Foreign Businesses', *The Star*, 27 April 2011, https://www.security.co.za/news/18203.

5   *City Press*, 'Campaign Against Foreign Township Traders Spreads', 14 May 2015, https://www.news24.com/news24/Archives/City-Press/Campaign-against-foreign-township-traders-spreads-20150430.

6   *Somali Association of South Africa and Others v Limpopo Department of Economic Development, Environment and Tourism* (48/2014) ZASCA 143 (26 September 2014).

7   Khulekani Magubane, 'Reveal Trade Secrets, Minister Tells Foreigners',
     Business Day, 28 January 2015, https://www.businesslive.co.za/archive/2015-
     01-28-reveal-trade-secrets-minister-tells-foreigners/.

8   Lindiwe Zulu, 'Laws Regulating Foreign Owned Spazas Must be Fast
     Tracked: Zulu', interview with Leanne Manas on *Morning Live*, SABC
     News, 27 January 2015., http://www.sabc.co.za/news/a/bfdc37004715b-
     f689b21bf686e648436/Laws-regulating-foreign-owned-spazas-must-be-
     fast-tracked:-Zulu-20152701. Accessed 4 March 2017.

9   Department of Trade and Industry, *National Informal Business Upliftment
     Strategy*, February 2014, 59.

10   *Somali Association of South Africa* case.

11   South African Government, 'Attacks against Foreign Nationals', media
     statement, 20 April 2015, https://www.gov.za/speeches/outbreak-violence-
     against-foreign-nationals.

12   *The Citizen*, 'SA Citizens Are Not Xenophobic – Jeff Radebe', 11 November
     2015, https://citizen.co.za/news/south-africa/government/2202783/south-
     africans-are-not-xenophobic-ramaphosa/.

13   Ad Hoc Joint Committee on Probing Violence against Foreign Nationals,
     Report on Probing Violence against Foreign Nationals, 20.

14   Ad Hoc Joint Committee on Probing Violence against Foreign Nationals,
     Report on Probing Violence against Foreign Nationals, 38–39.

Chapter 12: Infestation and Backlash

1   South African Police Service (@SAPoliceService), Twitter, 11 July 2018,
     https://twitter.com/sapoliceservice/status/1017038704244875265?lang=en.

2   Itumeleng Madumo Setshedi, Facebook, 12 July 2018, https://www.face-
     book.com/photo.php?fbid=10216558484934213&set=pb.1221371857.-
     2207520000.1549524235.&type=3&theater.

3   'Makula' is a derogatory term for a person of Indian descent.

4   #WhoIsYeezy (@katleho_Yeezy), Twitter, 28 July 2018, https://twitter.com/
     Katleho_Yeezy/status/1023201235531444225?ref_src=twsrc%5Etfw%
     7Ctwcamp%5Etweetembed%7Ctwterm%5E1023201235531444225&ref_
     url=https%3A%2F%2Fcitizen.co.za%2Fnews%2Fsouth-africa%2F1998917%
     2Fwatch-war-declared-against-my-friend-spaza-shops-selling-expired-
     products%2F.

5   Gopolang Chawane, 'WATCH: War Declared against "My Friend" Spaza
     Shops Selling Expired Products', *The Citizen*, 22 August 2018, https://citizen.

co.za/news/south-africa/1998917/watch-war-declared-against-my-friend-spaza-shops-selling-expired-products/.

6   Thembelihle Mkhonza, 'Consumer Commission Tackles "Potentially Harmful" Fake Food Products', *IOL News*, 27 August 2018, https://www.iol.co.za/news/south-africa/consumer-commission-tackles-potentially-harm-ful-fake-food-products-16765174.

7   *Thembisan*, 'WATCH: Fake, Expired Foods Removed from Tembisa Corner Shops', 30 August 2018, https://tembisan.co.za/74736/community-raids-foreign-owned-shops-selling-bad-food/.

8   *Thembisan*, 'WATCH: Fake, Expired Foods Removed'.

9   South African Government, 'Minister Aaron Motsoaledi on Allegations of Fake and Expired Food', media statement, 3 September 2018, https://www.gov.za/speeches/media-statement-minister-health-allegations-fake-and-expired-food-5-sep-2018-0000.

10   Karabo Ngoepe and Manyane Manyane, 'Fake Food Crunch', *IOL News*, 2 September 2018, https://www.iol.co.za/sundayindependent/news/fake-food-crunch-16850990.

11   The chairperson of the meeting replied that the person using the term 'was making an example, he was just using the word "flies"'.

Chapter 13: When Reasoning Rings Hollow

1   Edwin Ntshidi, 'Ramaphosa: Foreign Nationals Must Obey the Laws of South Africa', *Eyewitness News*, 15 September 2019, https://ewn.co.za/2019/09/15/ramaphosa-foreign-nationals-must-obey-the-laws-of-south-africa.

2   *Somali Association of South* Africa case, para 13.

3   The finding was based on a survey carried out in Motherwell township in Port Elizabeth involving 64 Somali and 65 South African spaza shop-keepers (Abdu Sh. Mohamed Hikam, 'An Exploratory Study on the Somali Immigrants' (Master's thesis, Nelson Mandela Metropolitan University, 2011), 75). In South Africa all businesses are obliged to register with the revenue service within 60 days of commencing operations, irrespective of whether or not they earn below the tax threshold.

4   Prologue by Lieutenant General AH Lamoer in South African Police Service, *Addendum to the Annual Report 2012/2013*, 2.

5   Valerie Cilliers, 'Court Rules on Spaza Shops', *Northern News*, 24 August 2012, http://www.noordnuus.co.za/details/24-08-2012/court_rules_on_spaza_shops/14634.

6   Valerie Cilliers, 'Court Rules on Spaza Shops'.

7   South African Police Service, *Annual Report 2007/2008*, 12.

8   Vicki Igglesden, *Case F22/1: Athlone Court* (Cape Town: 21 November 2011).

9   Igglesden, *Case F22/1: Athlone Court*, 2.

10   Igglesden, *Case F22/1: Athlone Court*, 2.

11   Unsigned agreement, 'Draft Mutual Agreement Between Local and Somali Traders in Gugulethu'.

12   Department of Trade and Industry, *National Informal Business Upliftment Strategy*, 59.

Chapter 14: The Problem as Legitimacy

1   Asiatic Inquiry Commission, *Report of the Asiatic Inquiry Commission* (Cape Town: Union of South Africa, 1921), 3.

2   Asiatic Inquiry Commission, *Report*, 9.

3   Asiatic Inquiry Commission, *Report*, 3.

4   Asiatic Inquiry Commission, *Report*, 30.

5   Pyong Gap Min, 'Middleman Entrepreneurs', in *The Routledge Handbook of Migration Studies*, ed. Steven J. Gold and Stephanie J. Nawyn (London and New York: Routledge, 2013), 145–152. Irwin D. Rinder, 'Strangers in the Land: Social Relations in the Status Gap', *Social Problems* 6, no. 3 (Winter 1958–1959): 258. Edna Bonacich, 'A Theory of Middleman Minorities', *American Sociological Review* 38, no. 5 (October 1973): 583.

6   Gap Min, 'Middleman Entrepreneurs'. Rinder, 'Strangers in the Land'.

7   Bonacich, 'A Theory of Middleman Minorities', 589.

8   Bonacich, 'A Theory of Middleman Minorities', 591.

9   Karen Manges Douglas and Rogelio Saenz, 'Middleman Minorities', in *International Encyclopedia of the Social Sciences*, 2nd ed., ed. William A. Darity Jr (New York: Macmillan Reference USA, 2008), 147.

10   Frantz Fanon, *The Wretched of the Earth* (New York: Grove Press, 1963). Mahmood Mamdani, 'Beyond Settler and Native as Political Identities: Overcoming the Political Legacy of Colonialism', *Comparative Studies in Society and History* 43, no. 4 (October 2001): 651–664.

11   Fanon, *The Wretched of the Earth*, 148.

12   President Jacob Zuma, speech at Grand Parade, Cape Town, 9 February 2016.

13   Lindiwe Zulu, 'Speech by the Minister of Small Business Development, Ms Lindiwe Zulu, at the Hookup Dinner 2nd Anniversary, Johannesburg',

1 August 2014, https://www.gov.za/speeches/minister-lindiwe-zulu-hookup-dinner-2nd-anniversary-1-aug-2014-0000.

14 Lindiwe Zulu, 'Minister Lindiwe Zulu: Small Business Development Dept Budget Vote 2015/16', speech, 20 May 2015, https://www.gov.za/speeches/minister-lindiwe-zulu-small-business-development-dept-budget-vote-201516-20-may-2015-0000.

15 Jonathan Crush, Abel Chikanda and Caroline Skinner, 'Migrant Entrepreneurship and Informality in South African Cities', in *Mean Streets: Migration, Xenophobia and Informality in South Africa*, ed. Jonathan Crush, Abel Chikanda and Caroline Skinner (Cape Town: Southern African Migration Programme, the African Centre for Cities and the International Development Research Centre, 2015), 1. Loren B. Landau, ed., *Exorcising the Demons Within* (Tokyo, New York, Paris: United Nations University Press, April 2012). Shireen Hassim, Tawana Kupe and Eric Worby, eds, *Go Home or Die Here: Violence, Xenophobia and the Reinvention of Difference in South Africa* (Johannesburg: Wits University Press, 2008).

16 Jean Pierre Misago, 'Disorder in a Changing Society'. Jean Pierre Misago, 'Politics by Other Means? The Political Economy of Xenophobic Violence in Post-Apartheid South Africa', *The Black Scholar* 47, no. 2 (2017): 40–53. Jean Pierre Misago, 'Political Mobilisation as the Trigger of Xenophobic Violence in Post-Apartheid South Africa', *International Journal of Conflict and Violence* 13 (2019): 1–10.

17 Lindiwe Zulu in Magubane, 'Reveal Trade Secrets, Minister Tells Foreigners'.

18 Asiatic Inquiry Commission, *Report*, 56.

Chapter 15: Regulating Trade

1 Human Rights Watch, *Shell-Shocked: Civilians Under Siege in Mogadishu* (New York: Human Rights Watch, 13 August 2007), https://www.hrw.org/report/2007/08/13/shell-shocked/civilians-under-siege-mogadishu.

2 Leila Samodien, 'ACDP Backs Call to Shut Down Somali Stores', *Cape Argus*, 8 September 2008.

3 Leila Samodien, 'ACDP Backs Call'.

4 Copy of agreement in author's possession.

5 Quinton Mtyala, 'Somali and Local Shopkeepers Strike a Deal on Peace', *Cape Times*, 20 August 2009.

6 South African Government, 'The Eastern Cape Provincial Government to Meet Residents of Nompumelelo Township', 19 July 2012, https://www.gov.za/eastern-cape-provincial-government-meet-residents-nompumelelo-township.

Chapter 18: Turning to Formality, 2012

1 Department of Home Affairs, *2018/2019 Annual Report*, 31 May 2019, 103, https://static.pmg.org.za/1/DHA_Annual_Report_201819_Text.pdf.
2 Johns, 'Myriad Laws on Foreigners "Must Change"'.
3 United Nations High Commissioner for Refugees, 'UNHCR Statistical Online Population Database', http://popstats.unhcr.org/#_ga=1.3026608.16 42008189.1414090050, accessed 12 December 2014.
4 Quinton Mtyala, 'Cele's Xenophobic Outburst', *Cape Times*, 7 October 2011, https://www.iol.co.za/news/celes-xenophobic-outburst-1152621.
5 United Nations High Commissioner for Refugees, 'Statistical Online Population Database'.
6 United Nations High Commissioner for Refugees, 'Statistical Online Population Database'.
7 African National Congress, *Peace and Stability: Policy Discussion Document*, March 2012, 5.
8 African National Congress, *Peace and Stability*, 6.
9 African National Congress, *Peace and Stability*, 6.
10 Clayton Barnes, 'Cut Number of Foreign Spaza Shops – ANC', *Cape Argus*, 25 June 2012, https://www.iol.co.za/news/politics/cut-number-of-foreign-spaza-shops-anc-1326536.
11 Department of Trade and Industry, *National Informal Business Upliftment Strategy*, 29.
12 SBP Business Environment Specialists, 'Current State of Legislation in South Africa: A country Overregulated and Undergoverned?', SBP Occasional Paper, August 2012, 4 and 6, http://smegrowthindex.co.za/wp-content/uploads/2012/08/SBP-alert-08.12_digital.pdf. *Eyewitness News*, 'DG Defends Business Registration Bill', 26 April 2013, https://ewn.co.za/2013/04/26/DG-defends-Business-Registration-Bill. Songezo Zibi, 'ANC Must Keep Its Promises', *The Herald*, 20 January 2014, https://www.pressreader.com/south-africa/the-herald-south-africa/20140120/281921655907642.
13 *Somali Association of South Africa* case.
14 *Somali Association of South Africa* case, para 43.

15 *Minister of Home Affairs and Others v Watchenuka and Others* (010/2003) [2003] ZASCA 142; [2004] 1 All SA 21 (SCA) (28 November 2003).

16 *Watchenuka* case, para 32.

17 *Watchenuka* case, para 32.

Chapter 19: Formalising Exclusion as the African Way

1   *The Citizen*, 'Foreign Owned Businesses Hampering Rural Growth – DTI', 10 September 2013, https://citizen.co.za/uncategorized/66033/foreign-owned-businesses-hampering-rural-growth-dti/.

2   Department of Trade and Industry, *National Informal Business Upliftment Strategy*, 22.

3   Khumbudzo Ntshavheni, 'Ntshavhe-ni: Businesses Owned by Foreign Nationals Need Regulating', interview on *eNCA*, 5 August 2019, https://www. youtube.com/watch?v=M-xLlwZ2BMY.

4   Gwede Mantashe, Media briefing on *ANN7*, 20 March 2016, https://www. youtube.com/watch?v=mCNnWrAjIcM, minute 45.

5   Victoria Ojeme, 'Inside the Politics, Diplomacy and Reality of Ghana's GIPC Levy on Foreign Traders', *Vanguard*, 27 August 2020, https://www.vanguardngr. com/2020/08/inside-the-politics-diplomacy-and-reality-of-ghanas-gipc-levy/.

6   Staff reporter, 'A/R: Open Our Shops Immediately or We'll March – Ghanaians Working In Nigerian Shops', Modern Ghana, 2 October 2020, https://www.modernghana.com/news/1033167/ar-open-our-shops-im-mediately-or-well-march.html. Timothy Ngnenbe, 'Ghanaian, Nigerian Spare Parts Dealers in Brawl Over Retail Trade', *Graphic Online*, 30 July 2020, https://www.graphic.com.gh/news/general-news/ghanaian-nigerian-spare-parts-dealers-in-brawl-over-retail-trade.html.

7   Abdullah Tijani, 'Ghana's Deportation of Nigerians is a New Chapter in a Very Ugly History that Must End', *African Liberty*, 6 March 2019, https:// www.africanliberty.org/2019/03/06/ghanas-deportation-of-nigerians-is-a-chapter-in-a-very-ugly-history-that-must-end/.

8   Ojeme, 'Inside the Politics'.

9   Immigration Ordinance 1947 (Laws of the Gold Coast) s 12, cited by W. Paatii Ofosu-Amaah, 'Restriction of Aliens in Business in Ghana and Kenya', *The International Lawyer* 8, no. 3 (July 1974): 458.

10 Ofosu-Amaah, 'Restriction of Aliens', citing P.T. Bauer, *West African Trade: A Study of Competition Oligopoly and Monopoly in a Changing Economy* (Cambridge: Cambridge University Press, 1954).

11 Rasheed Olaniyi, 'The 1969 Ghana Exodus: Memory and Reminiscences of Yoruba Migrants', International Migration Institute Conference Paper, 26 November 2008, 2.

12 Ebenezer O. Oni and Samuel K. Okunade, 'The Context of Xenophobia in Africa: Nigeria and South Africa in Comparison', in *The Political Economy of Xenophobia in Africa*, ed. Adeoye O. Akinola (Cham, Switzerland: Springer International Publishing AG, 2018), 41.

13 Shola Lawal, 'Ghana Must Go: The Ugly History of Ghana's Most Famous Bag', *Mail & Guardian*, 4 April 2019, http://atavist.mg.co.za/ghana-must-go-the-ugly-history-of-africas-most-famous-bag. Lynne Brydon, 'Ghanaian Responses to the Nigerian Expulsions of 1983', *African Affairs* 84, no. 337 (October 1985): 561–85.

14 Lawal, 'Ghana Must Go'.

15 Ofosu-Amaah, 'Restriction of Aliens', 459.

16 Maxwell Owusu, 'The Search for Solvency: Background to the Fall of Ghana's Second Republic, 1969–1972', *Africa Today* 19, no. 1 (Winter 1972): 57. Ofosu-Amaah, 'Restriction of Aliens', 473.

17 Brydon, 'Ghanaian Responses', 564.

18 Brydon, 'Ghanaian Responses', 564.

19 Owusu, 'The Search for Solvency', 60.

20 Lawal, 'Ghana Must Go'.

21 Brydon, 'Ghanaian Responses', 572.

22 Fanon, *The Wretched of the Earth*.

23 Fanon, *The Wretched of the Earth*, 157.

24 Edgar C. Taylor, 'Claiming Kabale: Racial Thought and Urban Governance in Uganda', Journal of Eastern African Studies 7, no. 1 (2013): 148.

25 *Scroll*, 'Indo-African History: Watch Idi Amin Defend the Decision to Kick Indians Out of Uganda', 27 October 2015, https://scroll.in/video/1138/indo-african-history-watch-idi-amin-defend-the-decision-to-kick-indians-out-of-uganda.

26 South African Government, White Paper on International Migration for South Africa, July 2017, 63.

27 Letter from UNHCR's acting regional representative to UNHCR implementing partners, dated 28 August 2015.

28 According to section 18 of the Act, asylum seekers can only work in the country if their visas are endorsed with the right to work. To obtain such an endorsement they must pass an 'sustainability determination process' showing that they can't support themselves. In the event that the department

endorses asylum seekers' visas with the right to work, relevant employers 'must furnish the Department with a letter of employment' within 14 days of asylum seekers taking up employment.

29   Edwin Ntshidi, 'Joburg Police to Monitor CBD after Violent Protests', *Eyewitness News*, 2 August 2019, https://ewn.co.za/2019/08/02/joburg-police-to-monitor-cbd-after-violent-protests.

30   David Bruce and Tanya Zack, 'Joburg Vendors vs Police: When a System Wears the Badge of the Law but Lacks Moral Authority', *Daily Maverick*, 5 August 2019, https://www.dailymaverick.co.za/article/2019-08-05-joburg-vendors-vs-police-when-a-system-wears-the-badge-of-the-law-but-lacks-moral-authority/.

31   Gauteng Premier David Makhura (@Davod_Makhura), 'Some foreign nationals who sell counterfeit goods and occupy buildings illegally in the Joburg CBD attacked our police with bottles and petrol bombs', Twitter, 1 August 2019, 9:06 p.m., https://twitter.com/David_Makhura/status/1157004670046547974?ref_src=twsrc%5Etfw%7Ctwcamp%5Etweetem-bed%7Ctwterm%5E1157004670046547974&ref_url=https%3A%2F%2Fwww.timeslive.co.za%2Fnews%2Fsouth-africa%2F2019-08-02-police-withdrew-from-street-battle-with-vendors-to-avoid-bloodbath-in-joburg-cbd%2F.

32   Luke Daniel, 'Makhura Vows to Retaliate Against "Foreigners" Who Attacked JHB Police', *The South African*, 2 August 2019, https://www.thesouthafrican.com/news/joburg-riots-makhura-vows-to-retaliate-against-foreign-nationals/.

33   Jan Bornman, 'Xenophobic Mob Rampages Through Joburg', *Daily Maverick*, 8 August 2019, https://www.dailymaverick.co.za/article/2019-08-08-xenophobic-mob-rampages-through-joburg/.

34   Bornman, 'Xenophobic Mob'.

35   Azarrah Karrim and Ntwaagae Seleka, 'UPDATE: Cele Condemns Violent Protests in Joburg, Briefs Makhura and Ramaphosa', *News24*, 2 September 2019, https://www.news24.com/SouthAfrica/News/sahrc-condemns-johannesburg-protests-calls-for-calm-20190902.

36   Femi Adesina, 'Xenophobic Attacks: President Buhari Dispatches Special Envoy to South Africa', *State House, Abuja, Nigeria*, 3 September 2019, https://statehouse.gov.ng/news/xenophobic-attacks-president-buhari-dispatch-es-special-envoy-to-south-africa/.

37   Peta Thornycroft, 'Five Dead as Mobs Burn Down Shops in "Anti-Foreigner" Riots in Johannesburg', *The Telegraph*, 3 September 2019, https://

www.telegraph.co.uk/news/2019/09/03/five-dead-mobs-burn-shops-anti-foreigner-riots-johannesburg/.

38 Cyril Ramaphosa, 'Address at the Joint Sitting of Parliament on the Crisis of Violence in South Africa, National Assembly, Cape Town (18/09/2019)', *Polity*, 18 September 2019, https://www.polity.org.za/article/sa-cyril-rama-phosa-address-by-south-african-president-at-the-joint-sitting-of-parlia-ment-on-the-crisis-of-violence-in-south-africa-national-assembly-cape-town-18092019-2019-09-19.

39 Qama Qukula, 'Govt Preparing New Laws to Restrict Foreign-Owned Business and "Protect Locals"', *Radio 702*, 26 September 2019, http://www.702.co.za/articles/361955/govt-preparing-new-laws-to-restrict-for-eign-owned-business-and-protect-locals.

40 Nigerian Investment Promotion Commission Act 1995, s 31.

41 Reuters, 'Zimbabwe to Replace Empowerment Law: Finance Minister', 1 August 2019, https://www.reuters.com/article/us-zimbabwe-economy-mining-idUSKCN1UR4X2.

42 Zanele Zama, 'Home Affairs Gazettes New Tougher Laws for Refugees and Asylum Seekers', *Radio 702*, 6 January 2020, http://www.702.co.za/arti-cles/371174/home-affairs-gazettes-new-tougher-laws-for-refugees-and-and-asylum-seekers.

43 Roni Amit, *Lost in the Vortex: Irregularities in the Detention and Deportation of Non-Nationals in South Africa*, Forced Migration Studies Programme Research Report, June 2010.

44 Qukula, 'Home Affairs Minister Aaron Motsoaledi Explains the New, Tougher Laws for Refugees and Asylum Seekers in South Africa', *Cape Talk*, *Today with Kieno Kammies*, 6 January 2020, http://www.capetalk.co.za/arti-cles/371160/new-tighter-laws-broaden-grounds-for-exclusion-from-refu-gee-status-motsoaledi.

45 Qama Qukula, 'Home Affairs Minister Aaron Motsoaledi'.

46 Thando Kubheka, 'SA Lockdown: Govt Working on Relief Package for Informal Sector', *Eyewitness News*, 26 March 2020, https://ewn.co.za/2020/03/26/sa-lockdown-govt-working-on-relief-package-for-infor-mal-sector.

47 South African Government News Agency, 'Guidelines for Spaza Shops Announced', 18 April 2020, https://www.sanews.gov.za/south-africa/guidelines-spaza-shops-announced.

Chapter 20: Pariahdom and Bare Life

1 Rinder, 'Strangers in the Land'.

2 Min, 'Middleman Entrepreneurs', 146.

3 Rinder, 'Strangers in the Land', 254.

4 Hannah Arendt, *The Human Condition*, 2nd ed. (Chicago: The University of Chicago Press, 1958). Michel Foucault, *The History of Sexuality Volume 1: An Introduction* (New York: Pantheon Books, 1978). Michel Foucault, *Society Must Be Defended: Lectures at the Collège de France 1975 to 1976* (New York: Picador, 1997). Giorgio Agamben, *Homo Sacer: Sovereign Power and Bare Life* (Stanford, California: Stanford University Press, 1998).

5 Arendt, *The Human Condition*, 29.

6 Foucault, *Society Must Be Defended*, 261–262.

7 Foucault, *Society Must Be Defended*, 243. Foucault, *The History of Sexuality*, 138.

8 Foucault, *Society Must Be Defended*, 256.

9 *Somali Association of South Africa* case, para 44.

10 Agamben, *Homo Sacer*, 123.

11 In 2003 the Supreme Court of Appeal in the *Watchenuka* case held that the right to dignity afforded by the Constitution excluded from 'its scope a right on the part of every applicant for asylum to undertake employment' (para 31–2). In *Union of Refugee Women and Others v Director, Private Security Industry Regulatory Authority and Others* 2007 (4) SA 395 (CC), the Constitutional Court also found that the right to choose a vocation did not 'fall within a sphere of activity protected by a constitutional right available to refugees and other foreigners'. Accordingly, the court held that legislation restricting asylum seekers and refugees from working in the private sector did not infringe the provision.

12 Timothy Fish Hodgsen argues that it was erroneous for the Supreme Court of Appeal and Constitutional Court to interpret the affirmative right of citizens 'to choose their trade, occupation or profession freely' in section 22 of the Constitution to mean that non-citizens do not have a similar or equivalent right. While not mentioned in section 22, non-citizens are not expressly excluded by the section, and their right to work could be empowered by other human rights provisions in the Constitution and international human rights law (workshop presentation titled 'International Perspectives' at the conference Migration, the Right to Work and Evidence: What Counts in Violent Times? organised by the Socio-Economic Rights Institute, African Centre

for Cities, and the London School of Economics and Political Science, 27 February 2020, Cape Town).

13 Hannah Arendt, *On Revolution* (London: Penguin Books, 1990), 118.

14 Jacques Rancière, 'Who is the Subject of the Rights of Man?', *South Atlantic Quarterly* 103, no. 2/3 (2004): 297.

15 Rancière, 'Who is the Subject of the Rights of Man?' Henk Botha provides a thorough analysis of Rancière's theory in relation to citizenship and rights in South Africa in 'The Rights of Foreigners: Dignity, Citizenship and the Right to Have Rights', *South African Law Journal* 130, no. 4 (2013).

16 Rancière, 'Who is the Subject of the Rights of Man?', 303.

Chapter 21: Pariah Justice

1 Arendt, *The Jew as Pariah*.

2 Hannah Arendt, *The Origins of Totalitarianism* (Orlando, Florida: Harcourt Brace & Company, 1948), 68.

3 Bernard Lazare, *Job's Dungheap* (New York: Schocken Books Inc., 1948), 85.

4 Lazare, *Job's Dungheap*, 85.

5 Lazare, *Job's Dungheap*, 44.

6 Lazare, *Job's Dungheap*, 82.

7 Steve Biko, *I Write What I Like*, ed. Aelred Stubbs, C.R. (Oxford: Heinemann, 1987), 49.

8 Biko, *I Write What I Like*, 28.

9 Lazare, *Job's Dungheap*, 100.

10 Arendt, *The Jew as Pariah*, 128.

11 Biko, *I Write What I Like*, 49.

12 Theodor Herzl, *Gesammelte Werke*, vol. 6, 462, cited in Arendt, *The Jew as Pariah*, 126.

Bibliography

Achiume, Tendayi. 'Beyond Prejudice: Structural Xenophobic Discrimination Against Refugees'. *Georgetown Journal of International Law* 45, no. 2 (2014): 323–381.

Ad Hoc Joint Committee on Probing Violence against Foreign Nationals. *Report of the Ad Hoc Joint Committee on Probing Violence against Foreign Nationals*, Africa: 19 November 2015. http://pmg-assets.s3-website-eu-west-1.amazonaws.com/151119Final_Report.pdf.

Adam, Heribert, and Kogila Moodley. *Imagined Liberation: Xenophobia, Citizenship, and Identity in South Africa, Germany, and Canada.* Stellenbosch: Sun Press, 2013.

Adesina, Femi. 'Xenophobic Attacks: President Buhari Dispatches Special Envoy to South Africa'. *State House, Abuja, Nigeria,* 3 September 2019. https://statehouse.gov.ng/news/xenophobic-attacks-president-buhari-dispatches-special-envoy-to-south-africa/.

African National Congress. *Peace and Stability: Policy Discussion Document.* March 2012.

Agamben, Giorgio. *Homo Sacer: Sovereign Power and Bare Life.* Stanford, California: Stanford University Press, 1998.

Alfaro-Velcamp, Theresa, Robert H. McLaughlin, Gahlia Brogneri, Matthew Skade and Mark Shaw. 'Getting "Angry with Honest People": The Illicit Economy in Immigrant Documents in Cape Town'. *Migration Studies* 5, no. 2 (July 2017): 216–236.

Alfaro-Velcamp, Theresa, and Mark Shaw. '"Please GO HOME and BUILD Africa": Criminalising Immigrants in South Africa'. *Journal of Southern African Studies* 42, no. 5 (September 2016): 983–998.

Amit, Roni. *Lost in the Vortex: Irregularities in the Detention and Deportation of Non-Nationals in South Africa.* Forced Migration Studies Programme Research Report, June 2010.

Amit, Roni. *Queue Here for Corruption: Measuring Irregularities in South Africa's Asylum System.* Johannesburg: Lawyers for Human Rights and the African Centre for Migration & Society, July 2015.

Arendt, Hannah. *On Revolution*. London: Penguin Books, 1990.

Arendt, Hannah. *The Human Condition*, 2nd ed. Chicago: The University of Chicago Press, 1958.

Arendt, Hannah. *The Jew as Pariah: Jewish Identity and Politics in the Modern Age*, edited by Ron Feldman. New York: Grove Press, 1978.

Arendt, Hannah. *The Origins of Totalitarianism*. Orlando, Florida: Harcourt Brace & Company, 1948.

Arendt, Hannah. 'What Is Freedom?' In *Between Past and Future*, by Hannah Arendt. New York: Viking Press, 1961.

Asiatic Inquiry Commission. *Report of the Asiatic Inquiry Commission*. Cape Town: Union of South Africa, 1921.

Barnard-Naudé, Jaco. 'Hannah Arendt's Work of Mourning: The Politics of Loss, "the Rise of the Social" and the Ends of Apartheid'. In *Remains of the Social: Desiring the Post-Apartheid*, edited by Maurits van Bever Donker, Ross Truscott, Gary Minkley and Premesh Lalu, 117–145. Johannesburg: Wits University Press, 2017.

Barnes, Clayton. 'Cut Number of Foreign Spaza Shops – ANC'. *Cape Argus*, 25 June 2012. https://www.iol.co.za/news/politics/cut-number-of-foreign-spaza-shops-anc-1326536.

Biko, Steve. *I Write What I Like*, edited by Aelred Stubbs, C.R. Oxford: Heinemann, 1987.

Bonacich, Edna. 'A Theory of Middleman Minorities'. *American Sociological Review* 38, no. 5 (October 1973): 583–5 94.

Bornman, Jan. 'Xenophobic Mob Rampages Through Joburg'. *Daily Maverick*, 8 August 2019. https://www.dailymaverick.co.za/article/2019-08-08-xenophobic-mob-rampages-through-joburg/.

Botha, Henk. 'The Rights of Foreigners: Dignity, Citizenship and the Right to Have Rights'. *South African Law Journal* 130, no. 4 (2013): 837–869.

Bruce, David, and Tanya Zack. 'Joburg Vendors vs Police. When a System Wears the Badge of the Law but Lacks Moral Authority'. *Daily Maverick*, 5 August 2019. https://www.dailymaverick.co.za/article/2019-08-05-joburg-vendors-vs-police-when-a-system-wears-the-badge-of-the-law-but-lacks-moral-authority/.

Brydon, Lynne. 'Ghanaian Responses to the Nigerian Expulsions of 1983'. *African Affairs* 84, no. 337 (October 1985): 561–585.

Carciotto, Sergio, Vanya Gastrow and Corey Johnson. *Manufacturing Illegality: The Impact of Curtailing Asylum Seekers' Right to Work in South Africa*. Cape Town: Scalabrini Institute for Human Mobility in Africa, 2018.

Chatterjee, Partha. *The Politics of the Governed: Reflections on Popular Politics*. New York: Columbia University Press, 2004.

Chawane, Gopolang. 'WATCH: War Declared against "My Friend" Spaza Shops Selling Expired Products'. *The Citizen*, 22 August 2018. https://citizen.co.za/news/south-africa/1998917/watch-war-declared-against-my-friend-spaza-shops-selling-expired-products/.

Chiumia, Sintha. 'FACTSHEET: How Many International Migrants Are There in SA?' *Africa Check*, 14 August 2016. https://africacheck.org/factsheets/data-migrants-numbers/.

Cilliers, Valerie. 'Court Rules on Spaza Shops'. *Northern News*, 24 August 2012. http://www.noordnuus.co.za/details/24-08-2012/court_rules_on_spaza_shops/14634.

City Press. 'Campaign Against Foreign Township Traders Spreads', 14 May 2015. https://www.news24.com/news24/Archives/City-Press/Campaign-against-foreign-township-traders-spreads-20150430.

Crush, Jonathan. 'The Perfect Storm: The Realities of Xenophobia in Contemporary South Africa'. *SAMP Migration Policy Series* no. 50. Cape Town: Idasa, 2000.

Crush, Jonathan, Abel Chikanda, and Caroline Skinner, eds. 'Migrant Entrepreneurship and Informality in South African Cities'. In *Mean Streets: Migration, Xenophobia and Informality in South Africa*, edited by Crush, Chikanda and Skinner. Cape Town: Southern African Migration Programme, the African Centre for Cities and the International Development Research Centre, 2015.

Crush, Jonathan, and Sujata Ramachandran. 'Xenophobic Violence in South Africa: Denialism, Minimalism, Realism'. *SAMP Migration Policy Series* no. 66. Cape Town and Waterloo, Ontario: Southern African Migration Programme and International Migration Research Centre, 2014.

Crush, Jonathan, Caroline Skinner and Manal Stulgaitis. 'Rendering South Africa Undesirable: A Critique of Refugee and Informal Sector Policy'. *SAMP Migration Policy Series* no. 79. Waterloo, Ontario: Southern African Migration Programme and International Migration Research Centre, 2017.

Crush, Jonathan, Godfrey Tawodzera, Cameron McCordic and Sujata Ramachandran. 'Refugee Entrepreneurial Economies in Urban South Africa'. *SAMP Migration Policy Series* no. 76. Waterloo, Ontario: Southern African Migration Programme and International Migration Research Centre, 2017.

Daniel, Luke. 'Makhura Vows to Retaliate against "Foreigners" Who Attacked JHB Police'. *The South African*, 2 August 2019. https://www.thesouthafrican.com/news/joburg-riots-makhura-vows-to-retaliate,-against-foreign-nationals/.

Davies, Rob. 'Minister Rob Davies Urges Orange Farm Small Businesses to Take Advantage of Economic Opportunities Provided by Government'. Speech, Orange Farm, Gauteng, 9 April 2013. https://www.youtube.com/watch?v=BGTvJWITSFg.

Department of Home Affairs. *2018/2019 Annual Report*. 31 May 2019.

Department of Trade and Industry. *National Informal Business Upliftment Strategy*. February 2014.

Dinbabo, Mulugeta F., Yanga Zembe, Sharon Penderis, Sergio Carciotto, Chris Nshimbi, Vanya Gastrow, Michael Nguatem Belebema, Jonas Nzabamwita, Kenny Chiwarawara, Maryan A. Ahmed, Murus Gidey Alemu and Leon Tshimpaka Mwamba. *Refugee and Asylum Seeking Representative Structures and Their Communities in South Africa*. Cape Town: Institute for Social Development and the Scalabrini Institute for Human Mobility in Africa, 2017.

Dodson, Belinda. 'Locating Xenophobia: Debate, Discourse, and Everyday Experience in Cape Town, South Africa'. *Africa Today* 56, no. 3 (Spring 2010): 2–22.

Douglas, Karen Manges, and Rogelio Saenz. 'Middleman Minorities'. In *International Encyclopedia of the Social Sciences*, 2nd ed., edited by William A. Darity Jr, 147–148. New York: Macmillan Reference USA, 2008.

Essa, Azad. 'South Africa's Soweto Tense after "Xenophobic" Attacks'. *Al Jazeera*, 23 January 2015. https://www.aljazeera.com/news/africa/2015/01/south-afri-ca-soweto-tense-xenophobic-attacks-150123044841532.html.

Eyewitness News. 'DG Defends Business Registration Bill'. 26 April 2013. https://ewn.co.za/2013/04/26/DG-defends-Business-Registration-Bill.

Fanon, Frantz. *The Wretched of the Earth*. New York: Grove Press, 1963.

Foucault, Michel. *Society Must Be Defended: Lectures at the Collège de France 1975 to 1976*. New York: Picador, 1997.

Foucault, Michel. *The History of Sexuality Volume 1: An Introduction*. New York: Pantheon Books, 1978.

Gastrow, Peter. *Lifting the Veil on Extortion in Cape Town*. Geneva: Global Initiative Against Organised Crime, 2021.

Gastrow, Vanya. 'Problematizing the Foreign Shop: Justifications for Restricting the Migrant Spaza Sector in South Africa'. *SAMP Migration Policy Series* no. 80. Waterloo, Ontario: Southern African Migration Programme and International Migration Research Centre, 2018.

Gastrow, Vanya, with Roni Amit. *Elusive Justice: Somali Traders' Access to Formal and Informal Justice Mechanisms in the Western* Cape. Johannesburg: African Centre for Migration & Society, 2012.

Gastrow, Vanya, with Roni Amit. *Lawless Regulation: Government and Civil Society Attempts at Regulating Somali Informal Trade in Cape Town*. Johannesburg: African Centre for Migration & Society, 2015.

Gastrow, Vanya, with Roni Amit. *Somalinomics: A Case Study on the Economic Dimensions of Somali Informal Trade in the Western Cape*. Johannesburg: African Centre for Migration & Society, 2013.

Grazer, Brian, and Charles Fishman. *A Curious Mind: The Secret to a Bigger Life*. New York: Simon & Schuster, 2015.

Hartley, Wyndham. 'Illegal Foreign Business Owners "A Soft Target for Criminals"'. *Business Day*, 9 February 2012.

Hassan, Abdullahi Ali. 'Enterprising Somali Refugees in Cape Town: Beyond Informality, Beyond the Spaza Shop'. Master's thesis, University of Cape Town, 2019. https://open.uct.ac.za/bitstream/handle/11427/31811/thesis_sci_2019_hassan_abdullahi_ali.pdf?sequence=1&isAllowed=y.

Hassim, Shireen, Tawana Kupe and Eric Worby, eds. *Go Home or Die Here: Violence, Xenophobia and the Reinvention of Difference in South Africa*. Johannesburg: Wits University Press, 2008.

Hikam, Abdu Sh. Mohamed. 'An Exploratory Study on the Somali Immigrants'. Master's thesis, Nelson Mandela Metropolitan University, 2011.

Human Rights Watch. *Shell-Shocked: Civilians Under Siege in Mogadishu*. New York: Human Rights Watch, 13 August 2007. https://www.hrw.org/report/2007/08/13/shell-shocked/civilians-under-siege-mogadishu.

Igglesden, Vicki. *Case F22/1: Athlone Court*. Cape Town: 21 November 2011.

IOL News. 'Minister Tackles Xenophobic Attacks'. 12 July 2010. https://www.iol.co.za/news/south-africa/minister-tackles-xenophobic-attacks-489525.

Johns, Lynette. 'Myriad Laws on Foreigners "Must Change"'. *Cape Argus*, 22 September 2011.

Joubert, Pearlie. 'Nafcoc Calls for Somali Purge'. *Mail & Guardian*, 5 September 2008. http://www.mg.co.za/article/2008-09-05-nafcoc-calls-for-somali-purge.

Karrim, Azarrah, and Ntwaagae Seleka. 'UPDATE: Cele Condemns Violent Protests in Joburg, Briefs Makhura and Ramaphosa'. *News24*, 2 September 2019. https://www.news24.com/SouthAfrica/News/sahrc-condemns-johannesburg-protests-calls-for-calm-20190902.

Khayelitsha Commission of Inquiry. *Towards a Safer Khayelitsha: The Report of the Commission of Inquiry into Allegations of Police Inefficiency and a Breakdown in Relations between SAPS and the Community in Khayelitsha*. August 2014.

Krusche, Petra and Vanya Gastrow. 'Somali Traders Could Pay the Price for Authorities' Failure to Uphold Basic Rights'. *Cape Times*, 31 August 2009.

Kubheka, Thando. 'SA Lockdown: Govt Working on Relief Package for Informal Sector'. *Eyewitness News*, 26 March 2020. https://ewn.co.za/2020/03/26/sa-lockdown-govt-working-on-relief-package-for-informal-sector.

Landau, Loren B., ed. *Exorcising the Demons Within*. Tokyo, New York, Paris: United Nations University Press, April 2012.

Landau, Loren B. 'Loving the Alien? Citizenship, Law and the Future in South Africa's Demonic Society'. *African Affairs* 109, no. 435 (April 2010): 213–230.

Lawal, Shola. 'Ghana Must Go: The Ugly History of Ghana's Most Famous Bag'. *Mail & Guardian*, 4 April 2019. http://atavist.mg.co.za/ghana-must-go-the-ugly-history-of-africas-most-famous-bag.

Lazare, Bernard. *Job's Dungheap*. New York: Schocken Books Inc. 1948.

Magubane, Khulekani. 'Reveal Trade Secrets, Minister Tells Foreigners'. *Business Day*, 28 January 2015. https://www.businesslive.co.za/archive/2015-01-28-reveal-trade-secrets-minister-tells-foreigners/.

Mamdani, Mahmood. 'Beyond Settler and Native as Political Identities: Overcoming the Political Legacy of Colonialism'. *Comparative Studies in Society and History* 43, no. 4 (October 2001): 651–664.

Mantashe, Gwede. Media briefing on *ANN7*, 20 March 2016. https://www.youtube.com/watch?v=mCNnWrAjIcM, minute 45.

Mbeki, Thabo. 'National Tribute in Remembrance of Xenophobic Attacks Victims'. Speech, Tshwane, Gauteng, 3 July 2008. https://www.polity.org.za/article/sa-mbeki-national-tribute-in-remembrance-of-xenophobic-attacks-victims-03072008-2008-07-03.

Min, Pyong Gap. 'Middleman Entrepreneurs'. In *The Routledge Handbook of Migration Studies*, edited by Steven J. Gold and Stephanie J. Nawyn, 145–152. London and New York: Routledge, 2013.

Minister of Home Affairs and Others v Watchenuka and Others (010/2003) [2003] ZASCA 142; [2004] 1 All SA 21 (SCA) (28 November 2003).

Misago, Jean Pierre. 'Disorder in a Changing Society: Authority and the Micro-Politics of Violence'. In *Exorcising the Demons Within*, edited by Loren B. Landau. Tokyo, New York, Paris: United Nations University Press, April 2012.

Misago, Jean Pierre. 'Political Mobilisation as the Trigger of Xenophobic Violence in Post-Apartheid South Africa'. *International Journal of Conflict and Violence* 13 (2019): 1–10.

Misago, Jean Pierre. 'Politics by Other Means? The Political Economy of Xenophobic Violence in Post-Apartheid South Africa'. *The Black Scholar* 47, no. 2 (2017): 40–53.

Mkhonza, Thembelihle. 'Consumer Commission Tackles "Potentially Harmful" Fake Food Products'. *IOL News*, 27 August 2018. https://www.iol.co.za/news/south-africa/consumer-commission-tackles-potentially-harmful-fake-food-products-16765174.

Moatshe, Rapula. 'Zuma: Marches Were Anti-Crime, Not Xenophobic'. *Pretoria News*, 25 February 2017. https://www.iol.co.za/news/politics/zuma-marches-were-anti-crime-not-xenophobic-7923422.

Mtyala, Quinton. 'Cele's Xenophobic Outburst'. *Cape Times*, 7 October 2011. https://www.iol.co.za/news/celes-xenophobic-outburst-1152621.

Mtyala, Quinton. 'Somali and Local Shopkeepers Strike a Deal on Peace'. *Cape Times*, 20 August 2009.

Ngnenbe, Timothy. 'Ghanaian, Nigerian Spare Parts Dealers in Brawl Over Retail Trade'. *Graphic Online*, 30 July 2020. https://www.graphic.com.gh/news/general-news/ghanaian-nigerian-spare-parts-dealers-in-brawl-over-retail-trade.html.

Ngoepe, Karabo, and Manyane Manyane. 'Fake Food Crunch'. *IOL News*, 2 September 2018. https://www.iol.co.za/sundayindependent/news/fake-food-crunch-16850990.

Nieftagodien, Noor. 'Xenophobia's Local Genesis: Historical Constructions of Insiders and the Politics of Exclusion in Alexandra Township'. In *Exorcising the Demons Within*, edited by Loren B. Landau. Tokyo, New York, Paris: United Nations University Press, April 2012.

Nieftagodien, Noor. 'Xenophobia's Local Genesis: Historical Constructions of Insiders and the Politics of Exclusion in Alexandra Township'. In *Exorcising the Demons Within*, edited by Loren B. Landau. Tokyo, New York, Paris: United Nations University Press, April 2012.

Ntshavheni, Khumbudzo. 'Ntshavheni: Businesses Owned by Foreign Nationals Need Regulating'. Interview on eNCA, 5 August 2019. https://www.youtube.com/watch?v=M-xLlwZ2BMY.

Ntshidi, Edwin. 'Joburg Police to Monitor CBD after Violent Protests'. *Eyewitness News*, 2 August 2019. https://ewn.co.za/2019/08/02/joburg-police-to-monitor-cbd-after-violent-protests.

Ntshidi, Edwin. 'Ramaphosa: Foreign Nationals Must Obey the Laws of South Africa'. *Eyewitness News*, 15 September 2019. https://ewn.co.za/2019/09/15/ramaphosa-foreign-nationals-must-obey-the-laws-of-south-africa.

Nyamnjoh, Francis B., ed. *Insiders and Outsiders: Citizenship and Xenophobia in Contemporary Southern Africa*. London and New York: Zed Books, 2006.

Ofosu-Amaah, W. Paatii 'Restriction of Aliens in Business in Ghana and Kenya'. *The International Lawyer* 8, no. 3 (July 1974): 452–477.

Ojeme, Victoria. 'Envoy Protests Inhuman Treatment of Nigerians in Ghana; 723 deported'. *Vanguard*, 20 February 2019. https://www.vanguardngr.com/2019/02/envoy-protests-inhuman-treatment-of-nigerians-in-ghana-723-deported/.

Ojeme, Victoria. 'Inside the Politics, Diplomacy and Reality of Ghana's GIPC Levy on Foreign Traders'. *Vanguard*, 27 August 2020. https://www.vanguardngr.com/2020/08/inside-the-politics-diplomacy-and-reality-of-ghanas-gipc-levy/.

Olaniyi, Rasheed. 'The 1969 Ghana Exodus: Memory and Reminiscences of Yoruba Migrants'. International Migration Institute Conference Paper, 26 November 2008.

Oni, Ebenezer O., and Samuel K. Okunade. 'The Context of Xenophobia in Africa: Nigeria and South Africa in Comparison'. In *The Political Economy of Xenophobia in Africa*, edited by Adeoye O. Akinola, 37–51. Cham, Switzerland: Springer International Publishing AG, 2018.

Owusu, Maxwell. 'The Search for Solvency: Background to the Fall of Ghana's Second Republic, 1969–1972'. *Africa Today* 19, no. 1 (Winter 1972): 52–60.

Patel, Khadija, Xolani Mbanjwa, Zinhle Mapumulo, Abram Mashego and Sipho Masondo. 'Soweto Unrest: "Cops Told Us to Loot"'. *City Press*, 25 January 2015. https://www.news24.com/SouthAfrica/News/Soweto-unrest-Cops-told-us-to-loot-20150125.

Plastow, Andrew. 'Spaza Shops, Xenophobia and Their Impact on the South African Consumer'. *Daily Maverick*, 22 June 2015. https://www.dailymaverick.co.za/opinionista/2015-04-20-spaza-shops-xenophobia-and-their-impact-on-the-south-african-consumer/.

Polzer, Tara, and Kathryn Takabvirwa. '"Just Crime"? Violence, Xenophobia and Crime: Discourse and Practice'. *SA Crime Quarterly*, no. 33 (September 2010): 1–10. https://www.ajol.info/index.php/sacq/article/view/101463.

Prince, Natasha. 'Men Left Trail of Death and Destruction'. *IOL News*, 5 March 2014. https://www.iol.co.za/news/men-left-trail-of-death-and-destruction-1656532.

Qukula, Qama. 'Govt Preparing New Laws to Restrict Foreign-Owned Business and "Protect Locals"'. *Radio 702*, 26 September 2019. http://www.702.co.za/articles/361955/govt-preparing-new-laws-to-restrict-foreign-owned-business-and-protect-locals.

Qukula, Qama. 'Home Affairs Minister Aaron Motsoaledi Explains the New, Tougher Laws for Refugees and Asylum Seekers in South Africa'. *Cape Talk*, *Today with Kieno Kammies*, 6 January 2020. http://www.capetalk.co.za/articles/371160/new-tighter-laws-broaden-grounds-for-exclusion-from-refugee-status-motsoaledi.

Ramaphosa, Cyril. 'Address at the Joint Sitting of Parliament on the Crisis of Violence in South Africa, National Assembly, Cape Town (18/09/2019)'. *Polity* 18 September 2019. https://www.polity.org.za/article/sa-cyril-ramaphosa-address-by-south-african-president-at-the-joint-sitting-of-parliament-on-the-crisis-of-violence-in-south-africa-national-assembly-cape-town-18092019-2019-09-19.

Rancière, Jacques. 'Who is the Subject of the Rights of Man?' *South Atlantic Quarterly* 103, no. 2/3 (Spring/Summer 2004): 297–310.

Reuters. 'Zimbabwe to Replace Empowerment Law: Finance Minister'. 1 August 2019. https://www.reuters.com/article/us-zimbabwe-economy-mining-idUSKCN1UR4X2.

Rinder, Irwin D. 'Strangers in the Land: Social Relations in the Status Gap'. *Social Problems* 6, no. 3 (Winter, 1958–1959): 253–260.

Samodien, Leila. 'ACDP Backs Call to Shut Down Somali Stores'. *Cape Argus*, 8 September 2008.

Sapa. 'The Body Count ...' *IOL News*, 12 June 2008. https://www.iol.co.za/news/south-africa/the-body-count-404220.

SBP Business Environment Specialists. Current State of Legislation in South Africa: A Country Overregulated and Undergoverned? SBP Occasional Paper, August 2012. http://smegrowthindex.co.za/wp-content/uploads/2012/08/SBP-alert-08.12_digital.pdf.

Scroll. 'Indo-African History: Watch Idi Amin Defend the Decision to Kick Indians Out of Uganda'. 27 October 2015. https://scroll.in/video/1138/indo-african-history-watch-idi-amin-defend-the-decision-to-kick-indians-out-of-uganda.

Seale, Lebogang. 'Groups Do Rounds Closing Down Foreign Businesses'. *The Star*, 27 April 2011. https://www.security.co.za/news/18203.

Somali Association of South Africa v Limpopo Department of Economic Development, Environment and Tourism (48/2014) ZASCA 143 (26 September 2014).

South African Government. 'Attacks against Foreign Nationals'. Media statement, 20 April 2015. https://www.gov.za/speeches/outbreak-violence-against-foreign-nationals.

South African Government. 'Minister Aaron Motsoaledi on Allegations of Fake and Expired Food'. Media statement, 3 September 2018. https://www.gov.za/speeches/media-statement-minister-health-allegations-fake-and-expired-food-5-sep-2018-0000.

South African Government. 'The Eastern Cape Provincial Government to Meet Residents of Nompumelelo Township'. 19 July 2012. https://www.gov.za/eastern-cape-provincial-government-meet-residents-nompumelelo-township.

South African Government. White Paper on International Migration for South Africa. July 2017.

South African Government News Agency. 'Guidelines for Spaza Shops Announced'. 18 April 2020. https://www.sanews.gov.za/south-africa/guidelines-spaza-shops-announced.

South African Police Service. *Addendum to the Annual Report 2011/2012*, 2012. https://www.saps.gov.za/about/stratframework/annual_report/2011_2012/saps_crime_stats_report_%202011-12.pdf.

South African Police Service. *An Analysis of the National Crime Statistics: Addendum to the Annual Report 2011/2012.*, 2012. https://www.saps.gov.za/about/stratframework/annual_report/2011_2012/saps_crime_stats_report_%202011-12.pdf.

South African Police Service. *An Analysis of the National Crime Statistics 2012/2013: Addendum to the Annual Report 2012/2013*, 31 August 2013. https://www.arrivealive.co.za/ckfinder/userfiles/files/national%20crime%20situation.pdf.

South African Police Service. *Annual Crime Report 2015/2016: Addendum to the SAPS Annual Report*, 2016. https://www.saferspaces.org.za/resources/entry/annual-crime-report-2015-2016-addendum-to-the-saps-annual-report.

South African Police Service. *Annual Report 2007/2008*, 29 August 2008. https://www.gov.za/sites/default/files/gcis_document/201409/saps-anrep-complete.pdf.

South African Police Service. *Annual Report 2008/2009.* 21 July 2009. https://www.gov.za/sites/default/files/gcis_document/201409/sapsanrep-0809.pdf.

South African Police Service. *Provincial Policing Needs and Priorities Report (PNP): Report for the Blue Downs Police Cluster 2016/17: 1–2 July 2016*, 2016. https://www.westerncape.gov.za/assets/departments/community-safety/policing_needs_and_priorities_report_blue_downs_cluster_16-17.pdf.

South African Police Service. *SAPS Western Cape Annual Report 2012/2013*, https://www.wcpp.gov.za/sites/default/files/SAPS_Ann_Rep_2012_2013[1].pdf.

South African Police Service. *SAPS Western Cape Annual Report 2013/2014.* https://www.westerncape.gov.za/files/department_of_community_safety_annual_report_2013_2014.pdf.

Southall, Roger. 'African Capitalism in Contemporary South Africa'. *Journal of Southern African Studies* 7, no. 1 (1980): 38–70.

Southall, Roger. 'The ANC & Black Capitalism in South Africa'. *Review of African Political Economy* 31, no. 100 (2004): 313–328.

Spiegel, Andrew. 'Refracting an Elusive South African Urban Citizenship: Problems with Tracking Spaza'. In *Limits to Liberation After Apartheid: Citizenship, Governance & Culture*, edited by Steven L. Robins, 190–205. Oxford: James Currey, 2005.

Staff reporter. 'A/R: Open Our Shops Immediately or We'll March – Ghanaians Working in Nigerian Shops'. *Modern Ghana*, 2 October 2020. https://www.modernghana.com/news/1033167/ar-open-our-shops-immediately-or-well-march.html.

Statistics South Africa. *Governance, Public Safety and Justice Survey: 2018/19.* Pretoria: STATS SA, 2019.

Statistics South Africa. *Victims of Crime Survey 2017/18.* Pretoria: STATS SA, 11 October 2018.

Steinberg, Jonny. 'South Africa's Xenophobic Eruption'. *ISS Paper* no. 169 (November 2008): 1–13.

Tawodzera, Godfrey, Abel Chikanda, Jonathan Crush and Robertson Tengeh. 'International Migrants and Refugees in Cape Town's Informal Economy'.

SAMP Migration Policy Series no. 70. Waterloo, Ontario: Southern African Migration Programme and International Migration Research Centre, 2015.

Taylor, Edgar C. 'Claiming Kabale: Racial Thought and Urban Governance in Uganda'. *Journal of Eastern African Studies* 7, no. 1 (2013): 143–163.

The Citizen. 'SA Citizens Are Not Xenophobic – Jeff Radebe'. 11 November 2015. https://citizen.co.za/news/south-africa/government/2202783/south-africans-are-not-xenophobic-ramaphosa/.

The Citizen. 'Foreign Owned Businesses Hampering Rural Growth – DTI'. 10 September 2013. https://citizen.co.za/uncategorized/66033/foreign-owned-businesses-hampering-rural-growth-dti/.

Thembisan. 'WATCH: Fake, Expired Foods Removed from Tembisa Corner Shops'. 30 August 2018. https://tembisan.co.za/74736/community-raids-foreign-owned-shops-selling-bad-food/.

Thornycroft, Peta. 'Five Dead as Mobs Burn Down Shops in "Anti-Foreigner" Riots in Johannesburg'. *The Telegraph*, 3 September 2019. https://www.telegraph.co.uk/news/2019/09/03/five-dead-mobs-burn-shops-anti-foreigner-riots-johannesburg/.

Tijani, Abdullah. 'Ghana's Deportation of Nigerians is a New Chapter in a Very Ugly History that Must End'. *African Liberty*, 6 March 2019. https://www.africanliberty.org/2019/03/06/ghanas-deportation-of-nigerians-is-a-chapter-in-a-very-ugly-history-that-must-end/.

Timberg, Craig. 'Not So Welcome in South Africa'. *Washington Post*, 1 October 2006. http://www.washingtonpost.com/wp-dyn/content/article/2006/09/30/AR2006093000982.html.

Turski, Marian. Speech, Auschwitz, Poland, 27 January 2020. https://www.france24.com/en/video/20200127-auschwitz-75-years-on-do-not-be-indifferent-says-death-camp-survivor-marian-turski.

United Nations High Commissioner for Refugees. 'UNHCR Statistical Online Population Database'. http://popstats.unhcr.org/#_ga=1.3026608.16420081 89.1414090050.

Verster, Ciska. 'Four Somali Shops Held Up in Past Week'. *False Bay People's Post, undated.* http://www.compcom.co.za/wp-content/uploads/2016/09/Vanya-Gastrow-Submission.pdf, date accessed 4 March 2017.

Weber, Max, Guenther Roth and Claus Wittich. *Economy and Society: An Outline of Interpretive Sociology.* Berkeley: University of California Press, 1978.

Western Cape Provincial Government. *Documenting and Evaluation Report: Masiphumelele Conflict Intervention August 2006–March 2007,* undated. Accessed 10 April 2021. https://www.westerncape.gov.za/text/2009/3/masiphumelele_conflict_intervention_report.pdf.

Xenowatch. 'About Us'. http://www.xenowatch.ac.za/about-xenowatch/. Accessed 29 May 2020.

Zama, Zanele. 'Home Affairs Gazettes New Tougher Laws for Refugees and Asylum Seekers'. *Radio 702*, 6 January 2020. http://www.702.co.za/articles/371174/home-affairs-gazettes-new-tougher-laws-for-refugees-and-and-asylum-seekers, 6 January 2020.

Zibi, Songezo. 'ANC Must Keep Its Promises'. *The Herald*, 20 January 2014. https://www.pressreader.com/south-africa/the-herald-south-africa/20140120/281921655907642.

Zulu, Lindiwe. 'Laws Regulating Foreign Owned Spazas Must Be Fast Tracked: Zulu'. Interview with Leanne Manas on *Morning Live*. *SABC News*, 27 January 2015. http://www.sabc.co.za/news/a/bfdc37004715bf689b21bf686e648436/Laws-regulating-foreign-owned-spazas-must-be-fast-tracked:-Zulu-20152701. Accessed 4 March 2017.

Zulu, Lindiwe. 'Minister Lindiwe Zulu: Small Business Development Dept Budget Vote 2015/16'. Speech, 20 May 2015. https://www.gov.za/speeches/minister-lindiwe-zulu-small-business-development-dept-budget-vote-201516-20-may-2015-0000.

Zulu, Lindiwe. 'Speech by the Minister of Small Business Development, Ms Lindiwe Zulu, at the Hookup Dinner 2nd Anniversary, Johannesburg'. 1 August 2014. https://www.gov.za/speeches/minister-lindiwe-zulu-hookup-dinner-2nd-anniversary-1-aug-2014-0000.

Zuma, Jacob. Speaking after the launch of Operation Phakisa, Johannesburg, 24 February 2017. https://www.news24.com/Video/SouthAfrica/News/watch-south-africans-arent-xenophobic-jacob-zuma-20170224.

Zuma, Jacob. Speech at Grand Parade, Cape Town, 9 February 2016.

Index

Page numbers in *italics* indicate photographs.

CPSIA information can be obtained
at www.ICGtesting.com
Printed in the USA
JSHW021501160922
30629JS00001B/68